The
Very Quick
Job Search

J. Michael Farr

Project Director: Spring Dawn Reader
Production Editor: Sara Hall
Cover Design: Mike Kreffel
Interior Illustration Arranged By: Mike Kreffel
Interior Design: Spring Dawn Reader
Proof Reader: Lisa Farr
Calligraphy: Sara Hall

The *Very* Quick Job Search—*Get a Good Job in Less Time*
©1991, **JIST Works, Inc.**, Indianapolis, IN

JIST Works, Inc.
720 North Park Avenue ●Indianapolis, IN 46202-3431
Phone: (317) 264-3720 ●FAX: (317) 264-3709

Library of Congress Cataloging-in-Publication Data
Farr, J. Michael.
    The Very Quick Job Search : get a good job in less time /
Mike Farr.
        p.   cm.
    Includes bibliographical references.
    ISBN 0-942784-72-3 : $9.95
    1. Job hunting—United States.   I. Title.
HF5382.75.U6F37   1991
650.14—dc20   91-12593
                                                          CIP

ISBN: 0-942784-72-3

If You Are in a Real Hurry to Find a Job...

When I first agreed to write this book, I had in mind a short book covering just the essentials of how to get a job in less time. If you have not already noticed, this is not a particularly short book. One thing just led to another and the result is a more thorough job search book than the title might lead you to believe. So if the title inspired you to buy this book because it was a "quick" read (which might be a reasonable assumption, based on its title), I would hate for you to feel misled. It isn't.

On the other hand, there is a lot in this book to help you feel that you got your money's worth. The techniques really can help you reduce your job search time by 50 percent or more. But, if you are in a particular hurry to get on with your job search, here are a few things I can suggest to move you on your merry way. Quickly.

1. Read Chapters one and two. The first chapter gives you important insights into our rapidly changing labor market and what it means to you. And I can assure you that it won't take you nearly as long to read it as it took me to write it. The second chapter provides the basics on how to find job leads. That is the one, if you are in a big hurry, that will help you the most. It will give you enough information to quickly improve your job seeking efficiency.

2. Read the last chapter. The last chapter, on organizing your job search, is not the least. If you want to get quick results, it is essential that you spend more time on your job search and get more interviews than the average job seeker. This chapter will show you how to organize your time and contacts to get results.

3. Review the chapters on interviewing skills. If you go out and get lots of interviews you will eventually get better at doing them. That's why I listed this as third on my list. Since interviews are where decisions are made to hire or not hire you, they are a particularly important part of the job search process.

4. Read the rest as time permits. Some of the chapters in this book will be more important to some people than others. I intended for you to begin at the beginning and build your job search skills and knowledge in a particular order. I think that each of the chapters provide important and useful information and I encourage you to read them all. But it is your book and you are an adult, so you are welcome to use it in any way you wish. You can even (heaven forbid) turn right now to the chapter on resumes. But if you do, you should know that others, who read at least the chapters I recommend in the first three suggestions above, will provide you with tough competition. They may, in fact, be working in their next job before you get your resume "just right."

You can read the essential chapters in this book this afternoon or evening and be looking for a job tomorrow. So my final suggestion for making your job search very "quick" is to make sure that, beginning tomorrow (or as soon as you are possibly able), you begin looking for your next job on a full-time basis. In my view, that means getting at least two interviews a day, five days a week. If you do that, the odds are good that you will have a job in much less time than average. And I won't have to feel bad about the title of this book.

❦ ❦ ❦ ❦

This is such a practical, "how to" book, that I thought it useful to consider job search issues in the more important context of what is really important in your life. So here is a quote from Ralph Waldo Emerson, a nineteenth century poet and philosopher, to ponder as you begin this book.

How do you measure success?
To laugh often and much,
To win the respect of intelligent people and the affection of children,
To earn the appreciation of honest critics and endure the betrayal
    of false friends,
To appreciate beauty,
To find the best in others,
To leave the world a bit better, whether by a healthy child, a
    redeemed social condition, or a job well done,
To know even one other life has breathed because you lived,
This is to have succeeded.

Table of Contents

Chapter Three—Identifying Your Skills - *The Key to Getting the Job You Want* . . 53

Chapter Eleven—Answering Problem Interview Questions 171

Chapter Twelve—Producing Superior Resumes 193

Introduction

About *The Very Quick Job Search*

This book is about getting a job. Lots of books claim to help you find a job, but this one is different. Besides showing you how to write a good resume and find job openings, it will:

Help you find a good job: This book will help you define and find "THE" job rather than just "a" job. This is an important issue since what you do for your work can be an important factor in how you feel about your life.

Help you find a job in less time: Some job search methods work better than others. Many thousands of people have used the techniques presented in this book to cut their job search time in half.

Show you how to negotiate for higher salary: There are a few things you can do when negotiating salary that can result in a significantly higher starting salary. It's easy enough to do and I will show you how.

Develop a skills language: Knowing what you are good at and being able to tell someone else is a very important life issue. Many people tell me that learning to identify their skills — and deciding how best to use them — was an important life experience for them. And, of course, it will help you in the interview process and throughout the job search.

All of this is a tall order. In writing this book, I have tried to keep things interesting, to emphasize the most important information and techniques, and to keep the book down to a manageable size. I hope you like it. More importantly, I hope that it helps you find a satisfying job and more meaningful life. In less time than you could have otherwise done. And that is why this book has been titled *The Very Quick Job Search*.

Why this Book Could be Worth Thousands of Dollars to You: The Economics of Career Planning and Job Search.

Here is a quote from a recent study titled "Workplace Basics" completed jointly by the U.S. Department of Labor and the American Society of Training and Development:

"Research shows that roughly half of the differences in earnings [between people] can be attributed to learning in school or on the job. Accidents of geography, career choices, and the selection of an employer account for the other half."

Another way to summarize their conclusion is to say that good career planning and job seeking skills can make a huge difference in how much you earn. Education and training also remain very important, of course. But even a good education or advanced technical skills are not enough if you don't know where or how to find the right jobs. And then, of course, there is the issue of finding a job you really like.

My own conclusion is that career planning and job seeking skills have now become essential survival skills in our new economy. They are that important. How well you plan your career and conduct your job search can make a tremendous difference in how much you earn, how rapidly you advance in your career, and how much you enjoy your work — and your life.

The High Cost of Looking for Work

Being out of work can be an expensive proposition. Besides the obvious costs of lost income while unemployed, there are less obvious psychological costs. For example, unemployed people have a higher incidence of stress-related illnesses; are more likely to have marital and other interpersonal problems; experience more alcohol and drug abuse and even experience higher death rates — the ultimate stress-related illness.

Using more effective job search skills can mean real money to you. For example, the average length of unemployment varies between 12 and 15 weeks and has gone as high as 20 weeks during times of high unemployment. For each $10,000 in annual salary you earn, that's $2,300 (for 12 weeks) to $2,850 (for 15 weeks) of lost income. Or much more. That is a substantial amount of money and anything that can reduce the time you need to find a job is like money in your pocket.

Salary negotiation is another area of the job search where knowing what to do at the right time can be worth thousands of dollars to you over the years. And the cost of underemployment in lower-paying jobs by people capable of more responsibility can become staggering over the years. For example, I recently interviewed a person for a job who had been working 50 hours a week for many years and making about half of what I thought her position should pay. She just got comfortable in her old job and hadn't gone out looking for another job for a long time. She lost enough income over the past five years to buy three new cars and a trip to Europe. And a down payment on a house.

But money is not everything. There is also the matter of finding the "right" job for you. It isn't easy to determine just what to look for but if you end up in a job you don't enjoy, you probably won't do well in it either. You also probably won't get promotions and raises like you might have otherwise. And you will probably end up looking for a job again because you will come to hate what you do.

So the stakes in your job search are quite high in both money and human terms. Yet most people spend more time shopping during the course of a month than planning their careers or learning how to look for a job. And for that reason, you should consider spending some time learning more about the career planning and job search process.

How Well Do the JIST Job Search Methods Presented in this Book Work?

There is no magic to getting a job. It requires hard work and a bit of luck. Too many people muddle through their job seeking without ever learning much about how to do it. And, as soon as they find a job, they certainly don't want to think about their unemployment experience. The result is that, too often, they don't learn much that they can apply to their next job search. What you need is someone to help you who knows lots more about this job search thing than you do. Or maybe you need a book.

There are lots of job search books but hardly anyone can offer any proof that their methods work better than others. And yet it seems to me that results are what count in your job search. At various points in this book I will ask you to come up with proof to support a key interview point, support a resume statement or, in some other way, provide proof that what you say you can do is true. So here is some proof of my credentials to write this book:

During the recession in the early 1980's, unemployment rates in many areas went well over 10 percent. That is as high as it has gotten in over 30 years, but in some areas it was much higher. My organization, JIST, had been operating successful job search programs since the early 1970s and was contracted to set up and run a demonstration job search program. The U.S. Department of Labor tracks the unemployment rates for the 200 largest cities in the U.S. and our project location, with lots of auto plant closings, went over 24 percent during the time we were there. That was the highest rate of any city in the entire United States at that time.

We were told by the government agency that hired us that there were no job openings. They knew because they had been looking for them without luck. We were to work with people who were unemployed but who were to receive no other services other than attending our job search program. We did no screening other than during a two-hour orientation session where we explained the program and asked them to attend only if they could commit themselves to a full-time job search and attend our program for six hours every weekday for four weeks or until they found a job. They were not compensated for attending. Following are some data and results from this program.

Average Length of Unemployment	14.5 months
% minorities:	50%
% women:	48%
Average age:	31.6

Results: 66 percent found jobs within 2.3 weeks of program initiation. Of those who attended the first two weeks without absence, 96 percent found jobs within 2.03 weeks.

These results are incredible but true. There was no magic to it, the jobs were there all along. Our job seekers were the ones who got them because they got to potential employers before the jobs were advertised and convinced the employer that they could do the job. The people waiting for a job to be advertised in the help-wanted section of the newspaper stayed unemployed.

You should know that these results were possible only because the JIST staff who operated the program were extremely talented and experienced. Debbie Featherston, who headed the team, is still with JIST and was one of its founders. That team of staff knew what they were doing and they know how to teach others to get results in a most difficult environment where jobs did not seem to exist at all. But these results are not unique and programs across the U.S. have obtained similarly positive results in difficult settings.

And now you have access to the same techniques. They are called the JIST Job Search Techniques and they are described in detail in this book. Together, these techniques represent a body of good common sense that has been developed and tested over many years. They can work if you make them work. Nothing more and nothing less. Making them work will, of course, be up to you.

A Few Words on "JIST" and I

You will notice the word "JIST" is used from time to time in this book. For example, you will learn about a "JIST Card" in chapter seven. And you may wonder what this word JIST means. For your information, "JIST" stands for Job Information & Seeking Training. The word "JIST" is a registered trademark and also refers to the organization, JIST Works, Inc., of which I am the president.

Over the years, JIST has become known for developing and publishing useful career planning and job search concepts and materials. JIST staff have trained over 10,000 job search instructors and my previous job search books have sold over 500,000 copies. JIST also published the very book you are reading.

I have a master's degree in counseling psychology and a background in industrial engineering (including efficiency studies) plus experience in working with groups. With all that, I still experienced the pain of unemployment and knew there had to be a better way to find jobs than the frustrating techniques I had used. Without any particular plan, I found myself directing programs where people needed help in finding jobs. And everything began to come together.

By the early 1970s I had developed a series of job search techniques and had used them with good results in a job search program I named JIST. Since then, I have continued to develop job search techniques that are easy to understand and that get results. Along the way, many job seekers have helped me stay away from approaches that looked good but that just did not work well. They have taught me much of what I know about job seeking by trying things out and letting me test and discard things that were not effective, were not easily communicated, or were not fun.

In addition to the good common sense that I have learned from presenting my ideas on job seeking to job seekers (an appropriately skeptical lot), I try to stay current on labor market trends and the all too little research that is available on the subject of job seeking. Robert Wegmann, who died in January 1991, has had an important influence on my thinking about the labor market and I will miss his counsel. Richard Lathrop has also helped me gain insight into the labor market and both he and Wegmann have written important books that are referenced in the first chapter of this book. The works of Bernard Haldane, John Crystal, and Richard Bolles have helped me develop some of the concepts I present in the career planning sections of this book. Now that I think of it, there have been hundreds of people who have taught me and helped me learn over the years. It just isn't possible to name them all but it has been a fun learning experience.

I hope that you enjoy this book. When you are done with it, after you have found your own job, pass it along to someone else or buy another one for them. That and your offering them a little bit of caring and support will let you become part of our underground movement to help each other find satisfaction in our careers and our lives. And, of course, reduce our lengths of unemployment to a minimum.

J. Michael Farr

Chapter One

Looking for Work in the New Economy

Things are not like they used to be. Our economy has changed so rapidly that, for most of us, our concepts about how to plan our careers — and how to find a job — are completely out of date. This can be a dangerous — and expensive — situation for most of us. The average person will change jobs far more frequently than their parents. They will also change their careers far more often than in the past. While there are a variety of reasons for this, the fact is that there are now huge negative economic consequences for those who are unprepared for our changed economy.

Think about it. At its simplest level, a job search now costs more money than it used to. The average length of unemployment is longer, varying between 12 and 20 weeks, depending on the rate of unemployment. Lost earnings and benefits during this time can be substantial. Even at modest salary levels, it adds up to thousands of dollars. Making things even worse is the fact that people change jobs more frequently now. Over an entire work life, the average cost of looking for work can be enough to buy a very nice car. Or yacht.

Even worse than the financial cost of a protracted job search are the long-term consequences of poor career planning: unhappiness, loss of self-esteem, missed promotions, and many other problems. The need for improved job search and career planning may not be obvious if you have not thought about it much. If that is the case for you, consider the details that follow.

The Bad News: Some Facts About the New Economy

Our economy has changed dramatically since the end of World War II. Even in the more recent years from the mid 1970s, change has been more rapid than most of us may realize. Newspaper articles and other media sources constantly present stories on the many economic and demographic changes now occurring. For example, most of us know that there are more women in the paid workforce than ever before and that the baby boomers are aging. But what does this all mean? And how do these changes affect me?

The fact is that literally every person who works now or plans to work in the next 20 years will be affected by a changed labor market. Following are some of the major trends.

Many People Experience Unemployment

At the end of 1990, there were 126 million people in the workforce and 5.8 percent of them were counted among the unemployed. About half of these people, 51.7 percent of the unemployed or 3.1 percent of the workforce, lost their jobs involuntarily. Of the remaining 2.7 percent who were unemployed, 1.5 percent are reentering the workforce, .8 percent are job leavers, and .7 percent are new entrants. That may not sound like much until you consider that about 17 percent of men and 12.5 percent of women in the workforce experience some unemployment during each year. That is about one in six workers.[1]

Some people are unemployed for long periods of time. During 1990, the average length of unemployment was 12.1 weeks. While half of all people found jobs in under 6 weeks, over 20 percent were unemployed longer than 15 weeks. And this does not count "discouraged workers," those who were unemployed but not actively looking. It is clear that many people suffer severe economic hardship from unemployment.[2]

People Change Jobs More Often

My father retired from an organization where he had worked for almost 30 years. It was one of the Fortune 500 companies and, believe it or not, they gave him a gold watch when he retired. That wasn't all that unusual a situation for people who retired in the 1960s and 70s. They tended to stay with an organization for many years.

It's different today. The average 35-year-old has changed jobs between six and seven times since they began working. Even those over 35 change jobs fairly frequently, on average of every three years or so.[3] That represents a lot of job changes over the average person's working life.

More Career Changes Expected

People change their careers more frequently now too. A change in careers is more significant than a job change since it involves changing from one occupational group to another. A teacher who moves into real estate sales is but one example.

It is now estimated that the average worker will change CAREERS from five to seven times.[4] Five to seven times! That is a lot of career changing. Changing technologies, more frequent job changing, more adults attending post-secondary training and educational programs, corporate "downsizing," and many other factors contribute to this trend.

Most Jobs Still not Advertised

It has been true for many years that most jobs are not advertised. Only about 15 percent of all people actually get their jobs through the want ads.[5] That leaves the other 85 percent or so of jobs, including most of the more desirable ones, to be filled in some other way. Even if you consider jobs available through other publicly accessible sources, such as the state-run Employment Service and private employment agencies, most jobs are still filled informally. Robert Wegmann's book, *Work in the New Economy*,[6] does a thorough job of looking into the available research on how people find jobs. He concludes that about 75 percent of all jobs are filled without ever being advertised or listed in any publicly available data bank or job posting.

Jobs Changing or Being Eliminated at a Rapid Pace

As you are surely aware, many thousands of manufacturing jobs have been eliminated in just the past decade. New technologies, foreign competition, consolidation and restructuring of large companies, and other factors have eliminated millions of manufacturing jobs since the mid-1970s.[7] Manufacturing jobs are not the only ones being affected either, with virtually no sector of the job market escaping the effects of rapid economic and technological change.

It may be that the factory is going the same way of the farm. Before the industrial revolution, over half of all people worked on farms. Now it is just 3 percent or so. Just as improved farm technology allowed more food to be produced with fewer workers, factories are becoming more productive as the result of improved technology. We are in the midst of a manufacturing technology revolution right now, which may eventually result in a small percentage of our workers producing all the goods we need.

It's a Far More Competitive Market

According to the U.S. Department of Labor, there were 20 million new workers added to the labor market between 1976 and 1988, a 30 percent growth rate. During this time the competition for available openings has sometimes been rather fierce. This has resulted in a higher average unemployment rate since the mid 1970s than in any period since World War II. Three groups have accounted for many of the new workers — women, baby boomers, and immigrants.

Women have been a major factor in the increase in our workforce. More of them work outside the home than ever before, and they stay in the labor market longer. For the first time in the history of this country, over 50 percent of women with young children work outside the home. Those who do have babies tend to return to work much sooner and in higher numbers than in the past. This trend will continue with three of every five new labor market entrants being female.[8]

While the baby boomers have mostly now entered the workforce, their large numbers have swelled the number of more experienced workers to unprecedented levels. New immigrants have also helped increase the number of available workers and will continue to do so. Since 1970, over 10 million legal immigrants have been absorbed into our labor market, plus an estimated eight to 12 million illegal immigrants.[9] While projected growth in the labor force is expected to moderate, another 18 million new workers are anticipated by the year 2000, a 15 percent increase. This slower but still substantial growth rate has been affected by the declining number of 16 to 24-year-olds entering the labor force. The average new worker will be older and more educated, on average, than in the past.

Fewer Jobs Exist in Large Organizations

While many more people have poured into the job market, larger companies have actually decreased the number of people they hire. Each year *FORTUNE* magazine provides data on the 500 largest corporations in America — the Fortune 500. Look at the following chart that shows the numbers employed by the Fortune 500. From 1979 to 1990, the Fortune 500 reduced the number of people they employed by over three million people. The percentage of the workforce they employed dropped from 18 percent to 11 percent during the same period. During this time, many large corporations "downsized" as the result of competitive pressures and new technologies. This downsizing continues, with 400,000 fewer workers in 1988, 200,000 fewer in 1989, and 324,000 fewer in 1990. The factories and refineries are simply more efficient, putting out more goods and services with fewer workers.

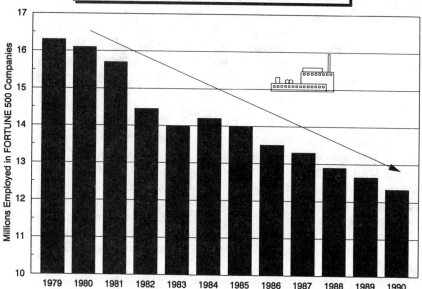

Besides the millions of factory workers who lost their jobs, the ranks of middle management were also greatly reduced over the past decade. Long-term employees from all levels of the corporate hierarchy were suddenly looking for work. With frequent layoffs, few new people were hired and far fewer opportunities for advancement were created.

More College Graduates Expected

As the baby boomers have moved through the educational system, unprecedented numbers have gone on to a rapidly expanded college system. More college-educated people have joined the workforce than ever before. Because the economy could not absorb them rapidly enough, many have ended up competing for jobs not normally held by college graduates. That resulted in others, without degrees, being bumped out of those jobs. And they, in turn, bumped out those with even less education. As a result, the educational level required for entry to many jobs has increased. Competition for entry-level jobs held by college graduates has also gone up during the employer's market of the 1970s and 80s through now, though future demand for college grads looks quite good.[10]

Good Paying, Low-Skill Jobs in Short Supply

Before 1975 or so, many high school graduates and even drop-outs could get a reasonably well-paying job at the local factory. With the downsizing of larger corporations, the loss of union dominance in many industries (from 1989 to 1990, the percent of union workers dropped from 16.4 to 16.1 and has been dropping for many years), and the overall huge reduction in manufacturing jobs, there are far fewer well-paying, low-skill level jobs. The relatively few such jobs that do open up are quickly filled by more experienced older workers or those with more seniority or training. Younger workers without technical training or college education are doing very poorly in today's economy. And for most of them, it's not going to get any better.

Education and Earnings Are Closely Associated

It is clear that people with lower educational attainment are not doing well in our new economy. Young males are now marrying later, for example, because most cannot afford families unless they obtain more education or become established in their careers. A college graduate earns over $10,000 a year more than a high school graduate. Over a decade, a college graduate's earnings will be between $100,000 and $150,000 more, enough to make a big difference in lifestyle and more than enough to pay off any cost of attending college. Over a lifetime, the difference in earnings is about a half million dollars.

Not only do those with more education earn more money, they are also more likely to be in the labor market. About 85 percent of women and 95 percent of men with college degrees are in the labor market as compared to 78 percent of male high school drop-outs and only 47 percent of female high school drop-outs.[11] This one-two punch of significantly lower earnings and lower labor market participation has profound effects on family income. Women with little education who are single heads of households are likely to have a particularly bleak economic future.

Following is a chart showing the average earnings for various family situations. The information comes from the Department of Labor's *Employment and Earnings* report and clearly shows the earnings differential for various family situations[12]. Note that these figures are average and that the effect of educational level would make them far more dramatic.

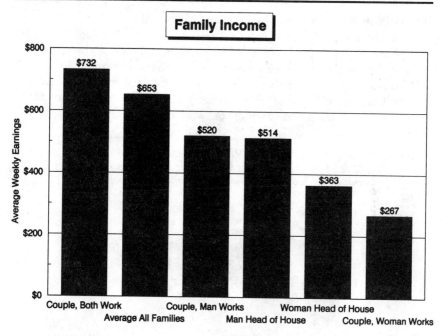

Family Income

College graduates tend to marry college graduates, and with more two income families, the family income of those with more education is much higher when compared to those with less education. It is a situation where the poor (and uneducated) get poorer and the rich (and educated) get richer. The solution is to obtain higher levels of education and academic achievement.

The Good News: Good Jobs Are Out There and You Can Learn to Find Them

Even though our economy has experienced a great upheaval, there is ample evidence that many people are doing quite well in it. Let's look at the trends in our economy having a positive side and examine ways to benefit from them.

There Are More Jobs Than Ever Before

Our economy has absorbed almost all of the new workers who have poured into it. As I mentioned earlier, many millions of new jobs have been created to employ the new workers who have come into the workforce since the mid 1970s. While our unemployment did go up during this time, it would have been much higher if not for the rapid expansion of our economy. Only during the recession of the early 1980s did the unemployment rate go above 9 percent. It has steadily decreased since then to rates, at times, well below 6 percent.[13]

Many New Jobs Are in Small Businesses

About two-thirds of all workers in the private sector work in small businesses. Small businesses, as defined by the U.S. Department of Labor, are those with 250 or fewer workers. These businesses are clearly the source of most of the new jobs in our economy. Look at the chart to below. It is based on information gathered by the U.S. Department of Labor from each state (the ES 202 form) and clearly shows the importance of smaller employers to our workforce.

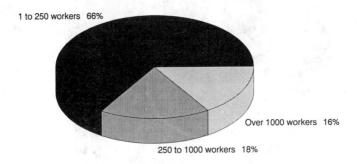

Where People Work - Most People Work in Small Organizations

1 to 250 workers 66%

Over 1000 workers 16%

250 to 1000 workers 18%

Distribution of Workers
According to Organization Size

An economist named David Burch has researched the job-generating ability of various sized businesses. His striking conclusion is that the smallest companies — those with 20 or fewer employees — are responsible for creating as many as 80 percent of the net new jobs.[14] While larger employers will remain an important source of employment, small businesses seem to be far more important in our new economy than ever before. They cannot be ignored as a major source of employment opportunities.

Service Jobs Are Growing Rapidly

Virtually all of the new jobs that have been created since 1960 have been in the service economy. The chart that follows shows the increase in the number of people working since 1940 as well as the numbers working in major segments of the economy.[15] Notice that government jobs have increased modestly during this time and manufacturing (goods producing) jobs have remained fairly stable. The growth has obviously been in the service industry.

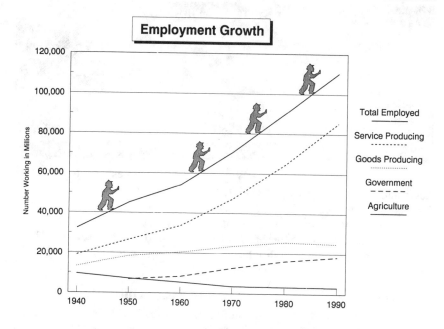

There is great misunderstanding about our becoming a "service" economy and what that means. Many people ask if we are becoming a nation of fast food workers being paid low wages. The answer is no, we are not. It is true that the number of people working in restaurants and retail stores has been going up. But these jobs are in what is called the "retail trade" sector of our economy.

About 75 percent of our workforce is now employed in the service sector and the percentage is expected to increase to about 78 percent by the year 2000. Only about 18 percent of these jobs are in retail trade. Here are the facts:

Trends in the Service-Producing Sector[16]				
	% Distribution of Total Employment		Growth 1988-2000	
	Actual 1988	Projected 2000	%	Number
Services, including education and hospitals	31.8	35.1	28.1	9,702,000
Retail trade	17.8	18.3	19.7	3,765,000
Government excluding local education and hospitals	8.3	7.6	6.6	589,000
Finance, insurance, and real estate	6.2	6.1	16.3	1,086,000

Trends in the Service-Producing Sector[16]				
	% Distribution of Total Employment		Growth 1988-2000	
	Actual 1988	Projected 2000	%	Number
Wholesale trade	5.7	5.7	15.1	908,000
Transportation, communications and utilities	5.2	4.9	9.9	548,000
TOTALS	75%		77.8%	

Jobs in what is technically called the "services" sector include occupations such as those in the health, business, education, and other services. This is the fastest growing sector of our economy and many of the jobs pay quite well. Doctors, lab technicians, optometrists, attorneys, accountants, and other specialists are some of the jobs included in this sector. These higher-paying and fast growth jobs also tend to require higher levels of skill and specialized training or education.

The Goods-Producing Sector Will Increase Only Slightly

Some sectors of the goods-producing industries will increase but the largest sector, manufacturing, will decline. This is in spite of an overall projected 15 percent increase for new job creation in the 1990s. It is clear that manufacturing jobs are declining in importance as a source of employment, even though some segments, such as plastic products, publishing, printing and medical-equipment related jobs are expected to increase. The table that follows provides projections for the goods-producing industries.

Trends in the Goods-Producing Sector[17]				
	% Distribution of Total Employment		Growth 1988-2000	
	Actual 1988	Projected 2000	%	Number
Construction	4.8	4.8	14.8	60,000
Agriculture, forestry, fishing	1.5	1.4	5.5	91,000
Manufacturing	18.0	15.4	-1.6	-314,000
Mining	.7	.6	-2.2	-16,000
TOTALS	25.0%		22.2%	-179,000

While the goods-producing sector is projected to shrink from 25 percent to 22 percent of the total jobs by the year 2000, service jobs are absorbing those losses and adding many more jobs. This is similar to what happened during what has come to be called the "industrial revolution" that occurred during the last century. Before then, well over half of the American workforce was in agriculture. Over the years, technological improvements reduced the percentage of workers on farms to about 3 percent, while those working in manufacturing increased dramatically. We may now be in the midst of a similar "service revolution" of similar magnitude. As manufacturing processes become more efficient and goods become more reliable, we will require fewer and fewer workers to produce and maintain the goods we need. Just as we have more food now than ever before with only a small percentage of our workforce producing it, we are moving towards fewer workers producing the manufactured goods we need.

Many New Jobs Pay Well — but Require More Education or Training

The average job in our economy pays over $22,000. To many, that is a higher amount than they would have guessed. Averages, however, can be misleading. If you separate the levels of compensation by education, a different picture emerges. In the chart titled "More Education = Higher Earnings" presented earlier in this chapter, you saw that the average high school graduate earns about $19,000 per year while the average college graduate earns about $33,000 per year. That is a considerable difference for the four years of additional education it took to obtain it. But remember that these are average earnings. People just starting out will often make considerably less and some will earn considerably more.

It is clear that average earnings go up with educational attainment. Some people with lower educational attainment do have higher than average earnings but dramatically fewer than those with higher levels of education. Earnings of those in the top 20 percent of income (about $31,000 per year or more) are also education-related as indicated in the chart that follows. Note that very few of those with a high school education or less are among the highest earners.

High Earnings by Level of Education[18]		
	Percent Earning Over	
	$600/week	$1,000/week
Less Than 4 Years of High School	6.0	0.6
4 Years of High School	11.9	1.5
1 to 3 Years of College	19.4	3.6
4 Years of College	34.9	10.3

High Earnings by Level of Education[18]		
	Percent Earning Over	
	$600/week	$1,000/week
5 or More Years of College	47.9	18.5
All Levels of Education Average	19.5	4.8

The types of occupations are related to education too. About 95 percent of those with 5 or more years of education are in professional specialty, managerial, technical and sales occupations while only 17 percent of those with less than four years of high school were. Generally, occupations that are growing rapidly also require higher educational attainment. For example, technicians, professionals, and executives/ administrators/ managers are the three fastest growing major occupational groups. All of these usually require education or training beyond high school. The occupations that are declining most rapidly include machine operators, fabricators, laborers and agriculture, forestry, and fishery workers. All of these groups have the highest proportion of workers with less than a high school education and also have the lowest earnings.

While some high school graduates do find well-paying jobs, they are becoming the exception. Some of these jobs include truck driver, secretary, data processing equipment repairers, police and firefighters, machinists, computer operators, tool and die makers and others. But many of these occupations also require substantial on-the-job training and considerable academic proficiency and talent.[19]

Chapter 6 will show you how to obtain additional information on various jobs, their anticipated growth rates, earnings, and entry requirements. If you are considering changing careers or want to advance to higher levels of responsibility in your current field, that chapter will be of particular interest.

Trade and Technical Training are Alternatives to a College Degree

More education clearly pays off in the job market but it should be noted that college is not the only route to higher earnings, since many trade, technical, sales and other fields offer similar benefits. A well-trained plumber, automechanic, chef, computer repair technician, police officer, tool and die maker, or medical technologist can all do quite well in our economy. These and many other occupations require one to two years of specialized training and some apprenticeship programs allow for on-the-job training. Outstanding people in sales, small business, management, self-employment and other activities can still do quite well without a college degree or technical training, though more education is often required to compete for the better positions. Plenty of jobs exist in large but slower-growing occupations.

While there is plenty of glamour in occupations that are growing rapidly, many jobs will continue to become available in occupations that are growing slowly or even declining. Jobs will become available to replace those who retire or leave for other reasons and opportunities will exist in virtually all areas for those with superior abilities, motivation and/or preparation.

More Education Pays Off in Other Ways, Too

It is clear that education and training pay off in higher average earnings. These people are in more demand in the job market. Look at the chart that follows to see how unemployment rates go down as educational attainment goes up.[20] People with more education not only earn more money but they also experience lower unemployment rates. This combination results in much higher average earnings and less economic disruption.

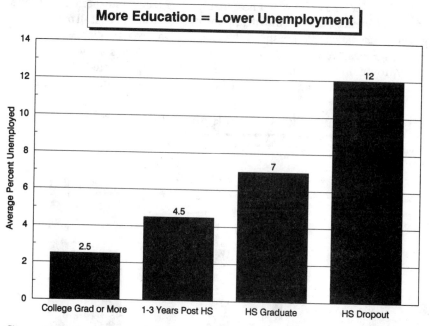

More Education = Lower Unemployment

Shortages are Anticipated in Many Jobs

Lower-paying jobs, such as those in the trade sector (food service workers, cashiers, etc.) have been typically filled by young people and those with few job-related skills and low educational attainment. In many parts of the country, employers cannot hire these workers at minimum wage any longer. A big reason is that there are fewer young people entering the job market. The number of new entrants peaked in 1979 and has continually decreased since. While immigrants and women without post high school education have taken many of these jobs, our rapidly expanding economy has generated more demand for people to fill these positions. In accord with the law of supply and demand, entry wages for these jobs are going up. Many of the fast-food chains are even actively recruiting older workers — a previously untapped source of employees.

Other occupations have also experienced or are anticipating shortages of qualified workers for a variety of reasons. As a result of expanded opportunities for women, fewer qualified women now seek jobs such as secretaries, nurses, teachers and other occupations that have traditionally employed many females. Shortages in these occupations now make them good occupational choices for qualified men or women.

Six of the fastest growing jobs between now and the year 2000 are expected to be in the medical area. Business services of all kinds are also expected to require more trained workers, as will technology-oriented jobs. Chapter 6 provides growth projections for various jobs and note that most of them are expected to require additional workers. But note also that, as mentioned earlier, almost all of the fastest growing occupations require special training or advanced education.

One measure of the demand for various skill levels of workers is the unemployment rate. In the previous section I presented the data on unemployment rates based on level of education. Following is a chart that

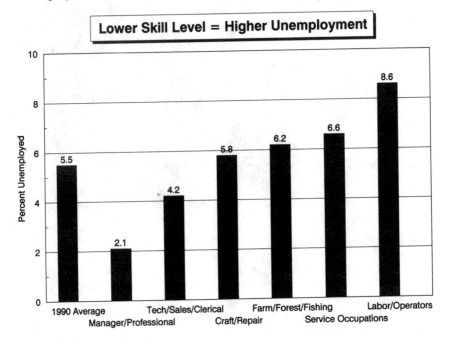

Lower Skill Level = Higher Unemployment

provides data on the unemployment rates for broad categories of workers.[21] Once again, it is clear that occupations requiring higher levels of training and education are in more demand.

The Bottom Line: Career Planning and Job Seeking Skills Give a Competitive Edge

More frequent job and career changes, less long-term security with any one organization, rapid technological change, and an ongoing demand for new job-related skills all point to continued disruption in the employment of most working people. For those who are unprepared, this can spell economic and personal disaster. New economic survival skills are needed for our new economy and you can ignore them only at your peril.

Change presents both problems and opportunities. While the new labor market realities do create problems for many people, there are, in my opinion, many ways that you can take advantage of the current job market — if you know how. The more important strategies for success in the new economy are presented in the section that follows. Other chapters in the book will give you many specific techniques for defining and getting the job you want.

Upgrade Your Job Skills and Keep Doing It

Too many people think that once they get their "credentials" they are set for life. Not so. No matter how much education or training you already have, you will need more to move ahead in your present job — or even to keep it.

It is increasingly important for people in all occupational areas to keep learning new things. Computers, for example, have revolutionized the way many people work. One study indicated that approximately 40 percent of all U.S. workers now use a computer for at least part of their day. Executives, accountants, secretaries, warehouse workers, accounting clerks, doctors, managers, cashiers and many others use computers on a regular basis. Over time, most jobs will incorporate computer and other new technologies.

If you are unfamiliar with a new technology that might affect your job, you should consider going back to school or learn to use it in some other way. Constantly look for ways to apply new techniques to your own job to increase your productivity. Finish that degree you have always wanted to get. Sign up for any relevant training related to your job. Be willing to try out new things. It is no longer enough to "put in your time" since the world will surely continue to change around you.

Avoid the "Boxes" in Your Life

Most people separate their life activities into the three major categories of playing, learning, and working. One way they do this is by age, emphasizing playing as the major activity for young children, learning and being educated for youth, working for adults and, finally, retirement and a return to playing again.

Richard Bolles, in a book titled *The Three Boxes Of Life*[22] has defined these three activities — playing, learning, and working — as the three boxes that too many people put themselves in. Instead, he suggests we should strive to incorporate playing, learning, **and** working into all aspects of our lives. Working, for example, can also be playing as well as an ongoing learning experience. Ideally, that is what good career and life planning should help you achieve — a balance between leisure, learning, and working rather than a separation.

Incorporate Life-Planning into Your Job Search

Your current priority may be to find your next job. That is a worthy objective and this book will show you a variety of techniques to accomplish that. But before you begin, take a bit more time to define more clearly what, precisely, you want and need from a job. And consider how that job might help you go where you want to go with your life. It will be time well spent.

Good career planning is extremely important but it should be done in the context of what you want to do with your life. How can you, for example, incorporate elements of pleasure and learning into your next job?

Develop Your Life-Long Skills

You will likely change jobs and careers again and again during your life. And whatever job skills you now have will need to be continually upgraded. This makes it increasingly important for you to know what you are particularly good at doing and develop those skills throughout your life.

Consider Small Organizations

More and more of us now work in small organizations. Over time, an increasing number of us will spend at least part of our working lives working in (or starting up) a small business. Smaller organizations offer excellent opportunities for young people to gain experience and for more experienced workers to apply their skills. And smaller organizations are now just as secure, on the average, as larger ones. They will become increasingly important as a source of jobs in the future. This book will help you learn job search techniques that are effective in finding jobs in small as well as larger organizations. If working in a small organization is a new idea to you, consider it.

Do Things You Enjoy Doing

Having been unemployed myself, I very well know that earning a living can sometimes be a difficult task. And over the years I have done many things that I did not enjoy to earn a living. But having fun or finding satisfaction with what we do with our lives is what it is all about. Get both if you can.

Chapter One Endnotes

On footnotes in general: I am not trying to write a scholarly work, so my footnotes will be informal throughout this book. I do try to keep up with current labor market information but consider myself a practitioner rather than a researcher. I am interested in techniques that help job seekers get better jobs in less time and much of my experience in this area has been gained by running job search programs rather than reading research studies. For this reason, some things that I KNOW work well are not referenced at all. They are my own techniques and observations on what works. Still, the research related to how the job market works is a very important part of knowing what works and I have included references where I thought it important.

1. Howe, Wayne, "Labor Market Dynamics and Trends in Male and Female Unemployment," *Monthly Labor Review*, published by the U.S. Department of Labor, 1990, vol. 113, no. 11. Data on unemployment rates come from the January 1991 edition of *Employment and Earnings*, published by the U.S. Department of Labor. The best data on job change comes from census data that is collected each month and published by the U.S. Department of Labor. The January 1991 edition of DOL's *Employment and Earnings* indicated that an average of 5.4 percent of the civilian labor market were unemployed in 1990. With the average duration of unemployment being 12.1 weeks, you can compute the percentage of people experiencing unemployment a year as 22 percent. That is a very high percentage of people experiencing unemployment, though about 40 percent of them are new labor market entrants or reentrants.

2 How often a person changes jobs is closely related to age and income, which is, in turn, related to educational level. An article titled "Occupational Tenure, Employer Tenure, and Occupational Mobility," published in the *Occupational Outlook Quarterly*, Summer 1990, provides a good review of how all this works. The mean duration on the job for 16 to 24-year-olds is only 1.9 years, while for 25 to 34-year-olds, it jumps to 5.4 years and goes to 10 years for 35 to 44-year-olds. Averages are considerably higher since they include people who change jobs very often and the mean, as used in the figures above, may be a more meaningful way to look at this.

3. Ibid.

4. A study by Ellen Sehgal titled "Occupational Mobility and Job Tenure in 1983," published in the *Monthly Labor Review* vol. 107, no. 10, indicated that over 7 percent of employed adults were changing careers that year — a rate of between 6 and 7 career changes during the average person's work life. More recent data published in the U.S. Department of Labor's

Occupational Outlook Quarterly Summer 1990 edition, in an article titled "Occupational Tenure, Employer Tenure, and Occupational Mobility" indicated that the average occupational tenure was 6.6 years. Over a work life of 45 years, that would result in 6.8 career changes.

5. Back in 1973, a series of questions were asked in the "Current Population Survey" of 60,000 households and is the most valid study on how people find jobs. The details were published by the DOL in 1975 and can be found in chapter 2 of this book. Later studies have confirmed this data, including a study by Camil Associates under a project funded by DOL.

6. Wegmann's book is titled *Work in the New Economy*, published by JIST Works, Inc. I was the editor for this book and have been a Wegmann fan for years. His book provides an extraordinarily thorough review of the trends outlined in this chapter with much more detail and supportive research. Dr.Wegmann has devoted himself to researching the labor market and how a job seeker can benefit from what he uncovers. I consider him to be THE expert on this topic. If you are interested in this topic, his is the best book that I can recommend.

7. The DOL also keeps track of where people work. While the economy has created over 30 million new jobs since 1970 and projects another 18 million in the 1990s, the manufacturing sector has not grown at all and is projected to decline slightly in the 1990s.

8. From the U.S. Department of Labor's *Occupational Outlook Quarterly*, "Outlook 2000," vol. 33, no. 3.

9. Wegmann, op.cit., cites a number of sources for this data.

10. There have been several articles on the plight of college graduates published in the *Occupational Outlook Quarterly*, published by the U. S. Department of Labor including one in the Fall 1990 edition.

11. From the *Monthly Labor Review*, published by the U.S. Department of Labor, vol. 113, no. 11, November, 1990.

12. This data is from the U.S. Department of Labor's *Employment and Earnings*, January 1991.

13. Ibid.

14. Burch, David, "The Job Generation Process," submitted to the U.S. Department of Commerce, 1979. Burch has also written numerous articles since then, including a series for *INC.* magazine that support the same findings.

15. *Employment and Earnings*, op.cit.

16. From the *Occupational Outlook Quarterly*, vol. 33, no. 3, Fall, 1989.

17. Ibid.

18. This information came from a good article on this topic titled "High-Earning Workers Who Don't Have A College Degree," published in the *Occupational Outlook Quarterly*, Fall, 1990.

19. Ibid.

20. *Employment and Earnings*, op. cit.

21. Ibid.

22. Bolles, Richard, *The Three Boxes of Life*, Ten Speed Press, 1981.

Chapter Two

Using Job Search Methods That Really Work

Looking for a job is hard work. If you are lucky, you may find one quickly. But finding even entry level jobs can take a long time if you don't know how.

The average adult spends three to five months finding a new job.[1] When unemployment rates are high, you can be out of work even longer. But some people find jobs faster than others, even in times of high unemployment. What do they do differently? While I'm sure the answers are sometimes complex, there are only two primary reasons why some people get jobs faster than others:

The Bottom Line:
What It Takes to Get a Job in Less Time

1. People who spend more time actually looking for work find jobs faster than those spending less time.

2. Some people get more interviews. And the more interviews you get, the more likely you are to get a job offer.

The bottom line is that people who spend more time on their job search and who get more interviews will usually get jobs faster. The average job seeker spends fewer than 15 hours a week looking for a job and gets fewer than two interviews. Part of the problem is that the traditional approach to the job search leads to many dead ends and rapid discouragement. Another part of the problem is that job seekers define an interview too narrowly. By doing this, they make obtaining an interview harder than it needs to be.

This chapter will deal with both of those problems. There are a variety of job search methods and some work much better than others. The most effective ones help you remain active in your job search and do not encourage you to wait until someone calls you. These techniques can dramatically increase the number of interviews you can get. They only work, of course, if you use them.

While this chapter does provide you with a variety of job finding techniques, additional methods found in later chapters will cover topics such as interviewing, making phone contacts, resumes, developing a job search schedule and more. When used together, these techniques do work.

Traditional vs. Nontraditional Job-Seeking Methods

Most people use a variety of techniques to find job openings. For example, one person might read want ads, fill out applications, and ask friends for leads. Each of these methods works for some people. Which methods are best for you? Let's look at various job-search methods to find out.

Traditional Job Search Methods

Traditional means it's the way people have "always" done things. That doesn't mean it's the best way, it's just the way that everyone knows. Traditional job search methods are not always the most effective ones, but some people do find jobs through them. One or more of these methods can result in your getting a good lead. Here are some frequently used traditional methods:

- Reading the help wanted ads in the newspaper
- Going to personnel offices and filling out applications
- Sending out resumes
- Going to the local Employment Service office
- Signing up with a private employment agency

Since so many people know about and use most of these methods in an active job search, let's take a closer look at them.

Traditional Job Search Method 1: The Help Wanted Ads

Since almost everyone who is looking for a job reads the want ads, they must be a good place to look for jobs, right? Not entirely. One of the very reasons they are **not** great sources for good job leads is that so many people do read them.

Let's do a little arithmetic to illustrate my point. The research indicates that about 10 percent of the workforce read the want ads.[2] In a city of 200,000 people, 130,000 people (about 65 percent) would be in the workforce and about 13,000 will be reading those ads. If there were 500 good ads for real jobs, that would be an average of 260 people per advertised job. For the jobs that say something like "good pay and benefits, no previous experience required," there are even more interested people. Let's say that twice as many people would be interested in this ad than normal. That would be 520 people who would be interested in that particular advertised job. If you were interested in that job, you would be about one-fifth of 1 percent of those interested, a slim chance indeed of getting that job. Figure out the odds for your own newspaper's distribution area. The competition is fierce!

As if that is not bad enough, another problem is that **most jobs are never advertised**. Various studies have found that about only 15 percent of all jobs are advertised, which leaves the other 85 percent that are not.[3] They are in the "hidden" job market, something you will learn more about soon.

While the odds are not in your favor, some jobs **are** advertised and this makes want ads worth looking at on a regular basis. Sunday and Wednesday newspapers have the most ads and you should look at all the ads on those days. The ones you are interested in may not be listed in an obvious way. An accounting job, for example, could be listed under "Accounting," or "Bookkeeper," or "Controller" or several other key words. Respond to any ad that sounds interesting, even if you don't have all the qualifications listed. Employers sometimes list things they do not require to limit the response. Another tip to increase your odds is to look at want ads that were placed in newspapers that are a month or so old. You can be certain that those organizations will need people with those same skills at some time in the future. Or perhaps the person they hired is not working out. Or maybe there is a similar job that might open up soon.

Why Employers Don't Like to Advertise

Employers don't advertise job openings for many reasons. The most common reasons are:

- They don't like to.
- When they do, it can be a lot of work.
- They often don't need to.

Let's look at each reason.

Employers don't like to advertise. When employers put an ad in the paper, they have to interview all sorts of strangers. Most employers are not trained interviewers and don't enjoy it. They have to interview job seekers who do their best to create a good impression. And they have to eliminate most of them by finding their weaknesses. It's not fun for either side.

Employers find that advertising can cause a lot of extra work. A business associate recently advertised for a receptionist and said 80 applicants responded. The large number of inquiries disrupted the phones and office routine and required considerable time to handle. All but five were screened out based on their applications and resumes. They interviewed five and got down to the final two, one of whom came in after hearing about the opening from the receptionist who was leaving. After all that work, they hired the job seeker who had never read the ad because they knew more about her from the recommendation they got from their trusted employee. Some organizations get hundreds or even thousands of applicants for each job opening. To the employer, they are all strangers that may or may not be telling the complete truth. And employers would really rather not have to interview strangers unless they have to.

Often, employers don't need to advertise. Most jobs are filled before advertising is needed. The employer may already know someone who seems to be right for the job. Or someone hears about the job and gets an interview before it is advertised. Often, employers hire someone who's been recommended to them by a friend or associate. Employers are much more comfortable hiring a person they know is good rather than someone they don't know at all. It's that simple.

Traditional Job Search Method 2: Personnel Offices and Application Forms

The personnel office is not a job seeker's best friend, and neither is an application form. When you think about it, just why does such an office exist, anyway? A person who works there might tell you that their job is to help their organization find qualified people to fill jobs by screening applicants. The question is, from the job seeker's point of view, who is getting screened? It's the job seeker — and it usually means getting screened out.

If you don't believe this, ask someone who has worked in a personnel office. They will tell you that for each person who is hired, 10 or more are not. Sometimes hundreds are screened out for each one hired. What makes this even worse is that personnel people don't actually **hire** anyone unless they will be working in personnel. They screen most job seekers out and then, if the position is still open, and **if** you weren't screened out, you get to meet the person who could eventually hire you. If you make it to the interview stage — and the chances are slim that you will — you are just one of several others being interviewed. This further reduces your chances of getting a job offer to maybe 5 percent or less.

While those odds seem terrible, they are even worse when you consider that many employers end up hiring someone who wasn't even referred by personnel. Jobs are often filled before personnel even knows they are open. I have hired many people while working within larger organizations and I know this to be a fact. I often would recruit informally for weeks before the position I was trying to fill worked its way through the formal channels and became posted in the personnel office. By then, I often had one or more good candidates who had the inside track on that job. The last thing I wanted was to get a lot of people referred to me from personnel. They would all be strangers, they would all try to manipulate me into thinking they were great, and they would take up a lot of my time.

If you still are skeptical, have you ever noticed how job seekers are treated in a personnel office? The furniture is usually inexpensive, sturdy, and uncomfortable. The walls are decorated with signs saying everything but "sit down and be quiet." But if the signs don't say that, the clerk might. When I was job seeking, I've had applications pushed at me with an announcement like, "Take one of those pencils and complete this application, then wait until someone can give you an interview." It makes you feel unimportant, doesn't it?

And one more thing — only larger organizations have personnel offices. Smaller organizations don't have them at all, nor do many branch offices of larger organizations. A job seeker who assumes that getting a job requires finding personnel offices will miss most of the jobs that are out there.

Filling Out Applications

Much of what I said about personnel offices applies to applications as well. Application forms are specifically designed to collect information that can be used to screen you out. And many smaller organizations don't even have them. It is always better to ask to see the person in charge than to ask to complete an application. Fill out an application if you are asked to, but don't expect it to get you an interview. I'll give you more details on completing applications in a later chapter.

Traditional Job Search Method 3: Sending Out Resumes

The resume has been around for ages. So have the "experts" who will advise you to send yours out by the hundreds. This approach does have its appeal — it seems easy, and almost every job search book recommends it. The problem is, it doesn't work very well. Like an application, a resume is the near-perfect tool for someone to screen you out. As a result, you should expect a **very** low response rate, in the neighborhood of 2 to 5 percent, if you mail out unsolicited resumes.

The effectiveness of sending out unsolicited resumes varies by industry and job. It might be that you have skills in short supply, like nursing, so sending out unsolicited resumes might work to get you interviews. But overall, it is clear that this is not an effective technique for most people.

In a study of resume effectiveness conducted by Deutsch, Shea and Evans, Inc., and titled "Technical Manpower Recruitment Practices," it took an average of 1,470 resumes for each job offer actually accepted using this method. That is not what I would consider good odds. Of course, you could be the exception, but for most people, sending out unsolicited resumes only helps support the post office. It is almost always better to contact the employer in person. Then send or bring your resume to the interviewer before the interview. Resumes will be covered in more detail in a later chapter.

Traditional Job Search Method 4: The Federal / State Employment Service

Required by Federal law, each state has a series of offices that provide assistance to job seekers in locating job openings. Going by different names in different states, these offices also administer the unemployment compensation program and are often referred to as the "unemployment office" as a result. You should also note that these agencies are publicly funded and **never** charge a fee.

Only about 5 percent of all workers get their jobs from this source. And most offices know of only about 5 percent of the existing job openings in their area. Richard Lathrop, in a book titled *The Job Market*, [4] found that only one in six who went to the employment service obtained a job there and only about half held those jobs for over 30 days. He also found that the jobs paid much lower than average. That all sounds very negative and I will show you better sources of job leads. But some offices, in some areas, are MUCH more active than in others, listing as many as 30 percent of the available openings in that area. Some states now provide job search workshops and other helpful services too.[5] Don't expect miracles but do consider a weekly visit. The staff sees hundreds of people a week, so ask for the same person each time. If you impress them, they might remember you when they see a good job opening being listed and refer you to it.

Traditional Job Search Method 5: Private Employment Agencies

Only about 5 percent of all people get their jobs through private' employment agencies. And only one in 20 who use them actually get their jobs through them.[6] To put it mildly, a 95 percent failure rate is not a good record.

These agencies also charge fees — often substantial ones — to either you or the employer. Fees range from 10 to 15 percent of your annual salary. For each $10,000 you earn a year, your fee will be between $1,000 and $1,500. Figure it out for your annual salary. That is a lot of money — entirely too much, I think, for most people to consider.

Don't expect much meaningful counseling from them either, especially if the employer pays the fees. It's obvious the agencies are working for **them**, not you. The people who work in private employment agencies are typically sales people who are paid a commission on the fees they earn. They are not career counselors, so you won't get much help if you have a problem (been fired, changing careers, etc.). What they will want is a quick fee, payable before you start your next job or soon after. And to get that, they may encourage you to accept a position that is less than you are qualified for.

You should also watch out for want ads placed by these agencies. There are lots of them in most papers. The advertised job may not exist, and they may try to refer you to another one paying less money. And NEVER sign an agreement without taking it home and studying it. Never. If you are pressured to sign, walk away.

Unless the employer pays the fee, using a private employment agency is not a good idea for most people. The exceptions might be if you have skills that are very much in demand or are working full-time and have a limited amount of time to look. Remember that most of the jobs they find are uncovered by calling up businesses listed in the *Yellow Pages* or by reading the want ads. You can do this yourself and keep the money. I'll show you how in this very book.

The Bottom Line: **Traditional Job Search Methods Encourage Inactivity**

Traditional job search methods all require you to depend on **someone else** to do something to let you know about an opening — put an ad in the paper, respond to your resume, look at your application and call you in for an interview, etcetera. They all force you to be passive, indirect, and dependent. I believe that these traditional job search methods foster a sense of helplessness and eventually hopelessness. While any one of the methods can and do work for some people, they represent, in total, only about one-third of the methods people use to actually get jobs. You can do much better.

The Hidden Job Market

Robert Wegmann has done extensive research on this subject. In his book titled *Work in the New Economy*,[7] he concludes that as many as 70 to 75 percent of all job openings are not "visible" to job seekers using traditional methods. Most jobs are not advertised. Only 15 percent of all people get their jobs through the want ads. Jobs available through private and government employment agencies are also considered public knowledge. Anyone can find out about them. But these **advertised** openings add up to only about 25 percent of all job openings. The other 75 percent or so are hidden from you if you use traditional job search methods. So **your** job search should be a search for these hidden jobs, in addition to the jobs that are advertised.

How Do People Really Find Jobs?

While you will hear varied opinions about how to look for a job, most job search advisors (and, sadly, many people who write job search books) seem unaware of some important facts — like just how people really **do** find jobs. By far the largest (and therefore the most valid) survey asking people how they found their jobs was taken by the U.S. Department of Labor in the mid-1970s. They surveyed 10.4 million people and published the results in Bulletin 1886, "Job-Seeking Methods Used by American Workers." People were asked which job search method they used to find their present job, or — if they were not employed — their most recent job. The following chart summarizes the findings along with those of another study by Camil Associates, under contract with the Department of Labor. Their study was based on a study of employers and did not include civil service job-holders. While the studies are not precisely the same, they do provide us with important information on how people find jobs.[8]

How People Find Jobs		
	Dept. of Labor %	Camil study %
Heard about opening from people I know:	28.4	34.0
Contacted employer directly:	34.9	29.8
Answered want ad:	13.9	16.6
Referred by private employment agency:	5.6	5.6
Referred by state employment service:	5.1	5.6
Referred by school placement office:	3.0	3.0
Took civil service tests:	2.1	N/A
Union hiring:	1.5	1.4
Other methods:	5.5	4.0
Examples: placed ads in journals; went to places where employers come to hire people; and so on.		

Let's take this data and organize it visually for more impact. The pie chart that follows is based on the averages of the two studies cited above. From it, you can clearly see that informal, nontraditional job search methods are a far more important source of openings than are those available through traditional sources.

Traditional vs. Informal Job Search Methods

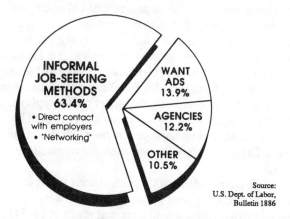

INFORMAL
JOB-SEEKING
METHODS
63.4%
• Direct contact
with employers
• "Networking"

WANT
ADS
13.9%

AGENCIES
12.2%

OTHER
10.5%

Source:
U.S. Dept. of Labor,
Bulletin 1886

This chart shows that only two job-seeking methods — direct contact with employers and getting leads from people you know — are used to find about two-thirds of all jobs. For these reasons, most of this chapter (and this book) emphasizes nontraditional or **informal** job-seeking methods. These are the methods that open doors to the hidden job market.

For Most People, "Luck" Is the Most Important Element in Their Job Search — but Should It Be?

In spite of all the books telling us how to read want ads and send out resumes, and in spite of the national "system" of private and public employment agencies, most people get their jobs by informal methods such as word of mouth or going directly to an employer. It is unfortunate however, that most have done so without any organized approach to it. The result is lost time — and time is money. Since very few people have any formal job search training, they waste much of their time using ineffective methods that needlessly lengthen their unemployment period and drain their confidence.

Some Job Search Theory

Well, you might say, all this is very enlightening, but just going around talking to people doesn't seem like a substantial job search method. It's true, there is more to it than that, and I will provide the details later in this chapter. But to understand just how to be most effective in your job search, I want you to understand a bit about the **why.**

Frictional Unemployment — Where the Job Search Action Is

Friction, according to the dictionary, is "a resistance to motion when two surfaces touch." According to the U.S. Department of Labor, a similar phenomenon occurs in the job market. Called "frictional unemployment," it is a situation where job openings exist and job seekers are looking for them but they cannot seem to hook up. The Department of Labor concludes that over 40 percent of all unemployment is due to this friction.

In *The Job Market*, author Richard Lathrop argues that 40 percent is a conservative estimate.[9] He also provides extensive supportive material indicating that frictional unemployment may be **the** most important factor in unemployment. In fact, he argues, frictional unemployment **is** unemployment since the longer it takes to find a job, the higher the unemployment rate. If you could reduce the average length of time it takes to find a job by just one day, it would reduce the number of unemployed by over 300,000 people. If you could reduce it by just 10 percent, it would have the same economic impact as creating 2.5 million jobs.

This may all seem somewhat theoretical until you realize that the major cause of frictional unemployment is that most job seekers do not know how to find the jobs that exist. Lathrop estimates that much of the lost time between jobs could be avoided if only the job seeker were taught more efficient job-search methods. He points to research that documents reductions of 50 to 75 percent in average unemployment length as a result of job search training. Lathrop concludes that the lack of a national policy to provide job search training is nothing short of a national scandal. I agree. It is relatively easy to increase your job-getting skills and a shame that it is not taught in more schools and programs.

More recent studies by the Department of Labor also acknowledge the increasing importance of unemployment due to friction. In a 1990 article published in the *Monthly Labor Review*, they indicated that 41 percent of the increase in the unemployment rate was attributable to the increased **frequency** of unemployment.[10] That is to say that, as more people have experienced at least some unemployment each year, the overall unemployment rate has also gone up. With more job and career changing and relatively higher unemployment rates, the implication for national policy is enormous but largely ignored.

The good news for you is that, once you learn the proper job search techniques, you can dramatically reduce the time it takes to find a job. In job-search programs that JIST has run, we have routinely decreased the time it takes to get a job to a matter of several weeks. Though these results are from a highly structured job search program, many people who use JIST methods cut their job search time in half.[11] Once you understand that jobs are out there for you that are not advertised — and that you qualify for these jobs — the next step is learning how to find them.

The Four Stages of a Job Opening[12]

There is a practical application to the idea of frictional unemployment. It comes in an examination of how a job opening comes to be. Jobs, you see, don't just open up one day with no notice. Someone typically knows a job might open up before it actually does. Often, these jobs get filled by someone before the job is advertised. But how do you find these openings if they're not advertised? Here is the answer: **you have to learn to find employers before they advertise the job you want.** To do this, you need to understand how most jobs become available.

I have found it useful to think of a job opening as a process that occurs over time. Thinking in these terms, I identified four major stages in a job opening. To help you understand this, look at the following illustration. Each of the four stages represents a distinct phase in the history of a job opening. The definitions for each of the four stages follow the illustration.

Before a job is filled, a series of events occur. Let's go through each stage of a job opening in more detail.

FOUR STAGES OF A JOB OPENING

	FIRST STAGE	SECOND STAGE	THIRD STAGE	FOURTH STAGE
	No job opening but employers always looking for good workers.	The need is clear; the insiders know; but no action is taken.	Job now "open"-- Referrals desired; applications being accepted	Ad is in the paper. The thundering horde appears.

Stage 1: **There Is No Job Open Now.** At some point in time, before a job is actually created or available, it does not exist. If you asked an employer if they had a job opening at this stage, they would say "No." Perhaps no openings are planned or all are occupied. In the conventional job search, there would be no basis for having an interview with this employer. And most job seekers will completely ignore the opportunities that exist in this situation. Yet, should an offer become available at any time in the future, persons who are **already** known to the employer will be considered before all others.

Stage 2: **No Formal Opening Exists, but One or More Insiders Know of a Possibility.** As time goes on, someone in an organization can usually anticipate a possible future job opening before one actually opens up. It could be the result of a new marketing campaign or product, an increase in business, an observation that someone is not doing well on the job or a variety of other things. It's not always the boss who knows either. In previous jobs, I have often known that a co-worker was looking for another job even though the boss did not. Or I wondered why that person didn't get fired. Typically, if you were to ask if there were any job openings at this stage of a job opening, you would be told "No" once again. In fact, there is no opening — yet. And most job seekers would keep on looking, not realizing that a job opportunity is right before them.

Stage 3: **A Formal Opening Now Exists, But It Has Not Been Advertised.** At some point in time, the boss will finally say that, yes, they have a job opening and that they are looking for someone to fill it. But, with few exceptions, days or even weeks go by before that job will be advertised. If you were to ask if there was a job opening at this stage, you might still get a "No," depending on who you ask. In larger organizations, even the personnel office doesn't get formal notice of an opening for days or weeks after the opening is known to people who work in the affected department. And they are unlikely to know of an opening in another department. In smaller organizations, of course, most staff would know of any formal openings. In either case, once a job opening finally reaches this stage, it is the first time a person using a conventional approach to the job search might get a "Yes" response.

Stage 4: **The Job Opening Is Advertised.** As more time goes by and a job opening does not get filled, it might be advertised in the newspaper, a sign hung in the window, the Employment Service notified, or some other action taken to make the opening known to the general public. This is the stage where virtually every job seeker can know about the opening and, if the job is reasonably desirable, a thundering horde of job seekers will now come after it.

What Does This Mean to You?

It means that you can be considered for a job opening long before a formal opening exists — and long before it is advertised. In fact, that is why most jobs are never advertised. Someone like you gets there before it needs to be. Employers don't like to hire strangers. They prefer to hire people they already know or who are referred to them by someone they know. Many are willing to talk to a job seeker even before they have a job opening — if you approach them in the right way. Once you know each other, of course, you are no longer strangers.

About 25 percent of the people who get hired become known to the employer before a job opening exists. Another 25 percent or so of those who get hired find out about the opening during the second stage of a job opening. These jobs are simply not available to someone using traditional job search methods. Only about half of all jobs make it to the third stage of a job opening.

During this stage the job is at least available to a job seeker using traditional methods. If that job seeker just happens to ask the right person at the right time and if there is a job opening they will, for the first time get a "Yes" response. During this third stage another 25 percent get their jobs. With 75 percent of the jobs getting filled during the first three stages, that leaves the remaining 25 percent that get advertised and, in other ways, made available to the public. This pattern illustrates the most important job search rule of all: **Don't wait until the job is open!** The best time to search for a job is before anyone else knows about it.

Most jobs are filled by someone the employer meets before a job is formally "open." So the trick is to meet people who can hire you before a job is available. Instead of saying "Do you have any jobs open?" say "I realize you may not have any openings now, but I would still like to talk to you about the possibility of future openings." With this simple approach many employers will say "Yes" instead of "No." Not all, but many.

More Bad News for Those Using Traditional Job Search Methods

Besides missing out on half the available job openings, there are other disadvantages to those using traditional job search methods. The first is that the jobs that remain unfilled by the third and fourth stages of a job opening tend to be less desirable or harder to fill. The best jobs are often gone by then. This is even more true for the jobs that are left unfilled long enough to get advertised. There are exceptions, of course, but the better jobs tend to get taken long before they are advertised.

Jobs that make it to the third and fourth stage of a job opening face another distinct disadvantage — they have more competition. This is particularly true for advertised jobs since there are often many applicants for these jobs. During these stages an employer has the task of screening out all but one of those who are interested. Virtually all of the applicants are now strangers who will manipulate the employer by "marketing" or "selling" themselves, which means emphasizing the positive and overlooking the negative. Employers know this, so they try to find out something "wrong" with each applicant in order to eliminate them from consideration. It is the nature of the game and it is not nice.

So the job search takes on a decidedly competitive and distasteful flavor for those seeking jobs in the third and, more so, in the fourth stage of a job opening. I am not saying you should not consider jobs that are advertised — you should — it's just that you need to find ways of finding **potential** openings before others do. Or, if you prefer, you can remain unemployed longer than you really need to.

A *New Job Search Concept:* You Can "Interview" Even Before a Job Opening Formally Exists

You may not have noticed that what I have done in the previous narrative is to redefine what an "interview" is. In the conventional job search, an interview is something you can obtain only when an employer has a clearly defined job opening that you qualify for. But that definition eliminates opportunities available during the first two stages of a job opening. Here is my new definition of an interview:

> *An interview is any face-to-face contact with a person who hires or supervises people with your skills — even if there is no job opening now.*

This definition is a very important one for you to remember because it allows you to "interview" all sorts of people who you would otherwise overlook in a job search. The rest of this book assumes this new definition of an interview. This mind set opens a world of possibility. And it can help you get a job in much less time than would be possible otherwise.

Finally, You Can Conduct an Active Job Search

The problem with traditional job search methods is that they encourage you to be passive. You send in a resume and hope someone else will call you back. You depend on an employer to place a help wanted ad — and hope you don't get screened out. You fill out an application and hope you get an interview. With virtually every traditional job search method, the odds are stacked against you.

I believe that traditional methods are designed to help the employer screen people out. They all create barriers to a job seeker getting in and talking to the person who is most likely to supervise a person with their skills. And they all assume that a prospective employer and a job seeker can't see each other unless there is a job opening. But now you know otherwise.

By narrowly defining who can talk to whom, traditional job search methods have the effect of encouraging people to believe that there are few jobs out there for which they are qualified. Private or governmental employment agencies know about only a small percentage of openings, so those who go there will never know of the 95 percent of jobs never listed there. Newspapers only list 15 percent (or fewer) of all openings and other sources are even worse.

After people use the traditional methods and nothing happens, they tend to believe that there is nothing more they can do. Eventually, they tend to sit at home becoming increasingly discouraged. The longer a person is unemployed, the fewer hours they tend to spend looking for a job. So even those who have good work habits, years of reliable work experience, and many skills begin to believe that there are no jobs out there and that they are undesirable.

In the rest of this book, you will learn about more effective and "nontraditional" job search methods. While each of the traditional techniques reviewed earlier DO work for some people, each should be used only as one of several methods. The techniques that follow will be far more effective for most people.

Warm and Cold Contacts: The Two Most Effective Job Search Methods

Warm contacts are what I call leads for job openings that come from people you know. Cold contacts are job leads from directly contacting people you don't know — employers in particular. If you remember the data on how people find jobs presented earlier in this chapter, you may recollect that warm contacts — from friends, and relatives — account for about one-third of all job leads. It is probably higher than that. More recent studies which asked job seekers for sources other than friends or relatives, found that other groups such as "business associates" and "acquaintances" provided leads as well. All personal referrals together probably account for about 40 percent of how people find jobs. That makes using personal contacts the most important job search technique of all.[13]

Leads developed from direct contacts with employers are also very important. About 30 percent of all job seekers find their jobs using this method. Together, these two techniques account for over two-thirds of all job leads. With a little practice, they may be the only job search techniques you need.

Warm Contacts: The Most Effective Job Search Method

The people who know you are the same people who are most likely to help you — if only they knew what to do. They typically **don't** know what to do and they aren't often asked. If they **are** asked to help a job seeker at all it is of the vague, "Tell me if you hear anything," variety. While this approach does work, people you know — your warm contacts — can and will be much more helpful if you learn to ask them to help you in more specific ways.

Begin by Defining the Groups of People You Know

To give you an idea of how this works, let's start by defining just who you know. These contact people are your "warm" contacts, as opposed to people you don't know, or "cold" contacts.

You know far more people than you may at first realize. To prove this, begin by listing the **types** or **categories** of people you know. For example, "people I used to go to school with," "neighbors," or "people I used to work with" are all groups of people with whom you might share something in common. To help you create your own list, review the list that follows, which includes categories that often come up in workshops I teach.

- Friends
- Former employers
- Classmates from grade school/high school etc.
- Members of my church
- Present or former teachers
- People in my athletic club
- Members of a professional organization I belong to (or could join—if you get the drift)
- Fraternity/sorority members

- Relatives
- Former co-workers
- Members of my political party — in and out of elected positions
- Members of my social club(s)
- Neighbors
- People I play sports with
- People who sell me things (at the store, insurance, etc.)

Now create your own list, using any of the groups from the list above as well as your own, and list them in the spaces below. I have already included the friends and relatives groups as almost everyone has some. Be as specific as possible in the categories you add.

Warm Contacts—Groups of People I Know	
Friends	Relatives

Warm Contacts—Groups of People I Know

_____   _____
_____   _____
_____   _____
_____   _____
_____   _____
_____   _____
_____   _____
_____   _____
_____   _____
_____   _____

People Do Get Jobs from People They Know

Job seekers often tell me they "don't know anyone" and they believe that most people get jobs because "they know someone." One of those assumptions is true, namely, that people very often do get jobs through someone they know. But job seekers are mistaken if they think they don't know people. To show you what I mean, let's take a few of the groups you listed in the preceding exercise and see how many people they represent.

Right now, if I asked you to take the first group on your list (which is "friends," since I put it there) and write a list that included everyone you are friendly with or who is even somewhat friendly to you, how many people would you guess that is? Ten? Twenty-five? Two-hundred?

Don't feel insecure here; some very good people just can't call a lot of people "friends." The truth is we all would be very fortunate to have just a few good friends during our lives. I'm looking for people who are "friendly" to you, not close friends. Jot that number on your list above, next to the "friends" entry. Estimate how many people are in each of the other groups and note your guess next to each entry. When you are finished, don't be surprised if your list is longer than you anticipated. It's not at all unusual for you to get hundreds of potential contact people this way. They don't all know about job openings, of course, but they are a place to start. And each contact on your list is a source of potential job leads.

Developing a Network of People You Know

I know from experience that leaving you with the idea that you know lots of people is not enough. To make this an effective job search technique, you will have to contact those people. To accomplish this, it is essential that you make — you guessed it — more lists.

For each group you listed in the previous section, starting with the one for friends, use a sheet of paper to make a separate list. On the first one, write as many friends' names as you can think of. Then do the same thing for relatives. When you have completed these two lists, you should have a significant number of names of people who know you. You can save the other lists to do later in your job search. You may only need the first two.

Networking Basics

Armed with your lists of friends and relatives, you have the beginning of a list of people who, in turn, can refer you to others. This is what is called "networking." Networking sounds sophisticated and complicated, but it's really a pretty simple idea. You use one person you know as a source to introduce you to one or preferably two other people you don't know. Like this:

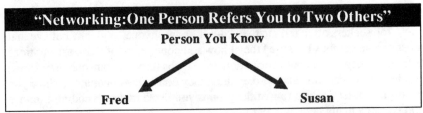

If you do the same thing with Fred and Susan (who you come to know after meeting them), and with the people **they** introduce you to and so on, this is what happens:

Incredible Arithmetic: the numbers of people you could contact this way are amazing. In this example, if you kept getting two referrals from each person, you would have 1,024 people in your network after only the tenth level. And that is starting with only one person!

The Six Rules of Successful Networking

Networking is a simple idea and it does work. It helps you meet potential employers you would not find using any other method. These employers may be a friend of a friend of a friend. And they will be willing to see you for this reason. Of course, not all of your contacts will be helpful to your job search, but there are some things you can do to increase this possibility. Here are the rules of networking:

Step 1: **Get Started.** The only criteria for a person to be in your network is that they talk to you. It would also be nice if they knew other people. Friends, relatives and other warm contacts are an ideal place to start, since they are usually very willing to help you if they can.

To set up a meeting, simply call your contact and say something like:

*"Hi there, Uncle Albert, I'm looking for a job and wonder if
you could help me out. When would be a good time for me to
come over?"*

While some short explanatory conversation is in order, your objective is to get an appointment. In a later chapter you will learn about a job search tool called a JIST Card and use this as a basis for making phone calls. These techniques will assist you in making more effective phone contacts but more on this later.

Step 2: **Present Yourself Well.** It is most important that whoever you see ends up thinking well of you. To increase the chances that they will, it helps to be friendly, well organized, polite, and interested in what they have to say. Even Uncle Albert doesn't **have** to see you.

Step 3: **Learn Something.** Be open to learn from your contacts, even if they don't know very much about your particular job search area. Do try, however, to keep things centered on your goal. Your goal, of course, is to get more job leads.

Step 4: **Get Two Referrals.** This is essential to developing a network, so don't give up until you have at least two names of other people who might help in your job search. You can get referrals from virtually anyone but only if you keep asking for them. I have developed three questions that will typically get you one or more referrals but often only after you ask the second or third question.

Three Essential Questions to Get Referrals

1. "Do you know of anyone who might have an opening for a person with my skills?" If no, then,

2. "Do you know of anyone else who might know of someone who would?" If still no, then,

3. "Do you know someone who knows lots of people?"

It is unusual to get a "No" if you ask all three questions. Any time you get a "Yes," write down the name of the referral and get enough details to contact them.

Step 5: **Follow Up on Referrals.** Call the people whose names you get in the referral process and say something like this:

> *"Hello, my name is Jean Porter, a friend of Fred Reader. He suggested I call and ask you for help. I am looking for a position as a retail sales manager and he thought you might be willing to see me and give me a few ideas . . ."*

The conversation pretty much takes care of itself from here on but do keep your phone conversation short. Remember that you want an interview in person, not over the phone. I'll give you more tips on making phone contacts in chapter 8.

One Thing Leads to Another

Once you make the first few contacts with people you know, you will quickly begin to be referred to people you don't know. The nature of the process encourages each person to refer you to someone who knows even more about the sort of job you want than they do. As you get referred along, you will begin to meet some very knowledgeable people who will tell you things you need to know. The more of them you see, the more you learn, and the better prepared you are.

With each level of referrals, you are also more likely to meet people who have the ability to hire you or who know someone who does. You are now in the hidden job market. Most of the people you meet this way do not have jobs open or are unlikely to hire someone like you. But they do know other people and are often willing to refer you to them — or tell someone else about you who, in turn, **does** have an opening. This is networking and it really does work.

How to Keep Things Moving in Referral Interviews

If you are shy and conversation does not come easily to you, here are a few questions you can ask in your referral interviews that should keep things moving:

- How did you get into this line of work?

- What are the things you like best (or least) about your work?

- Do you have any ideas how a person with my background and skills might find a job in this field?

- What trends do you see in this career field? How could I take advantage of them?

- What projects have you been working on that excite you?

- From your point of view, what problems are most important to overcome in this career area?

Step 6: **Write a Thank-You Note.** Sending someone a thank-you note is a simple act of appreciation. But hardly anyone does it. It is usually done as a social courtesy, but even then, it is a rarity these days. These two reasons alone justify sending thank-you notes to people who help you in your job search. They may have spent an hour or so interviewing you, given you the name of someone else to contact, or helped you in some other way. I believe that the job search can and should be conducted on a person-to-person level. Thank-you notes help reinforce this one-on-one relationship.

Thank-you notes also have practical benefits. The person who receives it is far more likely to remember you. They will perceive you as being thoughtful and well-organized. I have been told by hundreds of employers that they rarely or never get a thank-you note from the people they interview. They describe the people who **do** send them as being "thoughtful," "well-organized," "thorough," and in other positive terms. While thank-you notes will not get you a job for which you are not qualified, they will often help people remember you in a positive way. Thank-you notes can also help these referrals become an effective member of your network of people willing to help you. If they do know of a job opening, or meet someone who does, you will be remembered when others will not.

Cold Contacts: Direct Contacts with Prospective Employers

Many people need only use their warm contacts to develop a network that results in a job offer. It is wise, however, to use a **variety** of job search methods, including direct (or "cold") contacts with prospective employers.

There are two basic methods for making cold contacts. The first is using the phone to set up interviews with people who work in organizations that need a person with your skills. The second involves going to an organization and asking for an interview. Let me cover each of these methods in turn.

Using the *Yellow Pages* as a Source of Job Leads

If you think about it, the *Yellow Pages* telephone directory is the ideal source of prospective employers. Virtually every business, not-for-profit, and governmental organization is listed in this one place. Big organizations as well as the smallest of organizations are listed. And it is free. Even if you are considering looking for a job in a distant location, the *Yellow Pages* for that location is an important source of job leads.

Develop a Prospects List Based on the *Yellow Pages* Index

Look at the index that is usually in the front of the *Yellow Pages*. It lists the categories within which the various businesses and other organizations are listed. From "Abrasives" and "Accident & Health Insurance" through "Zoning Consultants," most *Yellow Pages* list hundreds of categories. And each category, of course, refers to a listing of organizations under that heading. The Yellow Pages is a gold mine of job leads once you know how to use it. Here are some tips to get the best effect.

1. Identify index headings. Go through each and every heading in the index of your *Yellow Pages* and, for each, ask yourself this question:

> **"Could this organization use a person with my skills?"**

The only possible answers are "Yes" or "No." There will be some strange options here, things you would never seriously consider, but humor me, and just answer yes or no for each listing.

2. Define which headings are of most interest. If your answer is "Yes," to a particular category, then you are to mark it with one of the following numbers:

1 = This type of organization sounds very interesting as a possible place to work.

2 = This type of organization sounds somewhat interesting.

3 = This type of organization does not appeal to me at all.

3. Identify specific prospects. Each and every index entry refers you to a section in the *Yellow Pages* which, in turn, lists specific organizations and businesses to contact. Each and every one of these individual listings is a potential target for you. Let's look at a way to identify which organizations you should contact.

The obvious place to begin would be the ones you rated with a "1" — those you were very interested in. But this may not be the best place to begin. If you are just beginning your job search it is often a good idea to improve your job-search skills with organizations where you have less to lose. Consider contacting organizations you listed as a "3" first. Even if you mess up these contacts you can't hurt yourself badly. If you are looking for a specialized job where few positions — and even fewer organizations — exist, it is also wise to start with your "3s" until your techniques improve. As you do this, though, you just may get a job offer. It happens often enough, even from the least likely of sources. And you just might want to consider such an offer, too.

In identifying specific places to contact, I have found it most effective to write down the name of each specific targeted organization on a simple list along with the phone number for each. Use a separate form for each general type of organization you identify in the index. For many jobs, there are hundreds (and in larger cities, perhaps thousands) of places you can identify using just this technique. The odds are excellent that one of them will hire you. And you only need one.

4. Make the call. In most cases, you can just pick up the phone and call. If you are calling a smaller organization, ask for the manager. In a larger organization, ask for the person in charge of the functional area you are interested in, like accounting, or computer operations, or whatever. Do **not** ask for the personnel department! Later in this book you will learn more about making effective phone contacts. There is a bit more to learn to make this all work well, but the basic techniques are quite easy and they do work.

Making Cold Telephone Calls Is Not Easy for Some People, but They Do Work

While a telephone call to a prospective employer is not easy for most people, ask yourself what is the worst thing that can happen to you. At worst, the employer might be annoyed that you called. They might even get angry and hang up on you. But my experience — and that of many job seekers who have used this technique — is that most employers don't mind at all. You see, they are interested in talking to good people, even if they don't have an opening when you call. Employers are people too — and they know from experience that they just might need someone soon.

Cold-Contacting in Person

Everywhere you go presents a potential source of job leads. I give you permission to drop in at businesses that look interesting. If you are interested in photography, drop in at a camera store. On your way to a job interview at 2 p.m., look for places along the way that might need someone with your skills. On your way home, when you don't have anything important to do anyway, stop in at these places. Managers in many small organizations will see you if you just drop in. Even managers in large organizations will often see you if you ask to see the person in charge. If this person is busy, get their name and ask when you should try again. Then call or go back and ask for them by name. Usually, people are willing to see you — even on short notice. If you're told they have no openings, say you would still like to talk about the possibility of future openings. Your JIST Card, which you will learn about later, is the perfect tool for these contacts, so always leave one with anyone you meet.

Small Organizations — Where Most of the Jobs Are

About two-thirds of all people work in small organizations. Most of the new jobs in our economy now come from small organizations and the opportunities there are often better than in large companies. Look at the following chart to see the importance of small organizations in your job search.[14]

Where People Work

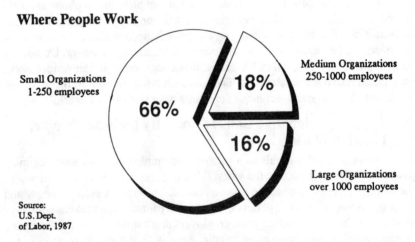

Small Organizations
1-250 employees

66%

18%

16%

Medium Organizations
250-1000 employees

Large Organizations
over 1000 employees

Source:
U.S. Dept.
of Labor, 1987

Many of the nontraditional methods presented in this chapter are most effective with smaller employers. This is the way our economy is headed. But the methods also work well with larger, more formal organizations, too.

You Can Now Get So Many Interviews That Keeping Track of Them Becomes Important

In case you haven't noticed, using these techniques can solve one of the major problems job seekers normally have — not having enough job leads or interviews. While that problem is solved if you use the job search methods I suggest, a new one is often created — having too many job leads to keep track of in your head. The only way to solve this new "problem" is to organize your contacts on paper. I know people who have used a computer to accomplish this, but for most job seekers, it is not a good enough reason to go out and buy one. Another very good system is based on 3-by-5-inch cards which have the advantage of being inexpensive, easy to get, and portable. In chapter 14, I'll show you how to use these index cards to build an effective system for organizing and tracking contacts.

Following Up on Job Leads

Throughout this book I will keep reminding you of the importance of following up on people you "interview" in your network. Following up is **very** important and here are two of the most important things you can do.

Send thank-you notes. Send an informal thank-you note to each and every person who provides significant help to you during your job search. It's just good manners. For example, after you call someone your friend referred you to, send them a thank-you note telling them how you appreciated the suggestions they gave you. Or if you arrange an interview, send a thank-you note telling them that you appreciated their willingness to see you. And surely send a thank-you note after an interview. I will mention thank-you notes throughout this book but you should know that, besides being polite, people remember those who send thank-you notes. Which surely will not hurt you.

Stay in touch. Stay in touch with the meaningful contacts you make during your networking. Ask them if it is OK to call them up every few weeks during your job search, then do so if it is OK (and it almost always is). If you sent them a thank-you note after your first contact, they will probably remember you fondly. When you call, let them know what happened from your following up with any referrals they gave you.

People in your network will hear of job openings that they did not know of when you last had contact. In a very real sense, they will know of jobs in the first, second or third stages of the job opening — long before they are advertised. Since they already know you, staying in touch with them is often a far more effective source of good job leads than making new contacts.

Civil Service Jobs

About 80 percent of all people who work support the 20 percent who earn their living in government-paid jobs.[15] Almost any job you can imagine can be found somewhere within the public sector: teachers, police, laborers, engineers, secretaries, managers, short-order cooks, librarians, etc. These jobs can be obtained from federal, state, province, county, city, township, and local government sources.

Most civil service jobs require you to meet certain criteria or to take tests in order to be considered. These procedures will definitely slow you down, so if you are in a hurry to find a job, this source is probably not for you. It takes months to be considered for some positions, and then more time to get an interview and there is often intense competition for the more desirable jobs. In spite of all this, it could be worthwhile to find out what jobs you may qualify for and how to apply for them.

In many areas, the white pages section of the phone book includes a special listing of government agencies. This section is usually on blue paper, making it, I suppose, the blue pages. Many potential places to apply are listed there but it may require some digging. You can use the white pages to look up listings under your city, county, state, province, parish, or town name. Most will have a general information number you can call to inquire about the agencies or departments which interest you. Larger governmental systems also typically have a centralized office that screens applicants and lists what openings they know about.

Who knows, the wait may be worth it.

More Good Job Search Methods

There are a lot of clever job seekers out there, so almost anything you can imagine has been tried by someone and has probably worked. Let's look at some of the more important of these other techniques.

School or Other Placement Office: A total of about 5 percent of all people get their jobs either from school placement programs or from referrals from teachers.[16] That may not sound like much, but it is almost as important a source as the employment service. There are some very good (and free) job search and placement programs operated by schools, government agencies, and other places. Some people even sign up for schools because of their records for helping graduates find jobs. If you have access to any such program, use it. Often, these services can be of excellent quality.

Take an Entry-Level Job: For example, if you want to manage a restaurant but you are short on experience, get a job as a waiter or waitress.

Take the jobs that are easy to get, then volunteer to help out at other, more responsible tasks. Ask to move up and keep after that goal.

Ask for the Job: Once you decide you are interested in a particular job, saying you want it is a way to communicate your enthusiasm for it. Be prepared to say exactly why you want that job and why you think you can handle it well. An employer is likely to be impressed with your enthusiasm for this particular job and assume you will be more energetic and committed to it. Say you want the job and you are more likely to get it. It's amazing how many people don't do this. Just say "I'm really interested in this position. When can I start?!" It makes a difference when it is true.

Define a Problem You Can Solve: If you look for them, opportunities for you to solve an employer's problem will often become obvious in your job search. Let's say you know something about marketing. During an interview, you become certain that you know how to substantially increase the sales of that organization. Go home and develop a simple written plan, including projected income and expenses, and set up a later interview to present your ideas. You could do this at any place you really wanted to work.[17]

The Armed Services: Don't overlook them as a source of training and employment. They are a major employer of young people and have a lot to offer, including funds for college.

Self-Employment: Often overlooked as a source of jobs, you could create your own. It's not easy, but some jobs — such as painting or consulting — cost very little to start. People with substantial management or professional experience often offer consulting services while continuing their job search. Some people successfully turn their unemployment into opportunities to start a business they have always dreamed of.

If you are considering this yourself, do be cautious. While some people succeed in starting up a profitable business, many more do not. The best way to approach this may be to define what sort of activity you want to be self-employed in and begin doing that part-time while employed elsewhere. Many hobbies help you develop the necessary skills to later avoid business failure. If you are now unemployed — or soon will be — see self-employment as a way to earn temporary income. Paint houses, do tax returns, or whatever else you know how to do to earn cash. The extra income will help get you through to your next "real" job.

If you know you want to be self-employed or start a particular type of business, it may also be wise to seek a job in your area of interest. Depending on the job, you can then gain the skills and contacts you need to succeed in it on your own.

Employment Contractors / Temporary Help: Under these headings in the *Yellow Pages* you will find organizations that can hire you for short-term jobs. Assignments can last from a day or two to many months. Some specialize in office help, others in accounting or other specialized areas. Several provide testing and training in such areas as word processing. These are good places to go if you need a source of income quickly. Another distinct advantage is that the job assignments often give you good work experience in a variety of work settings. It is not unusual, if you do a good job, to get job offers from the same employers to whom you were assigned as a temporary. Some employers routinely use these services to screen for good employees instead of using conventional hiring procedures.

Head Hunters: True head hunters look for you and are not interested in most job seekers. They are hired by employers to look for specific kinds of highly compensated people who are in short supply. Unless you are employed now in a responsible job, making good money and on your way up, they are not likely to be interested in you.

The Public Library

The library is a wonderful place for a job seeker. The research librarians there can help you find answers to the most difficult questions you might have. And it is quiet, free, and open evenings and weekends — the times you should reserve for the library.

A good library will have a variety of newspapers, professional journals, business directories, career information and job search books and other resources. Some even have typewriters and word processors to use and quiet places to research an organization's background between interviews. A library is a job seeker's friend. Look in the appendix of this book for additional resources that you can find at many libraries.

Now You Know How to Find a Job, But...

You now know far more than the average job seeker about finding job leads and getting interviews. With what you now know you can probably go out and find a job in less time. But there are other things for you to learn that will be of great value to you in your job search. For example, do you know precisely the **kind** of job you want? Most people have only a general idea. Will you be able to handle the tough interview questions you will be asked? Perhaps not as well as you might. Do you have a specific plan on how to spend your time each day during your job search? Very few people do.

The rest of this book prepares you for the job search in three ways. The first is by helping you to better understand yourself. Knowing who you are, what you have done, and what you are good at are important things to know. Once you explore yourself, you then need to consider what it is you want in a job. Not just any job should do, you see. When you have figured out the type of job you want, then — and only then — are you ready to learn more about job seeking techniques like interviewing, making phone contacts, writing resumes, organizing your time, and others. That is what the rest of this book is about — job search methods that work. You now know enough about finding job leads to go out and find one in less time. I hope you go out and find a great job before you finish this book. It happens...

Chapter Two Endnotes

1. The U.S. Department of Labor provides data on both the mean (average) and the median length of unemployment. Since some people take a very long time to find a job, it increases the arithmetic average length of unemployment of all workers. The median is where half the people find jobs in more and half in less time and is always shorter. At the time of this writing, the average length of unemployment is 12.5 weeks and the median is 6.2 weeks. Of course, these figures go up during periods of high unemployment and they do not count the statistics of "discouraged workers" (those who are unemployed but are not actively looking) nor of those who work part-time or are underemployed and who are looking for better jobs.

2. It's easy to justify that 10 percent of the workforce reads the want ads when you consider the unemployment rate plus the underemployed, discouraged workers, those thinking about entering the labor market, and those wanting to change jobs. When the unemployment rate is high it follows that more than 10 percent of the working population would read the want ads.

3. Miriam Johnson has authored a variety of important early papers on labor market issues. In this one she studied 200,000 want ads in 19 newspapers to reach her conclusions. The study was titled "The Role of Help Wanted Ads In Labor Market Intermediaries," National Commission For Manpower Policy, 1978.

4. In *The Job Market* (The National Center for Job-Market Studies, P.O. Box 3651, Washington, D.C., 20007), Richard Lathrop presents some interesting and well-researched data on this system.

5. Having the various state employment service offices provide job search assistance rather than simply referrals to the jobs they have listed, has been a controversial issue for years. Washington state's employment service has had innovative job search programs for years, going back to the early 1970s. Within the more recent past, Georgia's Department of Labor has been using many of the JIST techniques described in this book to teach groups of job seekers. Texas and other states are also now providing job

search training for unemployed people. In Wegmann's book, *Work in the New Economy,* he makes an excellent argument for the employment service to become the major source of such training since they are a place many job seekers routinely go. He presents a model job search program that should be considered as a matter of national policy.

6. Lathrop, op. cit.

7. Wegmann, op. cit.

8. The Bulletin 1886 data is aging gracefully but, with cuts in basic research funding at the federal level, there has been little newer data of such validity to replace it. What research I have seen has tended to support these findings, so I continue to use it as a data source. The Camil study was published in the late 1970s.

9. Lathrop, *The Job Market,* op.cit.

10. Howe, Wayne J., "Labor Market Dynamics and Trends in Male and Female Unemployment," *Monthly Labor Review,* November, 1990.

11. The preface of this book provided information on one program that JIST ran. In that program, during the high unemployment recession in 1982 and in the city with the highest unemployment rate in the country, my organization (JIST Works, Inc.) ran a job search project with the long-term unemployed. With an average length of unemployment of over one year, more than 90 percent found jobs within four weeks. This is not an isolated situation. Well-run job-search projects throughout the country have obtained similar, if not so outstanding, results. Your own job search, of course, could take longer or shorter than average. But it is clear that people who learn effective job search methods do find jobs faster, on average, than those who do not learn. Which is what this book is about.

12. The concept that a job opens in stages is mine. To make it easier to communicate, I have made it seem more predictable than it often is. I have also uniformly assigned 25 percent as the percentage of people who get jobs during each phase to make this a better teaching device. While it's probably not precisely 25 percent for each phase (I've never seen research organized in this way) I am quite certain that the numbers would be close to these estimates. What research there is supports this.

13. The data from Bulletin 1886 cited earlier in this chapter asked those surveyed if their leads were provided by "friends" or "relatives," among other sources. But they did not ask them if they found their job through an "acquaintance." If they had, subsequent research has indicated that the total percentage of job leads obtained from people they knew would be 40 percent or so. The Camil study, for example, found that 3.3 percent found their jobs through "business associates" in addition to the 30.7 percent who

had found their jobs through friends and relatives. Others who claimed their leads came from direct contact with employers, were in fact referred to that employer by someone they knew who was neither a friend nor relative.

14. The data in the chart comes from the U.S. Department of Labor. They define a small organization as one having fewer than 500 employees. Using that criteria, the percentages of people working in "small" organizations would have been even higher. Everything is relative, but I feel that 500 employees is too big to consider "small" and, so changed the criteria.

15. The precise number of people whose salary is paid by taxpayers is hard to obtain. There are about 18 million who actually work for state, local or federal governments. Plus the millions who work in the military. Plus teachers, social workers, people who work in the defense industry and everyone else whose salary is paid by tax dollars directly or indirectly. The total number would boggle the mind and is, I am quite sure, well over 20 percent of the workforce.

16. From the Camil study, mentioned earlier in this chapter.

17. Bernard Haldane developed this technique and it will be discussed more in chapter 10 on interviewing.

Chapter Three

Identifying Your Skills—

The Key to Getting the Job You Want

Knowing your skills is an important part of a successful job search. A variety of surveys have been conducted over the years to determine why some job applicants do better than others. According to a survey of employers, over 90 percent of the people they interview cannot adequately define the skills they have to support their ability to do the job.[1] They may **have** the necessary skills, but they can't communicate them.

In an exhaustive study titled "Job Search: A Review of the Literature," Steven Mangum cites a variety of research studies and concludes that "No single factor carries more negative connotations in the interview than an inability to communicate."[2] It is problem number one in the interview process.

For this reason, it is essential that you learn to identify and clearly communicate those skills which will be of most value to an employer. But knowing your skills is not "just" a job search issue. You also need to know them in order to select the job that you will most enjoy and have the best chance to do well in.

Skills — They May Not Be What You Think They Are

Webster's Dictionary defines a skill as an "ability to do something well, especially as the result of long practical experience." Like the definition of "love," there is much more to understanding skills than what a dictionary can tell you. Because knowledge of your own skills is such an important issue, it is worth one entire chapter in this book. And much more. But since one chapter is all there is, let's get started.

A Skill Is Something You Can Do

True enough. There are many skills that any of us could show someone else. These kinds of skills relate to performance of various kinds, like riding a bike or baking a cake. In turn, most of these types of activities can be broken down into "smaller" skills that must be used together to do the more complex tasks. For example, baking a cake seems simple enough to do, but only if you have some of the component skills. These might include: using measuring cups and other devices; reading a cookbook (and following directions); shopping for ingredients; using timing devices; using a stove properly; organizing the work area and others.

In turn, each of the above skills can be further broken down. For example, in order to use a stove, you would have to be able to read the numbers or words on the dial and be able to manipulate the dial with your fingers or toes, which requires fine motor coordination. You surely get the point. If you carefully analyze any task — even "simple" tasks — more skills are required than you would at first believe.

A Skill Can Also Be Something You Own, as Part of Your Personality

This can also be true. For example, some people just seem to be "organized." Others just seem to "get along well with others" or have "leadership abilities." Still others might be "creative thinkers" or "good writers." Such skills are more abstract than riding a bike or baking a cake, and it may be difficult to say just how you acquired them. Nevertheless, they are legitimate and important skills.

How Many Skills Do You Have?

Many people don't realize that everyone has hundreds of skills, not just a few. When I ask someone what skills they have, too often they say, "I can't think of any."

Some time ago, I was leading a workshop for a group of about 30 people and we were doing a series of group exercises to help each person in the group identify their skills. Most of the people in the group had been unemployed for a long time and they lived in a small town with an unemployment rate of about 15 percent. I asked one man in the group to tell me what he was good at. He couldn't think of one thing! I asked him some questions and found out that he had worked as a cabinet maker on the same job for over 15 years. He never missed a day of work and had been late once, over 10 years ago. He took pride in his work and had one of the lowest reject rates in his department of over 20 people. No skills?

Young people often underestimate their skills in the same way. So do women who have "just" been a homemaker and have "no work experience." So do some people who have had very responsible and well-paying professional positions. In my workshops over the years, countless job seekers have told me they have "no skills" when in fact, they have hundreds. And so do you.

The Three Types of Skills

Simple skills such as closing your fingers to grip a pen (which is not simple at all if you consider that miracle of complex neuromuscular interaction which computers have not quite been able to duplicate) are building blocks for more complex skills like writing a sentence and even more complex skills like writing a book.

Even though you have hundreds of skills, some will be more important to an employer than others. And some will be far more important to you in deciding what sort of job you want. So, to keep it simple, we will divide skills into the major categories described next.

The Skills Triad[3]

The skills you use can be divided into three major types: Adaptive, Transferable, and Job-Related.

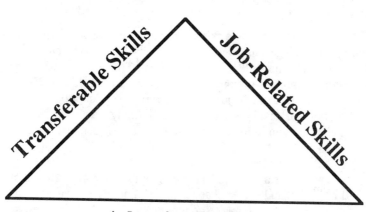

Adaptive Skills

Adaptive Skills / Personality Traits

These are skills you use every day to survive and get along. They are called adaptive or self-management skills because they allow you to adapt or adjust to a variety of situations. Some of them could also be considered part of your basic personality. Examples of adaptive skills valued by employers include getting to work on time, honesty, enthusiasm, and being able to get along with others.

Transferable Skills

These are general skills that can be useful in a variety of jobs. For example, writing clearly, good language skills, or the ability to organize things would be desirable skills in many jobs. These are called transferable skills because they can be transferred from one job — or even one career — to another.

Job-Related Skills

These are the skills people typically first think of when asked, "Do you have any skills?" They are related to a particular job or type of job. An auto mechanic, for example, needs to know how to tune engines and repair brakes. Typing or being able to read a micrometer are other examples of job-related skills.

The system of dividing skills into three categories is not perfect. Some skills could be considered personality traits, such as being trustworthy, dependable, or well-organized. There is also some overlap between the three skills categories that allows some skills, such as being organized, to be put in several categories. For our purposes, however, the Skills Triad is a very useful system for identifying skills that are important in the job search.

Identifying Your Skills

Adaptive and transferable skills are specific to you and perhaps **are** you. While they will change some over time, it is more likely to be an evolution, as you develop or use one skill more than another. This is one reason why these skills are more important to you as a person and as a job seeker. Your ability to transfer your skills to a new job or career will be very important. Even if you don't want or plan to change careers, it is likely you will be forced to. Technology is changing jobs so drastically that many jobs that exist now will not be here in 10 or 20 years. This will require you to continually learn new job-related skills to stay current.

People who have a good understanding of their adaptive and transferable skills will make job and career changes more smoothly and successfully than others. Knowing and being able to communicate your skills is a new survival skill that was not so important in the past. The material that follows will help you identify these key skills to use during your job search.

Your Adaptive Skills

On the following lines, list three things about yourself that you think make you a good worker. Take your time. Think about what an employer might like about you or the way you work.

1. _____

2. _____

3. _____

The skills you wrote were spontaneous. They define the way you see yourself and what you have to offer an employer. And they are among the most important things that an employer will want to know about you. Most (but not all) people write adaptive skills when asked this question. Whatever you wrote, these are important things to mention in the interview. Many job seekers do not think they are important enough to mention, but they are. In fact, presenting these skills well will often allow a job seeker with less experience to get the job over those with better credentials.

Adaptive Skills / Personality Traits Checklist

Below is a list of adaptive skills that I have developed over the years. The first group includes the basic adaptive skills I consider most important. The reason is that many employers will not hire someone if they are not certain that the job seeker has these skills. The remaining skills are important ones for many jobs and are often mentioned by both employers and job seekers. Look over the list and check the first blank for the adaptive skills you have and the second blank if you want to use these skills in your next job.

Adaptive Skills Checklist	
Basic Adaptive Skills (the minimum)	
__ Good attendance __	__ Honesty __
__ Arrive on time __	__ Following instructions __
__ Meet deadlines __	__ Get along with co-workers __
__ Hard-working, productive __	
Other Adaptive Skills	
__ Ambition __	__ Flexibility __
__ Patience __	__ Maturity __

Adaptive Skills Checklist	
Other Adaptive Skills	
___ Assertiveness ___	___ Dependability ___
___ Learning quickly ___	___ Completing assignments ___
___ Sincerity ___	___ High motivation ___
___ Solving problems ___	___ Intelligence ___
___ Friendliness ___	___ Creativity ___
___ Good sense of humor ___	___ Leadership ___
___ Physical strength ___	___ Enthusiasm ___
___ Good sense of direction ___	___ Persistency ___
___ Self-motivation ___	___ Accepting responsibility ___
___ Results-oriented ___	___ Asking questions ___
___ Pride in doing a good job ___	___ Willing to learn new things ___

Your Top Adaptive Skills

List in the margins or on a separate sheet, any adaptive skills you have that are not listed above. Then list the three adaptive skills you feel are most important for you to tell an employer about or that you most want to use in your next job.

1. _____

2. _____

3. _____

These three skills are one of the most important things you should remember from this book. They will be with you for the rest of your life and are EXTREMELY important to present to an employer in an interview.

Identifying Your Transferable Skills

Just as with adaptive skills, there are hundreds of transferable skills that you could list. Over the years I have developed the list that follows. It includes transferable skills that are particularly important to employers and that come up over and over again in my workshops. They are organized into clusters that may help you identify major types of jobs for which you are best suited — a topic I will cover in a later chapter.

As you review the list, pay particular attention to the list of "key" transferable skills since jobs that require these skills tend to pay more money. If you have one or more of these skills, it is clearly to your advantage to emphasize them in an interview — and to seek jobs that require them. On the first blank, check each skill you are strong in. Check the second blank if you want to use this skill in your next job. When you are finished, you should have checked 10 to 20 blanks.

Transferable Skills Checklist

Key Transferable Skills

__ Meeting deadlines __	__ Planning __
__ Speaking in public __	__ Controlling budgets __
__ Supervising others __	__ Increasing sales or efficiency __
__ Accepting responsibility__	__ Instructing others __
__ Solving problems __	__ Managing money or budgets __
__ Managing people __	__ Meeting deadlines __
__ Meeting the public __	__ Organizing or managing projects __

Other Transferable Skills:

Using My Hands, Dealing with Things

__ Assemble __	__ Make things __
__ Build __	__ Observe, inspect things __
__ Construct, repair buildings __	__ Operate tools and machinery __
__ Drive or operate vehicles __	__ Repair things __
__ Good with my hands __	__ Use complex equipment __

Dealing with Data

__ Analyze data, facts __	__ Investigate __
__ Audit records __	__ Keep financial records __
__ Budget __	__ Locate answers, information __
__ Calculate, compute __	__ Manage money __
__ Classify data __	__ Negotiate __
__ Compare __	__ inspect Record facts __
__ Count __	__ Observe,
__ Compile __	__ Research __

Transferable Skills Checklist

Key Transferable Skills

__ Detail-oriented __	__ Synthesize __
__ Evaluate __	__ Take inventory __

Working with People

__ Administer __	__ Patient __
__ Care for __	__ Persuade __
__ Confront others __	__ Pleasant __
__ Counsel people __	__ Sensitive __
__ Demonstrate __	__ Sociable __
__ Diplomatic __	__ Supervise __
__ Help others __	__ Tactful __
__ Insight __	__ Teach __
__ Interview others __	__ Tolerant __
__ Kind __	__ Tough __
__ Listen __	__ Trust __
__ Negotiate __	__ Understand __
__ Outgoing __	

Using Words, Ideas

__ Articulate __	__ Inventive __
__ Communicate verbally __	__ Logical __
__ Correspond with others __	__ Remember information __
__ Create new ideas __	__ Research __
__ Design __	__ Speak in public __
__ Edit __	__ Write clearly __
__ Ingenious __	

Leadership

__ Arrange social functions __	__ Motivate people __
__ Competitive __	__ Negotiate agreements __
__ Decisive __	__ Plan __
__ Delegate __	__ Run meetings __

Transferable Skills Checklist

Key Transferable Skills

___ Direct others ___   ___ Self-controlled ___

___ Explain things to others ___   ___ Self-motivated ___

___ Get results ___   ___ Solve problems ___

___ Mediate problems ___   ___ Take risks ___

Creative, Artistic

___ Artistic ___   ___ Music appreciation ___

___ Dance, body movement ___   ___ Perform, act ___

___ Drawing, art ___   ___ Play instruments ___

___ Expressive ___   ___ Present artistic ideas ___

Your Top Transferable Skills

Write in the margins or on a separate sheet any other transferable skills you have that were not listed. Then select the five top transferable skills you want to use in your next job and list them below.

1. _____

2. _____

3. _____

4. _____

5. _____

Identifying Your Job-Related Skills

Stressing the importance of adaptive and transferable skills in the job search does not mean that specific job-related skills are not also important. They are. Technical, professional, managerial, trade, and craft-oriented jobs often require substantial preparation and specific training. Many other jobs require knowledge of a specific industry or business that can only be learned on the job or by special training. The type of job you choose will determine the specific skills required.

Job-related skills may have been gained in a variety of ways including education, training, work, hobbies, or other life experiences. The next chapter will help you review elements of your personal history to help you identify job-related as well as other skills.

Knowing Your Skills Is the Basis for Your Job Search

Knowing what you are good at is an essential part of your job search. It will help you answer interview questions, write a resume, and complete applications. More importantly, knowing the skills you **like** to use can help you make a better decision about what sort of job you really want. Your jobs, careers, and personal situations will change, but your adaptive and transferable skills will be with you throughout your life. They are important for an employer to know, but even more important for you to know.

Meeting an Employer's Expectations[4]

Sidney Fine, a labor market expert who was the principal researcher for the U.S. Department of Labor's job classification system, has estimated that one-half of all jobs in North America could be learned by the average adult in two weeks or less.[5] To do so, they would use their adaptive and transferable skills to compensate for their lack of specific job knowledge and job-related skills. The point is, that if an employer has two job seekers with similar credentials, the one who makes a better impression will get the job. Both may have acceptable job-content and good adaptive and transferable skills, but the one who **presents** them well, all other things being equal, will get the job.

An important principle throughout this book is that the opinion of an employer **does** matter. In the interview, where their opinion matters most, I feel that there are three basic employers' expectations for you to meet. As luck would have it, it just so happens that the Skills Triad provides a useful way to understand how an employer makes hiring and screening decisions.

Expectation 1. Appearance: Do You Look Like the Type of Person Who Will Do Well in the Job?

Employers in one survey indicated that 40 percent of those they interview create a negative first impression by their appearance. I have listed this first since it is often so easy to correct this kind of problem and since, once you create a negative impression, it is most difficult to overcome.[6]

Employers react within a few seconds to people they first meet — just as all people do. If their initial reaction to you is negative, you probably will not be hired. In most situations they will react first to your adaptive skills, including whether you are on time to the interview, your dress and grooming, and your verbal skills, among others.

In an interview, if the employer feels you will not fit in or will not get along well with co-workers, you will not be hired — even if you have the experience to handle the job. Job seekers who can effectively present their ability to adapt to a new work situation often get jobs over people with more experience and training. I have seen this happen countless times. It is the better prepared job seeker who gets the job, not necessarily the better qualified one.

To further illustrate how important adaptive skills are to employers, note that most people who are fired or lose their jobs do so because of an inability to adapt and get along rather than an inability to do the job itself. Robert Half & Associates conducted a survey of personnel directors from the 1,000 largest U.S. corporations. Only 4 percent listed "not doing job" as the most disturbing employee behavior. Responses related to actual job performance totaled only 32 percent. The remaining responses related to poor adaptive skills. The most frequently noted problems were: lying and dishonesty (14%), absenteeism and tardiness (12%), arrogance and overconfidence (10%), and lack of dedication (6%).[7]

Expectation 2. Dependability: Can You Be Counted on to Get the Job Done?

Even if you have superior job-related skills, you won't get an offer unless the employer feels that you are a reliable sort who does not miss work, can be relied upon to get things done, and will hang around long enough to pay off their training investment.

Many interview questions are designed to probe this very issue. An employer will not hire a person who may move out of town soon, take another job (overqualified), has a history of leaving jobs, may have an attendance problem (alcoholism, sick kids?), has no family or friends living in town (will move soon), is late often or for any other reason can't be depended upon. Some of the issues may not seem fair for an employer to wonder about — and some are probably illegal to ask about — but are a legitimate concern to an employer. And it would be your concern as well, if you were hiring someone.

An employer is clearly not concerned with job-related skills here but in your adaptive skills and motivations for wanting to work. Once an employer is satisfied that you have acceptable adaptive skills, your transferable skills are often next in importance. Your ability to learn the new job quickly, for example, together with other desirable personal traits or skills will be more important than if you simply have the necessary experience. Most employers have learned that, despite whatever you already know, you will have to be retrained in their system. If a job seeker impresses the employer as disorganized, rigid, unmotivated, or lacking in other important transferable or adaptive skills, someone else with less experience may get the job. Your skill in organizing things could be more important to the employer in the long run than someone else's knowledge of a specific procedure.

Expectation 3. Credentials: Do You Have the Job-Related Skills, Experience, and Training?

Your education, training, and prior work experiences are weighted heavily by employers in determining whether you are capable of doing a particular job. These are obviously important but I have listed them third since they become important only if you don't get screened out based on the first and second criteria above.

People without the minimal job-related skills required for a job typically will not get an interview. But many employers will waive their requirements for education, training, and previous experience for the right candidate. That's why I have listed job-related skills third among the three employer expectations. This is not to say that job-related skills are unimportant, especially in certain professional or technical jobs. They are. For example, no matter how nice you are or how good you are with your hands (another transferable skill) you can't get a job as an airline pilot unless you know how to fly an airplane and have the appropriate credentials. This is a fact that I am very, very comfortable with since I'm on airplanes so much. But if you do meet the minimal criteria for a job **and** get an interview, you will be considered unless you create a negative impression based on expectations one and two.

The Skills Employers Want

As a way to illustrate that employers value adaptive and transferable skills very highly, I present to you the results of a 1989 study of employers conducted jointly by the U.S. Department of Labor and The American Association of Counseling and Development. According to that study, here are the top skills employers want in the people they hire:

1. Learning to learn.
2. Basic academic skills in reading, writing, and computation.
3. Listening and oral communication.
4. Creative thinking and problem solving.
5. Self-esteem and goal setting.
6. Personal and career development.
7. Interpersonal/negotiation and teamwork.
8. Organizational effectiveness and leadership.

Note that all are either adaptive or transferable skills. With that I can rest my case.

The rest of this book assumes that you know your key skills and will use them as a basis for developing career exploration and job seeking skills.

Chapter Three Endnotes

1. Mangum, Stephen, "Job Search: A Review of the Literature," Olympus Research Centers, Salt Lake City, Utah.

2. Ibid.

3. I really can't say who first began to divide skills into categories similar to those I list in this section. It's probably been a schema that has been around a long time. But I do take responsibility for the concept of the skills triad as articulated in this section as well as the various skills lists themselves.

4. I first used the concept of "Employers' Expectations" back in the mid 1970s when I found it a useful way to look at how employers evaluate people in interviews. There is evidence to support the importance of each expectation but I have arranged them in the order they are in for didactic reasons.

5. Dr. Sidney Fine, who was instrumental in developing the structure for classifying jobs now used by the U.S. Department of Labor, discussed this with me following a workshop he presented at the JIST Conference in 1980. He was the principal researcher for the *Dictionary of Occupational Titles*, published by the Department of Labor, which lists over 20,000 job titles.

6. The Endicott Study is one often used source to support this. Another study reaching the same conclusion is by Lundsden and Sharf titled "Behavioral Dimensions of the Job Interview," *Journal of College Placement*, Spring, 1974.

7. From a survey conducted by Burke Marketing Research and presented in a book by Robert Half titled, *Robert Half — On Hiring* (New York, Crown Publishers).

Chapter Four

Collecting the Details of Your Experience

Throughout your job search, you will need ready access to a large number of facts from your life's history. This chapter will help you organize those facts into a type of "data base." You can use this information in later chapters to select or research a job objective, complete applications and resumes, answer interview questions, and perfect many other job search skills.

Categories of your history to consider:

1. Education
2. Training
3. Work and Volunteer History
4. Other Life Experiences

The language of your skills that you developed in the last chapter will help you examine your background in this one. Knowing **which** things to emphasize from your life's history will be very important to you in your job search.

Emphasizing Your Accomplishments

When reviewing your history, remember the situations where you felt some joy or sense of accomplishment. Identify the skills you were using when you experienced these feelings.

Understand that an "accomplishment" could be something small, that only you know about. For example, perhaps you never won an award or do not consider yourself outstanding in any particular way. But you **did** figure out how to make an unauthorized announcement over your school's public address system, releasing everyone early on the last day of school in your senior year. (An action for which you did not get an award but that was quite creative.) Or you collected more canned food for the homeless than anyone else in your homeroom. Or whatever. Almost every month of your life there is something that you accomplish. These things are the basis for identifying your skills.

Here is an example of what one person selected as an accomplishment. I listed to the right of her story some of the skills needed to do what she described.

Accomplishment	Skills Needed
"Last summer my cousin got ill and could not run his concession at the city fair. Even though I had never run a concession before, I bought the supplies and handled all the details in time to open the stand the first day with only one day's notice! There are usually two people who run the stand, but without help I ran it myself. I served over 5,000 customers that week and took in over $20,000. That is an increase of 36 percent over last year. The profits were 50 percent over last year too because I bought supplies wholesale and in quantity. I worked 12-hour days but always opened on time."	• accepts responsibility • risk taker • problem solver • meets deadlines • good scheduler, prioritizer • efficient, fast • good customer contact, • interpersonal skills • gets results! • budgets money & time • good negotiator • saves money • hard worker • responsible

Do you see how one accomplishment, once you analyze it, can help reveal your skills? John Crystal, a pioneer in career planning, developed this way of analyzing skills many years ago. You may find it helpful to identify five or so things that you felt you did particularly well AND that you enjoyed doing. When you are done, write down in as much detail as you can, what you remember about each accomplishment. Then go back over each story and look for the skills you used. A pattern of similar skills being used again and again will usually develop in the things you do well and enjoy doing. These are probably the skills you are particularly good at and enjoy using most. And they are almost always adaptive or transferable skills.

Your Experience Data Base Worksheets

As you complete the various sections that follow, keep in mind that you are looking for skills you have demonstrated as well as your accomplishments. When possible, include numbers to describe your activities or their results. For example, saying "spoke to groups as large as 200 people," has more impact than "did presentations."

Use additional paper as needed to write drafts before writing final versions in this book. Use an erasable pen or pencil to allow for changes. In all sections, emphasize the skills and accomplishments that best support your ability to do the job you want.

Education Worksheets

Your education is a very important part in helping you define who you are. Consider the courses you took as well as any extracurricular activities.

High School Worksheet
Name of school(s)/years attended:
Subjects you did well in or might relate to the job you want:

High School Worksheet

Extracurricular activities/ hobbies/ leisure activities:

_____

_____

_____

_____

_____

_____

_____

Accomplishments/ things you did well (in or out of school):

_____

_____

_____

_____

_____

_____

After High School Worksheet

Name of school(s)/years attended:

_____

_____

_____

_____

_____

After High School Worksheet

Courses related to job objective:

_____

_____

_____

_____

_____

_____

_____

_____

Extracurricular activities/ hobbies/ leisure activities:

_____

_____

_____

_____

_____

_____

_____

Accomplishments/ things you did well (in or out of school):

_____

_____

_____

_____

_____

_____

After High School Worksheet

Specific things you learned or can do that relate to the job you want.

_____

_____

_____

_____

_____

_____

Post-High School Training Worksheet

List any training that might relate to the job you want. Include military and on-the-job training, workshops, or informal training such as from a hobby.

Training/ dates/ certificates:

_____

_____

_____

_____

_____

_____

Post-High School Training Worksheet

Specific things you can do as a result:

_____

_____

_____

_____

_____

_____

_____

Specific things you learned or can do that relate to the job you want.

_____

_____

_____

_____

_____

_____

_____

_____

Work and Volunteer History Worksheet

List your most recent jobs first, followed by previous ones. Include military experience and unpaid work here too. Both of these things are work and are particularly important if you do not have much paid civilian work experience. Create additional sheets to cover ALL of your significant jobs or unpaid experiences as needed. If you have been promoted, consider handling that as a separate job.

Whenever possible, provide numbers to support what you did: number of people served over one or more years; number of transactions processed; percent sales increase; total inventory value you were responsible for; payroll of the staff you supervised; total budget you were responsible for and other data.

As much as possible, mention results using numbers too. These can be impressive numbers when mentioned in an interview or resume.

Make copies of the worksheet I have provided or simply create your own worksheets on blank paper.

Job / Volunteer Worksheet

Name of organization: _____

Address: _____

_____

Employed from: _____to:_____

Job title(s): _____

Supervisor's name:_____

Phone number: _____

Machinery or equipment you used:

_____

_____

_____

_____

_____

Data, information, or reports you created or used:

_____

_____

_____

_____

_____

Job / Volunteer Worksheet

People-oriented duties or responsibilities to co-workers, customers, others:

_____

_____

_____

_____

_____

Services you provided or products you produced:

_____

_____

_____

_____

Reasons for promotions or salary increases, if any:

_____

_____

_____

_____

Details on anything you did to help the organization, such as increase productivity, simplify or reorganize job duties, decrease costs, increase profits, improve working conditions, reduce turnover, or other improvements. Qualify results when possible — for example, "Increased order processing by 50 percent, with no increase in staff costs."

_____

_____

_____

_____

Job / Volunteer Worksheet

Specific things you learned or can do that relate to the job you want:

_____

_____

_____

_____

_____

What would your supervisor say about you?

_____

_____

_____

_____

Other Life Experiences Worksheet

Think about any hobbies or interests you have had, family responsibilities, recreational activities, travel, or any other experiences in your life where you feel some sense of accomplishment. Write any that seem particularly meaningful to you below and name the key skills you think were involved in doing them.

Other Life Experiences Worksheet

Situation 1: _____

Details and skills used:

_____

_____

_____

_____

Other Life Experiences Worksheet

Specific things you learned or can do that relate to the job you want:

_____

_____

_____

_____

_____

Situation 2:_____

Details and skills used:

_____

_____

_____

_____

Specific things you learned or can do that relate to the job you want:

_____

_____

_____

_____

_____

Situation 3:_____

Details and skills used:

_____

_____

_____

_____

Other Life Experiences Worksheet

Specific things you learned or can do that relate to the job you want:

_____

_____

_____

_____

_____

Key Accomplishments and Skills to Tell an Employer

In this chapter, you had the opportunity to examine the job-related skills you have from education, work, and other life experiences. As you have surely noticed, these skills exist only in the context of your using your adaptive and transferable skills. Doing the activities I suggest in this chapter may have given you a few more adaptive or transferable skills to add to your list — or more insight into how you use them. Now it is time to consider which skills are likely to be most valuable to you and a prospective employer in a work situation. Answering the following questions may help.

Questions for Review

1. What are the most important accomplishments and skills you can present to an employer regarding your educational and training experiences?

_____

_____

_____

_____

_____

_____

_____

2. What are the most important accomplishments and skills you can present to an employer regarding your paid and unpaid work experiences?

_____

_____

_____

_____

_____

_____

_____

3. What are the most important accomplishments and skills you can present to an employer regarding your other life experiences?

_____

_____

_____

_____

_____

_____

If you find that your opinions about the skills you have or want to use on your next job have changed since the last chapter, that's OK. These are your lists and you can do anything you want with them. So feel free to go back and do those activities again as you learn new things or simply if you change your mind. Defining your skills and figuring out what to do with them is a process that is never completely done. In the next chapter you will use your skills knowledge in a new way to help define what sort of job you want — even if you already have a job objective.

Chapter Five

Defining Your Ideal Job

Defining your "ideal" job is a tricky business. There are over 20,000 job titles — far too many jobs for you or any one else to really know well.[1] Add to that the obvious variable of different work environments where people with the very same job title work. You might be delighted to work in one place (it being all that you could hope for in a great place to work) and entirely miserable working in another. Yet both could LOOK very much the same to a job seeker. And both could have the very same job title.

It seems clear that a job title, even a carefully considered one, is not enough to define an ideal job. There is more to it than that. But what, exactly, you might ask? A most interesting question whose answer, fortunately for you, has been considered by others who have come before you.

What People Want from Work

Let's begin by considering what working people say they want out of their jobs. Following are the results of a survey conducted by Louis Harris and Associates asking people to rate those things they considered to be very important in their work.[2]

What People Want From Work	
Response	% Rating This as Very Important
A challenging job	82
Good benefits	80
Good pay	74
Free exchange of information	74
Chance to make significant contributions	74
The right to privacy	62

In another survey conducted by Media General Associated Press, adults were asked to name the one thing they liked most about their work. Here are the top responses.[3]

Things People Like Most About Their Jobs	
Response	% Rating This as Very Important
The work itself	32
People at work	23
Money	12
Hours	7
Benefits	6
Boss	3
Other reasons	17

It should be obvious that there is more to defining the ideal job than simply what occupation it is. But the surveys above don't really give you enough information to use in planning a career. Fortunately, there is a way to approach this and it is presented in the very next section.

The Eight Components of an Ideal Job Description

Many experts have considered the elements involved in helping a person define a job that would be particularly well suited to them. Among the more helpful approaches is one that defines eight clusters of issues to consider in defining the ideal job. While a variety of people have contributed to the process that follows, John Crystal and Richard Bolles have articulated it most clearly in their writings.[4] The eight issues to consider are:

Components of an Ideal Job	
1. Skills Required	5. Location
2. Personal Values	6. Special Knowledge or Interests
3. Preferred Earnings	7. Work Environment
4. Level of Responsibility	8. Types of People You Like to Work with or For

All of these elements interact, so before you can define your ideal job, let's explore each of these factors in more detail.

Skills: What Skills Would You Prefer to Use?

Knowing what you are good at and which of these skills you would like to use in your next job is essential in developing a job objective. The previous two chapters should have given you a good sense of what skills you want to use on your next job. Review those chapters if you need to, then turn to the Ideal Job Worksheet towards the end of this chapter. After you have looked it over, record the skills you prefer to use on your next job in the appropriate section of the worksheet.

The Ideal Job Worksheet will be used in a similar way to record your preferences for each of the issues covered in the sections that follow. As you finish each section, record your preferences on the worksheet. When completed it will provide you an outline of your preferences for your ideal job.

Values: What Values Are Important in Your Work?

People work for many reasons. The checklist that follows will help you identify one or more of the values that others have identified as being important or satisfying to them in their work. It was developed by Howard Figler, author of *The Complete Job Search Handbook* and used in a book titled *Exploring Careers*, originally published by the U.S. Department of Labor.[5]

Work Values Checklist

This activity presents 33 common "satisfaction factors" that people get from their jobs.

Work Values Checklist

Begin by reading the entire list, then rate each item, using the scale that follows.

1 = Not Important at All   3 = Somewhat Important

2 = Not Very Important   4 = Very Important

___ **Help Society:** Contribute to the betterment of the world I live in.

___ **Help Others:** Help others directly, either individually or in small groups.

___ **Public Contact:** Have lots of daily contact with people.

___ **Work with Others:** Have close working relationship with a group. Work as a team toward common goals.

___ **Affiliation:** Be recognized as a member of an organization whose type of work or status is important to me.

___ **Friendship:** Develop close personal relationships with co-workers.

___ **Competition:** Pit my abilities against others. There are clear outcomes.

___ **Make Decisions:** Have the power to set policy and determine a course of action.

___ **Work Under Pressure:** Work in a situation where deadlines and high quality work are required by my supervisor.

___ **Power and Authority:** Control other people's work activities.

___ **Influence People:** Be in a position to change people's attitudes and opinions.

___ **Work Alone:** Do things by myself, without much contact with others.

___ **Knowledge:** Seek knowledge, truth, and understanding.

___ **Intellectual Status:** Be regarded by others as an expert or a person of intellectual achievement.

___ **Artistic Creativity:** Do creative work in any of several art forms.

___ **Creativity (general):** Create new ideas, programs, organizational structures, or anything else that has not been developed by others.

___ **Aesthetics:** Have a job that involves sensitivity to beauty.

___ **Supervision:** Have a job in which I guide other people in their work.

___ **Change and Variety:** Have job duties that often change or are done in different settings.

___ **Precision Work:** Do work that allows little tolerance for error.

___ **Stability:** Have job duties that are largely predictable and not likely to change over a long period of time.

Work Values Checklist

— **Security:** Be assured of keeping my job and a reasonable financial reward.

— **Fast Pace:** Work quickly, keep up with a fast pace.

— **Recognition:** Be recognized for the quality of my work in some visible or public way.

— **Excitement:** Do work that is very exciting or that often is exciting.

— **Adventure:** Do work that requires me to take risks.

— **Profit, Gain:** Expect to earn large amounts of money or other material possessions.

— **Independence:** Decide for myself what kind of work I'll do and how I'll go about it, not have to do what others tell me to.

— **Moral Fulfillment:** Feel that my work is contributing to a set of moral standards that I feel are very important.

— **Location:** Find a place to live (town, geographic area) that matches my lifestyle and allows me to do the things I enjoy most.

— **Community:** Live in a town or city where I can get involved in community affairs.

— **Physical Challenge:** Have a job with physical demands that are challenging and rewarding.

— **Time Freedom:** Handle my job according to my own time schedule; no specific working hours required.

When you are done, add to the above list any other values that are particularly important to you in the job you want, then list the top three in the appropriate place on the Ideal Job Worksheet towards the end of this chapter.

Earnings: How Much Money Do You Want to Make — or Are Willing to Accept?

It always surprises me how little thought most people give to how much money they want or expect to make. Answers like "I'll take any reasonable offer," is an invitation to trouble.

I remember a middle-aged executive who had made over $60,000 per year. He had been unemployed for some time and was quite depressed. When asked what he wanted to earn in his next job, he told me that he wanted to start at about $65,000 but that he really only **needed** $30,000 per year to maintain his lifestyle now that his kids were grown. I suggested he redefine his job objective to include jobs that he would really enjoy doing and not to screen out jobs paying less than $60,000 per year. He took a job paying $37,000 and loved it. He told me he would never consider going back to what he used to do — whatever the salary.

Pay is important, but relative. What you want to earn in your next job and in the future **will** affect your career choices. But some compromise is always possible. You should know in advance what you would accept as well as what you would prefer. Here are a few questions to help you define a salary range:

1. If you found the perfect job in all other respects (or were desperate), what would be the very least pay you would be willing to accept? (Hourly, weekly, or annual is OK.) _____

2. What is the upper end of salary that you could expect to obtain, given your credentials and other factors? _____

3. What sort of income would you need to pay for a desirable lifestyle? (However you want to define this.) _____

To get this, you may have to figure out what that lifestyle costs. If you are not sure, find someone who lives that way and have a chat with them. A research librarian can also help you find information on average expenses. Later in this book, I will show you how to find out how much various jobs pay, on the average, as well as tips for negotiating your salary to higher levels. But to be successful in your negotiations, you must start with a good idea of how much you want — and how much you are willing to accept.

Responsibility: **What Level of Responsibility Do You Prefer?**

If you want to earn lots of money but do not want to have much responsibility, you may be in for a rude awakening. Most jobs that pay well have more responsibility than those paying less. There are exceptions, of course, like being a rock star. But the competition is fierce, and there is often more responsibility and work than meets the eye. A general rule is that the higher up in an organization you are, the more you make. Here are some questions to help you consider how much responsibility you want (or are willing to accept) in your ideal job.

1. Do you like to be in charge of things?
2. Are you good at supervising others?
3. Do you prefer working as part of a team?
4. Do you prefer working by yourself or under someone else's guidance?

Location: **To Move or Not to Move?**

"Are you willing to relocate?" This is a very important question to answer now — before it comes up in an interview. There are often good reasons for wanting to stay where you now live but certain jobs and career opportunities are limited unless you are willing to move. For example, if you live in a small town, certain jobs exist only in small numbers, if at all. If you are willing to leave you may be able to find jobs with higher overall wages, a larger and more varied job market, or some other advantage. Even if you decide to stay where you are, there are still geographic issues to consider. How far are you, for example, willing to commute? Would it be more desirable for you to work on one side of town than another?

When you've looked at all the options, you can make a more informed decision. If you **prefer** to stay but are **willing** to go, a good strategy is to spend a substantial part of your job search time looking locally. If you are willing to relocate, don't make the common mistake of looking for a job "anywhere." That sort of scattered approach is both inefficient and ineffective. It is preferable to narrow your job search to a few key geographic areas and concentrate your efforts there.

One strategy is to identify where the best job opportunities exist for the sort of job you want. A research librarian can help you find this information. But this should not be your sole criteria for relocating.

The right job in the wrong place is **not** the right job. A better course, before you get desperate, is to define the characteristics of the place you'd like to live. For example, suppose you would like to live near the ocean, in a midsize city, and in a part of the country that has mild winters but does have four seasons. That leaves out many places, doesn't it? Or it may be as simple as wanting to live near your mom. As you add more criteria, there are fewer and fewer places to look — and your job search becomes more precise.

One way to do this is to consider the places you have already lived. Think about what you did and did not like about them. Use a sheet of paper to list the things you did like (on the left side) and did not like (on the right). This may help you identify the things you would really like to have in a new place. You should also go to your library to research a particular location you are considering or to just learn about the options. There are some excellent books that rate places to live and many other materials on this subject to browse through.

Knowledge and Interests: What Special Knowledge or Interests Would You Like to Use or Pursue?

You have all sorts of prior experience, training, and education that can help you succeed on a new job. Formal education, special training and work experience are obviously important, but leisure activities, hobbies, volunteer work, family responsibilities and other informal activities can also help define a previously overlooked job possibility.

To help you consider alternatives, use a separate sheet of paper to make a list of the major areas in which you: **(1)** have received formal education or training, (2) are well-versed due to some prior work or non-work experience, or (3) are very interested, but don't have much practical experience.

Once you have made your list, go back and select the three areas that are most interesting to you. These could give you ideas for jobs that you might otherwise overlook. If you already have a job objective and it does not include one of your top three choices, don't toss out that experience yet. For instance, if you are looking for a job as a warehouse manager, but you selected your hobby of making pottery as one of the three, can you think of a possible job combining the two? Perhaps distributing pottery supplies or managing some part of a pottery business would be more your cup of tea than just managing any sort of warehouse.

Work Environment: What Sort of Work Environment Would You Prefer?

I don't like to work in a building without windows and I do like to get up and move around occasionally. While most of us can put up with all sorts of less-than-ideal physical work environments, some things are more important than others.

Once again, defining the things that you did **not** like about previous work environments is a good way to help you define what you prefer. So think of all the places you've worked or gone to school and write down the things you didn't like about those environments. Then redefine them as positives, as in the following example. When you have completed the list for each job you've had (use extra sheets if necessary), go back and select the five environmental preferences that are really important to you. Here is one example of such a worksheet to help you get started.

Job: Accountant for the I.R.S.	
Things I Did Not Like About the Workplace	**Environment I Would Like in My Next Job**
too noisy	quiet workplace
no variety in work	lots of variety in work
no windows	my own window
parking was a problem	my own air strip (just kidding)
too much sitting	more activity
not people-oriented	more customer contact
indoors in nice weather	more outside work
too large a business	smaller business

People: What Types of People Would You Prefer to Work With?

An important element in enjoying your job is the people you work with and for. If you have ever had a rotten boss or worked with a group of losers, you know exactly why this is so important. But what someone else defines as a good group of people to work with might not be good for you. You could argue that there is no way to know in advance the types of people you will end up having as co-workers. But then you have nothing but luck to help you if you haven't already given any thought to the subject. The following exercise will help you do just that.

Think about all your past jobs (work, military, volunteer, etc.) and your co-workers on those jobs. As in the sample worksheet above, write down the things you **didn't like** about your co-workers, then redefine them into qualities you'd **like** to see in your workmates. When your list is complete, go back and identify the types of people you would really like to work with in your next job. Then select the three qualities that are most important to you.

Putting Together Your Ideal Job Definition

Use this section to bring together the various elements of your ideal job in one place. This helps you deal with all the information in a more memorable way. If you have not already done the activities suggested earlier in this chapter, I urge you to do so now. Fill in your top choices for each of the categories in the appropriate spaces below.

The Ideal Job Worksheet

Fill in each section of this worksheet. The questions correspond to the eight preferences that were described earlier in this chapter.

1. What job-related skills do you prefer to use?

_____

_____

_____

_____

_____

_____

_____

The Ideal Job Worksheet

Adaptive skills: _____

_____

_____

_____

_____

_____

Transferable skills: _____

_____

_____

_____

_____

_____

2. What values would you prefer to use or pursue?

_____

_____

_____

_____

_____

_____

_____

3. What range of earnings would you prefer?

_____

_____

_____

_____

_____

_____

The Ideal Job Worksheet

4. What level of responsibility would you prefer?

_____

_____

_____

_____

_____

_____

5. What location would you prefer?

_____

_____

_____

_____

_____

_____

6. What special knowledge or interests would you like to use or pursue?

_____

_____

_____

_____

_____

7. What type of work environment would you prefer?

_____

_____

_____

_____

_____

The Ideal Job Worksheet

8. What types of people would you prefer to work with or for?

_____

_____

_____

_____

_____

_____

Once you have assembled the components of your ideal job, consider the possibilities. Your task in the job search is to find a job that comes as close as possible to meeting the criteria you have selected. If you conduct a creative job search, you won't be looking for a job but for the job. Of course, some compromise between the ideal and what you accept may be needed. But the closer you can come to finding a job that meets your preferences, the better job it will be for you.

This chapter has not provided you with a job title but it does give you a variety of places to start your job search. In the next chapter, you will learn how to find out about specific job titles to consider in your job search. Your knowledge of what you want in your ideal job can help you in deciding what types of jobs to look for.

Chapter Five Endnotes

1. The *Dictionary of Occupational Titles*, published by the U.S. Department of Labor, lists over 20,000 different job titles. Many of them, of course, are quite obscure. My favorite is "chicken eviscerator." I am told it takes a lot of guts to do this job.

2. These and other reports were cited by Richard Plunkett in a book titled *Supervision: The Direction of People at Work*, published by Allyn and Bacon, 1989.

3. Ibid.

4. In the 1940s and 50s, Bernard Haldane was involved in helping people figure out what they wanted to do with their careers and their lives. I consider his work, including his book *Career Satisfaction And Success* as important early contributions. In the 1960s, John Crystal had evolved an

elegant system for individual career and life planning that was studied by Richard Bolles. The two of them collaborated on a book titled *Where Do I Go From Here With My Life?*, Ten Speed Press, 1974, still available. Later, Bolles wrote a book titled *What Color Is Your Parachute?*, Ten Speed Press, revised yearly. That book has become the all-time best selling career planning book. Bolles and Crystal started a movement that has come to be called "Life/Work Planning." That is the basis for the approach used in this chapter, though my iteration here is very brief. If you want more, try *Parachute*. I have also written books titled *The Right Job for You* and *Job Finding Fast* that provide more detailed activities on the eight preferences defined in this chapter.

5.   A revision of *Exploring Careers* has since been published by JIST Works, Inc., in 1990 and the worksheet is included in that work. Dr. Figler is a career consultant, presenter and author located in Orangevale, California. *The Complete Job Search Handbook* is a wonderful book, published by Henry Holt &Co.

Chapter Six

Researching Specific Job Titles

If you are not at all certain of what sort of job to look for, this chapter will help you obtain information on alternatives. But many job seekers already have a general idea of the kind of job they want. If you are among this group, you still have much to gain in knowing how to research various job titles.

Why Job Seekers Need to Explore Alternatives

By this time, some career or job possibilities have probably occurred to you. If you are already sure of what career field you want to work in, there are probably details about that career that can benefit you in your job search. For example, can you name the specific skills most often needed in that particular field? What are **related** job titles you may qualify for? What are the advancement opportunities? What is an average pay range for jobs in that field?

You may be overlooking many jobs for which you are qualified but don't know about. Anyone who has ever been unemployed knows that they have to be flexible in considering alternatives. As you have discovered, you have many adaptive and transferable skills that can be used in various occupations, even though your experience may be in another field or industry. A good manager, for example, can be effective in a variety of management positions and in a variety of industries.

Often, what you don't know about a specific job can be learned quickly enough. Of course, many jobs **do** require you to have job-related skills, experience, or training related to that job, but many job seekers with inferior credentials get jobs over more qualified applicants based on how they present themselves in an interview. And, of course, if **you** get to talk to the right person and your competition does not, they won't even have a chance against you. So do consider jobs that you may not have previously considered. You will learn how to do this in the sections that follow.

Looking at the Most Popular Jobs

While there are over 20,000 job titles, most people work in a relatively small number of these. In fact, about 85 percent of all workers are employed in about 250 of the most popular jobs described in the U.S. Department of Labor's book titled the *Occupational Outlook Handbook.*[1]

The 250 jobs are arranged into 12 occupational clusters used by the U.S. Department of Labor. This arrangement will make it easier for you to identify jobs requiring related skills, training or experience.

I have also provided information on how many people are employed in each of the listed jobs, as well as projections for growth through the year 2000. While this is important information to have, it should not be used to select a job objective. Some jobs are expected to grow more rapidly than others and may offer you excellent career opportunities. But even in jobs where little growth is expected, new jobs are opening as employees retire or go on to other jobs. Even when they have slower projected growth rates, occupations employing large numbers of people will often offer more job openings than smaller, faster growing occupational groups. It would be equally unwise to pick a "hot" job — one with a much higher-than-average growth rate — just because it was growing rapidly. If it took you several years to acquire the necessary skills and experience, there might be a surplus of job seekers by the time you are prepared for that hot job.

Many of the 250 jobs listed in this chapter will require more experience, education, training, or responsibility. Those that do will usually pay better. But some lower paying jobs could allow you to enjoy your work more. If you're interested in a job you don't qualify for now, don't eliminate it too quickly. Consider an entry-level job in the same field. Or get additional training or education. A lower paying job now may lead to increased earnings in the future.

An Overview of the Major Occupational Clusters

The U.S. Department of Labor organizes all jobs into 12 major clusters of similar occupations. This section includes brief descriptions of each of these clusters as well as some information on their projected growth. Look over the clusters and identify those that you are interested in for further exploration or those clusters where you have previous expereince or training.

Executive, Administrative, and Managerial Occupations: Employment in this cluster is expected to increase 22 percent, from 12.1 to 14.8 million. Growth will be spurred by the increasing complexity of business operations and by large employment gains in trade and services — industries that employ a higher than average proportion of managers.

Employment in management-related occupations tends to be tied to industry growth. Thus jobs for employment interviewers are projected to grow much faster than the average, in line with the expected growth in the personnel supply industry.

Hiring requirements in many managerial and administrative jobs are rising. Work experience, specialized training, or graduate study will be increasingly necessary. Familiarity with computers is a "must" in a growing number of firms, due to the widespread use of computerized management information systems.

Professional Specialty Occupations: Employment in this cluster is expected to grow 24 percent, from 14.6 to 18.1 million jobs. Much of this growth is a result of rising demand for engineers; computer specialists; lawyers; health diagnosing and treating occupations; and preschool and elementary and secondary school teachers.

Technicians and Related Support Occupations: Workers in this group provide technical assistance to engineers, scientists, and other professional workers as well as operate and program technical equipment. Employment in this cluster is expected to increase 32 percent, from 3.9 to 5.1 million, making it the fastest growing in the economy. It also contains the fastest growing occupation—paralegals. Employment of paralegals is expected to skyrocket due to increased utilization of these workers in the rapidly expanding legal services industry.

Marketing and Sales Occupations: Employment in this large cluster is projected to increase 20 percent, from 13.3 to 15.9 million jobs. Demand for real estate brokers, travel agents, and securities and financial services sales workers is expected to grow much faster than the average due to strong growth in the industries that employ them. Many part- and full-time job openings are expected for retail sales workers and cashiers due to the large size, high turnover, and faster than average employment growth in these occupations. The outlook for higher paying sales jobs, however, will tend to be more competitive.

Administrative Support Occupations, Including Clerical: This is the largest major occupational group. Workers in these occupations perform the wide variety of tasks necessary to keep organizations functioning smoothly. The group as a whole is expected to grow 12 percent, from 21.1 to 23.6 million jobs. However, technological advances are projected to decrease the demand for stenographers and typists, word processors, and data entry keyers. Others, such as receptionists and information clerks, will grow much faster than the average, spurred by rapidly expanding industries such as business services. Moreover, because of their large size and substantial turnover, clerical occupations will offer abundant opportunities for qualified jobseekers in the years ahead.

Service Occupations: This group includes a wide range of workers in protective services, food and beverage preparation, and cleaning and personal services. These occupations are expected to grow 23 percent, from 18.5 to 22.7 million, because a growing population and economy, combined with higher incomes and increased leisure time, will spur demand for all types of services.

Agriculture, Forestry, and Fishing Occupations: Workers in these occupations cultivate plants, breed and raise animals, and catch fish. Although demand for food, fiber, and wood is expected to increase as the world's population grows, the use of more productive farming and forestry methods and the consolidation of smaller farms are expected to result in a 5 percent decline in employment, from 3.5 to 3.3 million jobs.

Mechanics, Installers, and Repairers: These workers adjust, maintain, and repair automobiles, industrial equipment, computers, and many other types of equipment. Overall employment in these occupations is expected to grow 13 percent — from 4.8 to 5.5 million — due to increased use of mechanical and electronic equipment. One of the fastest growing occupations in this group is expected to be automotive body repairers, reflecting the growth in the number of lightweight cars that are prone to collision damage. Telephone installers and repairers, in sharp contrast, are expected to record a decline in employment due to laborsaving advances.

Construction, Trades, and Extractive (Mining) Occupations: Overall employment in this group of occupations is expected to rise from 4.0 to 4.7 million, or 16 percent. Virtually all of the new jobs will be in construction. Employment growth in construction will be spurred by new projects and alterations to existing structures. On the other hand, continued stagnation in the oil and gas industries and low growth in demand for coal, metal, and other materials will result in little change in the employment of extractive workers.

Production Occupations. Workers in these occupations set up, install, adjust, operate, and tend machinery and equipment and use handtools and hand-held power tools to fabricate and assemble products. Employment is expected to decline 2 percent, from 12.8 to 12.5 million. More efficient production techniques—such as computer-aided manufacturing and industrial robotics—will eliminate some production worker jobs. Many production occupations are sensitive to fluctuations in the business cycle and competition from imports.

Transportation and Material Moving Occupations: Workers in this cluster operate the equipment used to move people and equipment. Employment in this group is expected to increase 12 percent, from 4.6 to 5.2 million jobs. Employment of busdrivers and truckdrivers will grow as fast as the average, while employment of material moving equipment operators is expected to grow more slowly due to greater use of automated materials handling equipment in factories and warehouses. Railroad transportation workers and water transportation workers are projected to show a decline in employment.

Handlers, Equipment Cleaners, Helpers, and Laborers: Workers in this group assist skilled workers and perform routine, unskilled tasks. Employment is expected to increase only about 2 percent, from 4.9 to 5.0 million jobs as routine tasks are automated.

The 250 Most Popular Jobs and Their Projected Growth[2]

Tips for Using the List

Look closely at the jobs within the occupational clusters that most interest you or where you have related education or experience. If you already have a job objective, look for that job and any related jobs within the same cluster. You can also use a simple prioritizing system to identify interesting job alternatives. Mark each job using the criteria that follow, then use this list as a basis for additional career exploration.

1 = Very Interested   2 = Somewhat Interested   3 = Not Interested

The data in the chart that follows is based on U.S. Department of Labor projections through the year 2000. The listed jobs cover over 85 percent of the jobs in our workforce.

The Most Popular Jobs and Their Projected Growth of Employment

	Estimated Growth in Thousands	%
EXECUTIVE, ADMINISTRATIVE, AND MANAGERIAL OCCUPATIONS		
___ Accountants and auditors	963	23
___ Administrative services managers	217	26
___ Budget analysts	62	17
___ Construction and building inspectors	56	14
___ Construction managers	187	26
___ Cost estimators	169	15
___ Education administrators	320	19
___ Employment interviewers	81	40
___ Engineering, science, and data processing managers	258	32
___ Financial managers	673	19
___ General managers and top executives	3,030	16
___ Government chief executives and legislators	69	3
___ Health services managers	177	42
___ Hotel managers and assistants	96	28
___ Industrial production managers	215	18
___ Inspectors and compliance officers, except construction	130	14
___ Management analysts and consultants	130	35
___ Marketing, advertising, and public relations managers	406	26
___ Personnel, training, and labor relations specialists and managers	422	22
___ Property and real estate managers	225	19
___ Purchasing agents and managers	458	14
___ Restaurant and food service managers	524	28
___ Underwriters	103	29
___ Wholesale and retail buyers	207	6
Professional Specialty Occupations		
___ Engineers	1,411	25
___ Aerospace engineers	78	13
___ Chemical engineers	49	16
___ Civil engineers	186	17
___ Electrical and electronics engineers	439	40

The Most Popular Jobs and Their Projected Growth of Employment

	Estimated Growth in Thousands	%
— Industrial engineers	132	18
— Mechanical engineers	225	20
— Metallurgical, ceramic, and materials engineers	19	13
— Mining engineers	5	6
— Nuclear engineers	15	3
— Petroleum engineers	17	7
Architects and Surveyors		
— Architects	86	25
— Landscape architects	19	29
— Surveyors	100	12
Computer, Mathematical, and Operations Research Occupations		
— Actuaries	16	54
— Computer systems analysts	402	53
— Mathematicians	16	19
— Operations research analysts	55	55
— Statisticians	15	22
Life Scientists		
— Agricultural scientists	25	21
— Biological scientists	57	26
— Foresters and conservation scientists	27	8
Physical Scientists		
— Chemists	80	17
— Geologists and geophysicists	42	16
— Meteorologists	6	30
— Physicists and astronomers	18	12
— Lawyers and Judges	622	30
Social Scientists and Urban Planners		
— Economists and market research analysts	36	27
— Psychologists	104	27
— Sociologists	N/A	N/A
— Urban and regional planners	20	15
Social and Recreation Workers		
— Human services workers	118	45
— Social workers	385	29

The Most Popular Jobs and Their Projected Growth of Employment

	Estimated Growth in Thousands	%
___ Recreation workers	186	19
Religious Workers		
___ Protestant ministers	429	N/A
___ Rabbis	3.5	N/A
___ Roman Catholic priests	54	N/A
Teachers, Librarians, and Counselors		
___ Adult and vocational education teachers	467	12
___ Archivists and curators	16	17
___ College and university faculty	846	3
___ Counselors	124	27
___ Kindergarten and elementary school teachers	1,359	15
___ Librarians	143	10
___ Secondary school teachers	1,164	19
Health Diagnosing Practitioners		
___ Chiropractors	36	N/A
___ Dentists	167	13
___ Optometrists	37	16
___ Physicians	535	28
___ Podiatrists	17	35
___ Veterinarians	46	26
Health Assessment and Treating Occupations		
___ Dietitians and nutritionists	40	28
___ Occupational therapists	33	49
___ Pharmacists	162	27
___ Physical therapists	68	57
___ Physician assistants	48	28
___ Recreational therapists	26	37
___ Registered nurses	1,577	39
___ Respiratory therapists	56	41
___ Speech-language pathologists and audiologists	53	28
Communications Occupations		
___ Public relations specialists	91	15
___ Radio and television announcers and newscasters	57	19

The Most Popular Jobs and Their Projected Growth of Employment

	Estimated Growth in Thousands	%
— Reporters and correspondents	70	16
— Writers and editors	219	25
Visual Arts Occupations		
— Designers	309	28
— Photographers and camera operators	105	19
— Visual artists	216	27
Performing Arts Occupations		
— Actors, directors, and producers	80	30
— Dancers and choreographers	11	19
— Musicians	229	10
TECHNICIANS AND RELATED SUPPORT OCCUPATIONS		
Health Technologists and Technicians		
— Clinical laboratory technologists and technicians	242	19
— Dental hygienists	91	18
— Dispensing opticians	49	31
— EEG technologists	6	50
— EKG technicians	18	10
— Emergency medical technicians	76	13
— Licensed practical nurses	626	37
— Medical record technicians	47	60
— Nuclear medicine technologists	10	30
— Radiologic technologists	132	66
— Surgical technicians	35	56
Technologists, Except Health		
— Aircraft pilots	83	31
— Air traffic controllers	27	15
— Broadcast technicians	27	-31
— Computer programmers	519	48
— Drafters	319	12
— Engineering technicians	722	28
— Library technicians	54	9
— Paralegals	83	75
— Science technicians	232	19
— Tool programmers, numerical control	8	26

The Most Popular Jobs and Their Projected Growth of Employment

	Estimated Growth in Thousands	%
MARKETING AND SALES OCCUPATIONS		
___ Cashiers	2,310	13
___ Counter and rental clerks	241	28
___ Insurance sales workers	423	14
___ Manufacturers' and wholesale sales representatives	1,883	23
___ Real estate agents, brokers and appraisers	422	17
___ Retail sales workers	4,571	20
___ Securities and financial services sales representatives	200	55
___ Services sales representatives	481	45
___ Travel agents	142	54
ADMINISTRATIVE SUPPORT OCCUPATIONS		
___ Adjusters, investigators and collectors	961	18
___ Bank tellers	522	5
___ Clerical supervisors and managers	1,183	12
___ Computer and peripheral equipment operators	316	29
___ Credit clerks and authorizers	229	27
___ Financial record processors	2,849	1
___ Billing clerks and related workers	421	0
___ Bookkeeping, accounting and auditing clerks	2,251	1
___ Payroll and timekeeping clerks	176	-2
___ General office clerks	2,519	18
___ Information clerks	1,316	34
___ Hotel and motel desk clerks	113	26
___ Interviewing and new accounts clerks	237	18
___ Receptionists	833	40
___ Reservation and transportation ticket agents and travel clerks	133	28
___ Mail clerks and messengers	259	10
___ Material recording, scheduling, dispatching and disributing occupations	2,889	12
___ Dispatchers	202	14
___ Stock clerks	2,152	12
___ Traffic, shipping and receiving clerks	535	10

The Most Popular Jobs and Their Projected Growth of Employment

	Estimated Growth in Thousands	%
— Postal clerks and mail carriers	665	6
— Record clerks	886	5
— Brokerage clerks and statement clerks	96	3
— File clerks	263	10
— Library assistants and bookmobile drivers	105	6
— Order clerks	293	-2
— Personnel clerks	129	9
— Secretaries	3,373	17
— Stenographers	159	-23
— Teacher aids	682	21
— Telephone, telegraph and teletype operators	330	15
— Typists, word processors and data entry keyers	1,416	-6
SERVICE OCCUPATIONS		
Protective Service Occupations		
— Correction officers	186	41
— Firefighting occupations	291	10
— Guards	795	32
— Police, detectives and special agents	515	13
Food and Beverage Preparation and Service Occupations		
— Chefs, cooks and other kitchen workers	2,755	21
— Food and beverage service occupations	4,458	24
Health Service Occupations		
— Dental assistants	166	19
— Medical assistants	149	70
— Nursing aides and psychiatric aides	1,298	31
Personal Service and Building and Grounds Service Occupations		
— Animal caretakers, except farm	92	16
— Barbers	46	0
— Childcare workers	670	30
— Cosmetologists and related workers	649	13
— Flight attendants	88	39
— Gardeners and groundskeepers	760	24
— Homemaker-home health aides	327	63
— Janitors and cleaners	2,895	19

The Most Popular Jobs and Their Projected Growth of Employment

	Estimated Growth in Thousands	%
___ Private household workers	902	-5
AGRICULTURE, FORESTRY, FISHING AND RELATED OCCUPATIONS		
___ Farm operators and managers	1,272	-19
___ Fishers, hunters, and trappers	54	10
___ Timber cutting and logging workers	106	-10
MECHANICS, INSTALLERS, AND REPAIRERS		
___ Aircraft mechanics and engine specialists	124	16
___ Automotive body repairers	214	26
___ Automotive mechanics	771	16
___ Commercial and industrial electronic equipment repairers	79	17
___ Communications equipment mechanics	113	-16
___ Computer and office machine repairers	128	35
___ Diesel mechanics	269	16
___ Electronic home entertainment equipment repairers	44	13
___ Elevator installers and repairers	13	17
___ Farm equipment mechanics	54	1
___ General maintenance mechanics	1,,080	19
___ Heating, air-conditioning and refrigeration mechanics	225	17
___ Home appliance and power tool repairers	76	0
___ Industrial machinery repairers	463	16
___ Line installers and cable splicers	231	-4
___ Millwrights	77	17
___ Mobile heavy equipment mechanics	108	14
___ Motorcycle, boat, and small-engine mechanics	58	13
___ Musical instrument repairers and tuners	8	8
___ Telephone installers and repairers	58	-20
___ Vending machine servicers and repairers	27	1
CONSTRUCTION, TRADES, AND EXTRACTIVE OCCUPATIONS		
___ Bricklayers and stone masons	167	16
___ Carpenters	1,106	16
___ Carpet installers	56	21

The Most Popular Jobs and Their Projected Growth of Employment

	Estimated Growth in Thousands	%
— Concrete masons and terrazzo workers	114	17
— Drywall workers and lathers	152	17
— Electricians	542	18
— Glaziers	49	18
— Insulation workers	65	19
— Painters and paperhangers	431	16
— Plasterers	27	8
— Plumbers and pipefitters	396	18
— Roofers	123	19
— Roustabouts	39	1
— Sheet-metal workers	97	19
— Structural and reinforcing ironworkers	91	19
— Tilesetters	26	22
PRODUCTION OCCUPATIONS		
Assemblers		
— Precision assemblers	354	-26
— Blue-collar worker supervisors	1,797	7
Food Processing Occupations		
— Butchers and meat, poultry and fish cutters	368	8
— Inspectors, testers and graders	676	-6
Metalworking and Plastic-working Occupations		
— Boilermakers	25	9
— Jewelers	35	16
— Machinists	397	9
— Metalworking and plastic-working machine operators	1,405	-3
— Metalworking machine operators	1,252	-6
— Steel workers	8.9	-19
— Numerical-control machine-tool operators	64	9
— Tool and die makers	152	4
— Welders, cutters and welding machine operators	424	-7
Plant and Systems Operators		
— Electric power generating plant operators and power distributors and dispatchers	45	14

The Most Popular Jobs and Their Projected Growth of Employment	Estimated Growth in Thousands	%
___ Stationary engineers	36	-1
___ Water and wastewater treatment plant operators	76	14
Printing Occupations		
___ Bindery workers	73	11
___ Compositors and typesetters	86	1
___ Lithographic and photoengraving workers	67	18
___ Printing press operators	239	15
Textile, Apparel, and Furnishings Occupations		
___ Apparel workers	1,104	-7
___ Shoe and leather workers and repairers	32	0
___ Textile machinery operators	310	-12
___ Upholsterers	73	11
___ Woodworking occupations	375	9
Miscellaneous Production Occupations		
___ Dental laboratory technicians	51	10
___ Ophthalmic laboratory technicians	26	28
___ Painting and coating machine operators	159	5
___ Photographic process workers	67	21
TRANSPORTATION AND MATERIAL MOVING OCCUPATIONS		
___ Busdrivers	506	17
___ Material moving equipment operators	1,010	4
___ Railroad transportation workers	106	-16
___ Truckdrivers	2,641	14
___ Water transportation occupations	49	-12
HANDLERS, EQUIPMENT CLEANERS, HELPERS, AND LABORERS		
___ All workers in this group	4,894	2

Using The *Occupational Outlook Handbook*

All of the jobs listed in this chapter are described in a book titled the *Occupational Outlook Handbook* (*OOH*), published by the U.S. Department of Labor. The *OOH* is the most widely used source of basic information on jobs and is available at most libraries. A bookstore version of the *OOH* is also now available, titled *America's Top 300 Jobs*.[3] Because of the importance of the

OOH as a basic reference for career planning and job seeking, I feel it is important for you to become more familiar with it.

The *OOH* describes each of the 250 jobs listed earlier in this chapter and each description includes the following categories:

- Nature of the Work
- Working Conditions
- Employment
- Training, Other Qualifications and Advancement

- Job Outlook
- Earnings
- Related Occupations
- Sources of Additional Information

While the *OOH* job descriptions are a brief one to two pages in length, they are full of information and facts that can be of great value to you. The book is updated every two years and the newest edition has current information on salaries, growth projections and other details. I feel strongly that the *OOH* is a book that you should get your hands on. While most libraries will have a copy, it will probably be in the reference section and not available for check out. The bookstore version of the *OOH* titled *America's Top 300 Jobs*, may be in the library's circulation section or you can order one from most bookstores.

Use the *OOH* to Get Specific Career Information and Prepare for an Interview

One way to use the *OOH* is to obtain background information on an occupational area that interests you. After reading the job description, you may decide it is worth more exploration. The *OOH* is also useful in preparing for a job interview. Once you know what sort of job you will be seeking, **carefully** review the *OOH* descriptions for related jobs. They provide a wealth of information on the required skills, salary ranges, and other details that can help you tremendously in your interviews.

One other excellent use for the *OOH* relates to your adaptive and transferable skills. As you discovered earlier in this book, you have many transferable skills from past experiences that you can use again in the future. Use the *OOH* to look up jobs you have held earlier. Almost always, some skills required to do well in that job are also necessary for the job you now seek. Note all skill words listed for your new job and look for similar ones in previous jobs. Suddenly, something you did in the past can take on a whole new importance!

As an example, let's assume that at one time you waited on tables. You now want to look for a position in sales. In your interviews, you had not planned on mentioning your restaurant experience because it didn't seem to relate. Well, guess what? It can. If you look at the *OOH* descriptions for waiters and waitresses, you will find references to the need for skills similar to those required for sales, "...an even disposition is also important," and "...successful waiters and waitresses genuinely like people, provide good service, and make customers feel comfortable."

In an interview situation, armed with such information, you could now make this statement: "In a previous job, I worked with large numbers of customers — over 1,000 per week. I learned to take care of their needs quickly and efficiently while maintaining a friendly and professional manner." Compare that to "I used to wait on tables," and you can begin to appreciate the power of communicating your skills in this way.

There are many similar examples between almost any two jobs. It may be helpful to review the job which interests you and list all the skills necessary to do it well. Similar lists could be created for previous jobs to help identify transferable skills.

Other Sources of Career Information

Following are a variety of resources you can use to get additional information or help in your career planning or search for career information.

America's Top 300 Jobs. This is a special version of the *Occupational Outlook Handbook* that can be found in many bookstores. It is published by JIST Works, Inc., the same people who published the book you are now reading. Except for the title, cover design and the first few pages, it has the exact same content as the *OOH* published by the U.S. Department of Labor.

The *Guide For Occupational Exploration.*[4] The *GOE* provides a method of narrowing down broad interests of the many specific jobs within each major category. It lists over 12,000 jobs by occupational cluster, interests, abilities, and traits required for successful performance. In addition, each job is cross-referenced in useful ways. You can look up jobs by industry, types of skills or abilities required, values, related home/leisure activities, military experience, education required, or related jobs you have had. The U.S. Department of Labor published the earlier edition of this book and a later edition was published by a private source. Most larger libraries will have one of these editions available.

The *Dictionary of Occupational Titles.*[5] While the *GOE* allows you to locate thousands of job titles in a variety of helpful ways, it does not describe these jobs. The *DOT* does provide brief descriptions for each of the jobs listed in the *GOE* and is the only book to do so. Also published by the U.S. Department of Labor, the *DOT* can be found in most large libraries. It is a very large book (over 1,400 pages) and is not particularly easy to use but, combined with the *GOE*, provides the most thorough system of organizing jobs available.

The *Enhanced Guide for Occupational Exploration.*[6] This book combines useful elements of both the *GOE* and the *DOT*. It uses the *GOE*'s structure for organizing jobs into major interest areas and cross-references jobs in similarly helpful ways. But it also provides descriptions for each of the jobs it lists. One book can do this by excluding the many jobs that employ few people or are highly specialized. The 2,500 jobs it does include cover 95 percent of the jobs in the workforce and few people will miss those that are not listed. In fact, I think that the excluded 10,000 jobs tend to get in the way of finding the ones that most people actually work in. This book is published by JIST, the same people who published the book you are now reading.

The Public Library. Most libraries have books and other resource materials on a variety of careers. Ask the librarian for help in finding information about the jobs that interest you. If you have narrowed your job search to one or two fields, there are a variety of good (and some not-so-good) books at your library or bookstore. One excellent series, Career Horizons, is published by VGM. It is well-written, easy-to-read, and provides current information on over 50 occupations.

Career Counselors. If you have access to free career counseling from a school you have attended, consider yourself fortunate and set up an appointment. There are also excellent career counselors who work in various community organizations and in private practice. Look in the *Yellow Pages* for the places they may work. Be forewarned though: just because they say they do career counseling does not mean they are good. If they won't tell you their fees, it's probably best to stay away. And avoid anyone who uses high pressure tactics or charges total fees in excess of a week's pay or so.

People. Ask friends, relatives, and others to tell you what they know about the jobs that appeal to you. They may also know about other jobs that would be right for you. Once you get interested in a type of job, find someone who has this kind of job. Ask them what they do or don't like, how they got started, and what advice they can give you about getting a job in that area.

Work in That Field. The best way to explore long-term career alternatives is to get a job in that career. Often, you can find entry-level jobs that don't require special training. You would then be in a good position to decide to stay there, get additional training, or try something else.

Questions You Should Be Able to Answer Before Beginning Your Job Search

Beginning with the next chapter, the rest of this book is about GETTING a job. But before you begin looking, it is essential that you (1) can clearly state what sort of a job you want, and (2) know what kinds of skills and experiences are needed to do well in that job.

Even if you decide to change your job objective later, it is very important that you decide on a temporary one now. Much of what follows in this book assumes that you have at least a temporary job objective. You should be able to answer each of the questions that follow. Consider writing out your responses to each before you go to the next chapter.

1. What is the general type of job you want?

2. What specific job or job titles are most appropriate for you to look for now?

3. What top adaptive and transferable skills do you have that this job requires?

4. What specific job-related skills or knowledge do you have that directly relate to doing this particular job?

5. What special training or education do you have that directly supports your doing this job well?

6. Does the job require you to use any special tools or equipment? If so, what experience do you have in using them?

7. What specific work experiences similar duties, tasks, responsibilities, etc. relate to your doing this job well?

8. What else can you offer that supports your doing this job well?

Unless you can answer all of the above items thoroughly, you are not ready to conduct a truly effective job search. If necessary, seek help from the other sources I've mentioned, but do settle on a career objective before you begin your job search.

Chapter Six Endnotes

1. New revisions of the *Occupational Outlook Handbook* are published by the U.S. Department of Labor every other year. The book is in the public domain and republished by several private sources including JIST Works, Inc.

2. I assembled the information in this chart from two sources. The jobs themselves are those described in the *Occupational Outlook Handbook*. The data on the numbers of people employed in each occupation comes from the "1990-91 Job Outlook In Brief," published in the DOL's *Occupational Outlook Quarterly*. The data used is for 1988 employment and is the latest data available from the DOL at the time of this publication. The percentage growth comes from the same source and is a projection of anticipated growth through the year 2000 from the base year of 1988.

3. While the *OOH* is available in most libraries, it is not particularly easy to get a copy for yourself as few bookstores carry it. JIST does publish it too,

ours being cheaper than the government edition even though the content is the same. We publish *America's Top 300 Jobs* because we feel the *OOH* is the best book on career information available, and its information should be readily available in bookstores. In our own way, we like to think that we are doing our patriotic duty in bringing the excellent work of the DOL to a broader audience...

4.   The original edition of the *GOE* was published by the Department of Labor in 1979. It is still available and is the one found in most libraries. A revision, under the direction of Drs. Thomas Harrington and Arthur O'Shea, came out in 1985. Published by the Forum Foundation and distributed by JIST, it is a much improved edition with many useful features but not as widely available.

5.   At the time this book goes to press, the "current" edition of the *Dictionary of Occupational Titles* is one published way back in 1977. The most recent supplement, including new job descriptions and other changes was published in 1986. JIST distributes both. A new edition of the *DOT* may be published in 1992 or so.

6.   The *Enhanced Guide for Occupational Exploration* is the result of much work by Marilyn Maze and Donald Mayall who have compiled a unique data base of career information over the years. Based mostly on Department of Labor data, the information has been marketed as computer software and report-generating software by CIASA, Inc., located in Berkeley, California. I wrote the introductory chapters and helped edit and publish the book.

Chapter Seven

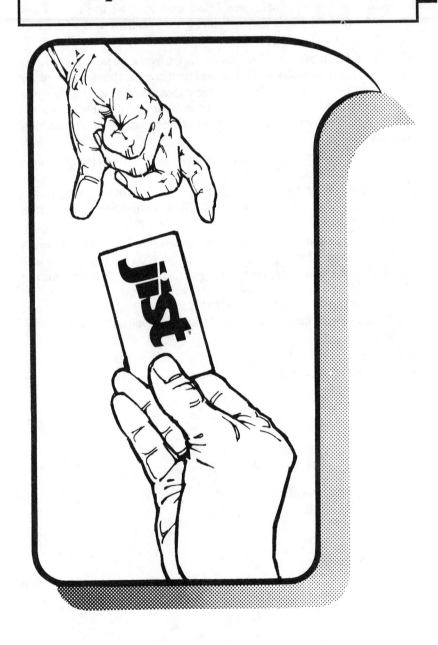

Creating JIST Cards
— *A New Job Search Tool*

To best understand a JIST Card I want you to begin by looking at one. As you do, respond to what you read as an employer might. Imagine that you are an employer and can hire someone to help manage a small business. You may or may not have a job opening now. A job seeker will soon present some information to you and I want you to simply react to it.

```
John Kijek                        Home: (219) 232-9213
                                  Message: (219) 637-6643
Position Desired: Management position in a small-
to medium-size organization.
SKILLS: B.A. in business plus over five years experience
in increasingly responsible management positions. Have
supervised as many as 12 staff and increased
productivity by 27% over two years. Was promoted twice
in the past three years and have excellent references.
Started customer follow-up program that increased sales
by 22% within 12 months. Get along well with others and
am a good team worker.
Willing to travel and can work any hours
Hardworking, self-motivated, will accept responsibility
```

My Questions to You Are These:

1. Do you feel good about this person?
2. Would you be willing to see him if you had a job opening?
3. If he asked, would you be willing to see him even if you did not have a job opening?

Most People Are Willing to Set Up an Interview

What you just read is called a JIST Card. JIST stands for **Job Information and Seeking Training**. It is a name used to identify a series of job-search techniques I developed in the early 1970s and is now the name of the organization that I work for, JIST Works, Inc.

A JIST card is a 3-by-5-inch card you can use like a mini-resume or business calling card. The card is usually printed commercially so you have plenty to use during your job search. Most people can read a typical JIST Card in fewer than 30 seconds. Yet, in that short period of time, most people react in a positive way to what they read. I know because I constantly survey those who attend seminars I give and over 95 percent react positively to reading their first JIST Card. In fact, most people who read it say they would interview such a person — based on just this much information.

Since I first developed this job search tool in 1972, it has been used by many thousands of job seekers of all kinds with great success. It works because it presents the essentials an employer wants to know.

A few people do react negatively to it, saying that it does not present enough information or that the person sounds **too** good. It is true that it does not present much information. Certainly not enough to hire someone — but neither does a resume. Its brevity is its advantage. It is the only job search tool I know of that can create a specific positive impression that relates to what a job seeker can do — and can be communicated in 30 seconds or less. You will also find that, as a job search tool, the JIST Card can help you get results in a way no other job search tool can.

Some Ways You Can Use a JIST Card

With a track record of 15 years, JIST Cards have been used in many creative ways. I have seen them posted on a grocery store bulletin board in Texas, on a table at a hairdresser's salon in southern California, even had friends tell me they found them under their windshield wiper after going to a movie. But here are some of the best uses.

Give to friends and relatives. The odds are good that the people who know you best could not describe what you can do as clearly as a JIST Card can. Give them several to pass along to people they know who might, in turn, give it to someone who knows of a job opening. Friends and relatives are a major source of job leads and you can quickly get hundreds of your cards into circulation this way. This can expand your network and increase the results dramatically.

As a business card. Since it is small, you can give your JIST Card to almost anyone you meet during the time you are looking for a job. One example was a job seeker who gave a handful of JIST Cards to his insurance agent who put them in his waiting room where customers could see them. This resulted in several phone calls from employers and one job offer. This is an excellent way to equip your network contacts with a tool that they can use to help you.

Send to an employer before an interview. Think about it. Send an informal note thanking someone for setting up an interview with you and enclose a JIST Card. It's just enough to arouse their interest.

Enclosed with a thank-you note after an interview or phone contact. Sending an informal thank-you note is simply good manners. Enclosing a JIST Card is good sense. It's just one more way to tell the prospective employer about yourself and give them a tool for contacting you. I also know that this approach has often resulted in the person sending the thank-you note getting the job over those with better credentials.

Attached to an application. When you have to complete an application (knowing as you do that it is not a good way to get an interview), attaching a JIST Card will allow the viewer to quickly get a positive overall impression. It can't hurt.

Attached to a resume. Unlike a resume, you can read a JIST Card in 30 seconds. It provides a clear and direct presentation of what you want and what you can do. It can also help give the reader a positive perception of you as they get into the details of your resume.

As the basis for a telephone presentation. With just a few changes, the JIST Card can be easily adapted to use as a telephone script for obtaining interviews. I'll show you how this is done in the next chapter.

As a source for answering interview questions. Small as it is, a well-prepared JIST Card includes a variety of things you can use as the basis for answering interview questions. For example, in response to the question "Why don't you tell me about yourself?" you might say "You might want to know that I am a hard worker..." Or you can select almost any key skill, experience, or accomplishment statement from your JIST Card and use it as the basis for answering many interview questions. In fact, even though the JIST Card is an effective job search tool, I believe that its greatest value is the way it forces us to get to the essence of what we have to offer an employer. It can foster a sense of identity and self-definition that comes through in an interview. I have seen it happen and know that it is true.

The Anatomy of a JIST Card

A JIST Card doesn't contain many details, but consider what John Kijek's card (the sample card at the beginning of this chapter) does include:

Identification: John's name is given.

How to Be Contacted: John lists two phone numbers. An employer will almost always call rather than send a letter. By giving the number of a reliable friend who will take messages, John can usually be reached.

Related Education and Training: His JIST Card lists his education related to the job he wants.

Length of Experience: John lists his total length of work experience as well as the fact that he was promoted.

Skills: This section tells what John can do and how well he can do it. These are job-related skills. John also mentions several important transferable skills such as his ability to supervise others and get results.

Preferred Working Conditions: John lists two preferences for the type of work he wants. Both of these are positives.

Good Worker Traits: John lists adaptive skills that would be important to most employers.

And he does all this on a 3-by-5-inch card! If you didn't see it here you may not have believed it possible to do all this in such a small format, but there it is.

Sample JIST Cards

Here are some more sample JIST Cards. To save space, they are less than full-size and vary from those for entry- level jobs (for persons just out of school) to those for professionals and other occupations. Study them and use any ideas that help you with your own card.

Sandy Zaremba   Home: (512) 232-7608
                                   Message: (512) 234-7465

Position: General Office/Clerical

Over two years work experience plus one year of training in office practices.
Type 55 wpm, trained in word processing operations, post general ledger,
handle payables, receivables, and most accounting tasks. Good
interpersonal skills and get along with most people. Can meet deadlines
and handle pressure well.

Willing to work any hours

Organized, honest, reliable, and hardworking

Joyce Hua   Home: (214) 173-1659

Leave message: (214) 274-1436

Position Desired: Programming/Systems Analyst

Skills: Over 10 years combined education and experience in data processing & related fields. Competent in programming in COBOL, FORTRAN, RPG II, BASIC PLUS, and data base management on DEC and Prime computers. Extensive PC and network applications experience. Have supervised a staff as large as seven on special projects and have a record of meeting deadlines. Operations background in management, sales, and accounting.

Desire career-oriented position, will relocate

Dedicated, self-starter, creative problem solver

Paul Thomas   Home: (214) 173-1659

Leave Message: (214) 274-1436

Position: Research Chemist, Research Management in a small- to medium-size company

Skills: Ph.D. in Biochemistry plus over 15 years of work experience. Developed and patented various processes having current commercial applications worth many millions of dollars. Experienced with all phases of lab work with an emphasis on chromatography, isolation and purification of organic and biochemical compounds. Specialized in practical pharmaceutical and agricultural applications of chemical research. Have teaching, supervision, and project management experience.

Personal: Married over 15 years, stable work history, results and task oriented, ambitious, and willing to relocate.

Richard Straightarrow   Home: (602) 253-9678

Answering Service: (602) 257-6643

Objective: Electronics installation, maintenance & sales

Skills: Four years work experience plus two year A.A. degree in Electronics Engineering Technology. Managed a $300,000/yr. business while going to school full-time, with grades in the top 25%. Familiar with all major electronics diagnostic and repair equipment. Hands-on experience with medical, consumer, communications, and industrial electronics equipment and applications. Good problem-solving and communication skills. Customer service oriented.

Willing to do what it takes to get the job done.

Self-motivated, dependable, learn quickly

Juanita Rodriquez   Home: (639) 247-1643
                                      Message: (639) 361-1754

Position Desired: Warehouse Management

Skills: Six years experience plus 2 years of formal business coursework. Have supervised a staff as large as 16 people and warehousing operations covering over two acres and valued at over $14,000,000. Automated inventory operations resulting in a 30% increase in turnover and estimated annual savings over $250,000. Working knowledge of accounting, computer systems, time & motion studies, and advanced inventory management systems.

Will work any hours

Responsible, hardworking, and can solve problems.

Deborah Levy   Home: (213) 432-8064

                                      Messages: (213) 888-7365

Position Desired: Hotel Management

Skills: Four years experience in sales, catering, and accounting in a 300 room hotel. Associate's degree in Hotel Management plus one year with the Boileau Culinary Institute. Doubled revenues from meetings and conferences. Increased dining room and bar revenues by 44%. Have been commended for improving staff productivity and courtesy. I approach my work with industry, imagination, and creative problem-solving skills.

Enthusiastic, well-organized, detail-oriented

Jonathan Michael   Home: (614) 788-2434

                                      Message: (614) 355-0068

Objective: Management

Skills: Over 7 years of management experience plus a B.S. degree in Business. Managed budgets as large as $10 million. Experienced in cost control and reduction, cutting over 20% of overhead while business increased over 30%. Good organizer ad problem solver. Excellent communication skills.

Prefer responsible position in a medium to large business

Cope well with deadline pressure, seek challenge, flexible

Tips on Creating Your Own JIST Cards

There is no doubt that the JIST Card is an effective new tool in the job search. Employers respond positively to them and they can be used in ways a traditional resume cannot. But you may also find that they are more difficult to create than they at first appear. The reason is that they are sophisticated in their simplicity.

In order to create a good JIST Card you must know yourself very well, know what sort of job you are looking for, and be able to sort through all your personal information to find the few words that best describe your ability to do that job. It is also essential that every statement on your JIST Card be both accurate and true. Copying someone else's just won't do.

Writing an effective JIST Card may require some time on your part. The tips that follow should help you create each section of the card. As you assemble your own, consider asking others for feedback before you create your final version.

Your Name

Don't use nicknames or initials if possible. Keep it simple and don't include your middle name unless you go by that name.

Phone Numbers

Unless you have an answering machine, always include two phone numbers. This will allow an employer to contact you at a second number should the first one be busy or is not answered. Ask a friend or relative if you can list their phone number as an alternate and to take down any messages. Include your area code, since you never know how widely your JIST Cards might get distributed.

Job Objective

Don't be too narrow in your job objective. Avoid job titles by saying "general office" rather than "receptionist," "accounting" rather than "controller," or "data processing" rather than "programmer" if you would consider a variety of jobs. If you **are** more specific in your job objective, try to avoid a job title but give other details. For example, say "management position in an insurance-related business" or "working with children in a medical or educational setting."

Don't limit yourself to entry-level jobs if you have the potential or interest in doing more. If you say "office manager," instead of secretary, or "business manager" instead of "supervisor," you just might get the better job. If you are not too sure of your ability to get a higher paying job, it is still best to keep your options open. Say "office manager" or "responsible secretarial position," for example.

Length of Experience

You want to take advantage of **all** the experience you have that supports your job objective. If you are changing careers, have been out of the work world for awhile, or do not have much work experience, you will need to use other experiences to convince the employer you can do the job. Depending on your situation, here are some examples of things you might include:

Paid Work. You can list any work you were paid to do. Experience related to the job you are now looking for is best, of course, and should be emphasized if you have it. But the work does not have to be similar to the job you are looking for now. Working in a fast food place while you went to school can count and so can a job in an unrelated career.

Volunteer Work. You can include volunteer work as part of your experience total. Consider this if you don't have very much paid work experience. The fact that you were not paid is not all that relevant and does not need to be mentioned until later.

Informal Work: If your paid work history is scanty, you can also include work you did at home or as an unpaid hobby. It is best if this work relates to the job, but it doesn't have to. For example, if you worked on cars at home and want to be an auto mechanic, there is an obvious connection. You may have experience taking care of younger brothers or sisters. Or working in the family business. Use this experience if your job-related paid work experience is weak.

Related Education and Training: Any training or education that might help you should be mentioned. Job-related classes in high school, in the military, in college, or any other setting can be used.

To figure out your total experience, complete the following table. Write either years or months (if you don't have much experience) in the spaces beside each question.

Your Total Experience Includes:	
1. Total paid work experience:	_____
2. Total volunteer work experience:	_____
3. Total informal work experience:	_____
4. Total related education or training:	_____
Total Experience:	_____

Other Tips for Writing Your Experience Statement

Because everyone has a different background, no single rule can be given for everyone. Here are some tips for writing your own experience statement.

If you have lots of work experience: If part of your work experience is not related to the job you want now, you can leave it out. For example, if you have 20 years of experience, say "Over 15 years of work experience" or include just the experience that directly relates to this job. This keeps the employer from knowing how old you are, should you be concerned about this.

If you don't have much paid work experience: You need to include everything possible. If you have no paid work experience in the field you want to work in, emphasize training and other work. For example, "Nearly two years of experience including one year of advanced training in office procedures."

Remember to include the total of all paid and unpaid work as part of your experience. Include all those part-time jobs by saying "Over 18 months total work experience..."

If your experience is in another field: Just mention that you have "Four years work experience" without saying in what.

If you can cite raises and promotions: If you earned promotions, raises or have other special strengths, this is certainly the time to say so. For example, "Over seven years of increasingly responsible work experience including three years as a supervisor. Promoted twice."

Education and Training Statement

Depending on your situation, you can combine your education and training with your experience (as in one of the examples just discussed) or list it separately. Don't mention it at all if it doesn't help you. If you have a license, certification, or degree that supports your job objective, you may want to mention it here, too. For example: "Four years of experience plus two years of training leading to certification as an Emergency Medical Technician."

Skills Section

In this section you list the things you can do. You might mention any job-related tools or equipment you can use if that is appropriate. Use the language of the job to describe the more important things you can do. It is best to use some numbers to strengthen what you say and emphasize results. Instead of saying "Skills include typing, dictation," (and so on) say "Type 60 wpm accurately and take dictation at 120 wpm."

Emphasize results: It is too easy to overlook the importance of what you do unless you organize it correctly. Add up the numbers of transactions you handled, the money you were responsible for, the results you got. Some examples:

- "Expanded sales territory to include over seven new states and increased sales by $1,500,000."

- A person with fast-food experience might write "Handled over 50,000 customer contacts with total sales over $250,000, quickly and accurately." (These figures are based on a five-day week, 200 customers a day for one year, and an average sale of $5.)

- Someone who ran a small store could say "Responsible for managing a business with over $250,000 in sales per year. Reduced staff turnover by 50 percent by introducing employee training and retention program."
- Present a successful fund-raising project as: "Planned, trained, and supervised a staff of six on a special project. Exceeded income projections by 40 percent."

Also include in this section one or more of your transferable skills that are important for that job. A manager might mention their ability to train and supervise others, a receptionist might add "Good appearance and pleasant telephone voice." It is certainly OK to give numbers to support these skills, too. A warehouse manager might say "Well-organized and efficient. Have reduced expenses by 20 percent while orders increased by 55 percent."

Preferred Working Conditions

This is an optional section. You can add just a few words — one line at most — to let the employer know what you are willing to do. Do not limit your employment possibilities by saying "Will only work days" or "No travel wanted." It is better to leave this blank than give anything negative. Look at the sample JIST Cards for ideas. Then write your own statement.

Adaptive Skills

List three or four of your key adaptive skills. Choose skills that are important in the job you are seeking.

Writing and Production Tips

The best way to write a JIST Card is to begin with longer versions until your content is getting pretty clean. Then edit, edit, edit. When you are working with such a small format, every word has to count. Use short, choppy sentences. Get rid of any word that does not directly support your job objective. Add more information if your JIST Card is too short. Then read your card out loud to see how it sounds.

After you have edited it down, ask someone else to help you with the final version. It is amazing to see how many typographical errors slip onto these little cards. (Hey, did you notice that there is a typo in Jonathan's sample JIST Card earlier in this chapter?) An employer might notice such an error and it will not create a positive impression. Here are some other tips for creating the final version.

Formatting: You can type individual JIST Cards — or even hand write them — but it is much better to have them printed in large quantities. Four copies of the same card can fit on one standard sheet of 8-1/2-by-11-inch paper. Make sure your final version is error-free and typed on a good typewriter or printed on a letter quality printer if using a computer-based word processor. Never use a dot-matrix printer or poor quality typewriter.

Making Copies: Take the final version to a local print shop and have at least a hundred sheets printed. That will get you 400 JIST Cards, once they are cut. The cost for printing and cutting the cards should be $30 or so. You can also get them photocopied in smaller quantities for a reasonable price at many quick print shops with copy machines. If you do this, make certain that you get excellent copy quality and use a good quality paper.

Typesetting: Many print shops can also type or typeset your JIST Cards for an extra fee. It may be worth this to get a professional appearance. Also note that typesetting allows you to put more content on your card if you feel you need to.

Paper: I recommend you use a light card stock in a buff, off-white or pastel color such as light blue or gray. Most print and copy shops will have a selection of card stock to show you.

Design: Some of the sample JIST Cards have been typeset and use different typefaces and simple design elements such as lines. Keep yours simple and uncluttered. Many people also coordinate their resume and JIST Card design for a professional appearance. Some have also had them typeset like a true business card sometimes using both sides or having a folded style card format. Be creative if you wish but keep it functional and brief.

You Have to Use JIST Cards for Them to Work

Once you have your JIST Cards, use them! Give them away freely because they will not help you get a job if they sit on your desk. To avoid delay, you may want to start with a few typed JIST Cards reproduced on a photocopy machine. The better ones can come as you have time to improve them. But before you get a chance to, they may just help you get a job...

Chapter Eight

Dialing for Dollars

The telephone is a wonderful invention and using it is one of the most efficient ways of looking for work. You don't spend any time traveling, and you can talk to lots of people in a very short time. In one morning, for example, you can easily talk to more than 20 employers once you learn how.

In fact, many job seekers get more interviews by using the phone than with any other method. You can call people you already know to get interviews or referrals. You can follow up with leads you get from want ads or stay in touch with prospective employers and with people in your network who might hear of openings. And you can contact employers whose names you get from the *Yellow Pages*.

As I tell you about using the telephone to get interviews, remember that, in an earlier chapter, I defined an interview in a new way. An interview can now be any face-to-face contact with a person who might use a person with your skills — whether or not they have a job opening.

This chapter shows you some very effective ways to use the telephone to find job openings and set up interviews.

Using Your JIST Card as the Basis for Phone Contacts

You can base your phone calls on the content of your JIST Card. Look at the following example to see how John Kijek, the person presented in the sample JIST Card in the previous chapter, used his JIST Card to develop a phone script. As you read the phone script that follows, imagine that you are an employer who hires people with these skills. Would you be interested in interviewing this person?

The Transformation of John Kijek

"Hello, my name is John Kijek. I am interested in a management position in a small- to medium-size organization. I have a B.A. in business plus over five years experience in increasingly responsible management positions and have supervised as many as 12 staff whose productivity increased by 27 percent over two years. During a three year period I was promoted twice and have excellent references. I initiated a customer follow-up program that increased sales by 22 percent within 12 months. I also get along well with others, am a good team worker and am willing to travel or work any hours as needed.

"I am hardworking, self-motivated, and willing to accept responsibility. When may I come in for an interview?"

Most People Respond Well to a Short Phone Contact

Before you go on, consider how you might feel about a person who called you — an employer — with this approach. If you needed someone like this, would you give John an interview?

Most people say they **would** give him an interview if they had an opening. Not everyone, but most. For this reason, reading a phone script based on your JIST Card is a very effective way to use the telephone.

You should also notice that the script used above takes most people 30 seconds or less to read. And, once you get to the prospective employer, that is about how long it would take to say it out loud. In just that short time, you present a great deal of information. Based on many years of experience, the JIST Card/ phone script approach has been carefully constructed to reduce the opportunity for an employer to interrupt you (remember, it is only 30 seconds) and it does not allow for a "no" response.

As I will show you later in this chapter, you can adapt your phone script for use in calling people you know as well as in making cold contacts to employers. In both situations, the telephone can be used as a time efficient tool for finding jobs in the hidden job market.

I have run job search programs where phone scripts based on JIST Cards were used. Thousands of people have used this technique and most find that it takes 10 to 15 cold contact phone calls to get one interview. That may sound like a lot of rejection but it takes less than an hour to make that many calls. And how many job search methods are you aware of with that kind of a track record?

Overcoming Fear of Phoning Contacts

You may find it hard to use the phone in the way I suggest. Many people do. They think it is "pushy" to call someone and ask for an interview. Before you decide this technique is not for you, think about why you are afraid. What is the worst thing that can happen to you? Most calls take only a minute or so. And most employers don't mind talking to a person they might be interested in hiring.

These calls do require you to overcome some shyness, but they are really quite easy to do. Start with people you know. Then call the people they refer you to. Soon you will find that most people are happy to help you. Even people you just picked from the *Yellow Pages* will typically treat you well. The experience of thousands of job seekers is that very few people will be rude to you. And you probably wouldn't want to work for someone who is rude anyway.

The Five Parts of a Phone Script

The phone script that I will show you assumes that you will contact a person who does not know you and who may or may not have a job opening. An example of this situation would be if you were making cold calls to organizations listed in the *Yellow Pages*. Later you can adapt your script to the situation but, for now, I suggest that you begin by writing a script in the specific way I outlined below. This approach has been carefully created based on years of experience and it is effective.

I have divided the script into the following five sections. Write your own narrative on your own worksheet as suggested in the material that follows.

1. **The Introduction:** This one is easy. Just write "Hello, my name is" and fill in your name as if you were introducing yourself.

2. **The Position:** Always begin your statement with "I am interested in a position as..." and write in your job objective. It takes you only about 30 seconds to read your phone script, and you don't want to get rejected before you begin. So don't use the word "job" in your first sentence. If you say you are "...looking for a job..." or anything similar, you will often be interrupted. Then you will be told there are no openings. For example, if you say "Do you have any jobs?" the person you are talking to will often say "No." And you will have come to a screeching halt in less than 10 seconds. Remember that, in the new definition of an interview, you

are not looking for a job opening, you simply want to talk to people who have the ability to hire a person with your skills - even if they don't have a job opening.

If the job objective from your JIST Card sounds good spoken out loud, then add it to your worksheet. If it doesn't, change it around a bit until it does. For example, if your JIST Card says you want a "management/supervisory position in retail sales," your phone script might say "I am interested in a management or supervisory position in retail sales."

3. **The Hook:** The skills section of your JIST Card includes length of experience, training, education, special skills related to the job, and accomplishments. Use this information in your phone script. Rewriting the content from this part of your JIST Card may take some time. The sentences in your phone script must sound natural when spoken. You may find it helpful to write and edit this section on a separate piece of paper before writing the final version on your script worksheet. Then read the final version out loud to hear how it sounds. Also read it to others and continue to make improvements until is sounds right.

4. **The Clincher:** Simply take the last section of your JIST Card, containing your key adaptive skills, and make these key traits into a sentence. For example, "reliable, hard working, and learn quickly" from a JIST Card might be written in a phone script as "I am reliable, hard working, and I learn quickly." These are some of your most important skills to mention to an employer and putting them last gives them the most power.

5. **The Goal:** Your goal is to get an interview. In the example I used earlier in this chapter, the final statement was "When can I come in for an interview?" and that is what I suggest you write on your own script. The reason is that it tends to work. If you said, for example, "May I come in for an interview?" (or "Could you please, please, let me come in to talk with you?") that allows the employer to say "No." And you don't want to make it easy for the employer to say no. They can, of course, do that on their very own, without your assisting them.

Tips for Completing Your Phone Script

Use one or more sheets of paper to write out the script you will use in your telephone contacts. Consider the tips that follow carefully. Then use the information on your JIST Card as the basis for writing each section of your phone script.

Write exactly what you will say on the phone. A written script will help you present yourself effectively and keep you from stumbling around for the right word. Avoid the temptation (I know that you are resisting this) to "wing it" without a script. It just won't work as well. Trust me.

Keep your telephone script short. Just present the information an employer would want to know about you, then ask for an interview.

Write your script the way you talk. Since you have already completed your JIST Card, use it as the basis for your telephone script. Your JIST Card uses short sentences and phrases, and you probably wouldn't talk that way. So add some words to your script to make it sound natural when you say it out loud.

Use the words I use. As you write your script, avoid being too creative. I developed the specific words used in the samples presented in the "Five Parts of a Phone Script," over many years and suggest you use them as they are presented. For example, do not write or say "Good morning, my name is _____" since that will build a bad habit, which you will realize all too late on one overcast afternoon. Really, I have learned the best words to use through years of making mistakes and there is no need for you to make the same ones. Start my way, you can change it to your way after you have mastered mine.

Practice it out loud. I know that your neighbors may think you are nuts but reading your script out loud etches it into your being in a way that reading it to yourself can not do. It has something to do with neural pathways and brain stuff. Or maybe something more spiritual having to do with the way we define ourselves. Or both. But the fact is, reading an honestly prepared phone script out loud helps you accept that all this good stuff about you is true. And later, that will help you in an interview.

Tips for Making Effective Phone Contacts

Now that you have developed your phone script, you need to know how to use it effectively. Here are more tried and true tips:

Get to the hiring authority. You need to get directly to the person who would supervise you. When contacting a larger organization, avoid the personnel department. Unless you want to work in personnel, you wouldn't normally ask to talk to someone in that department. Depending on the type and size of the organization you're calling, you should have a pretty good idea of the title of the person who would supervise you. For example, in a small business you might ask to speak to the "person in charge." In a larger one, you would ask for the name of the person who is in charge of a particular department.

Get the name of a person. If you don't have the name of the person you need to speak to, ask for it. For example, ask for the name of the person in charge of the warehouse if that is where you want to work. Usually, you will be given the name and your call will be transferred to him or her immediately. When you do get a name, get the correct spelling and write it down right away. Then you can use their name in your conversation.

Get past the secretary. In some cases, secretaries or receptionists will try to screen out your call. If they find out you are looking for a job, they may transfer you to the personnel department or ask you to send an application or resume. Here are two things you can do to avoid getting screened out by the secretary:

1. **Call back:** If you get screened out on your first try, call back a day later and say you are getting ready to send some correspondence to the person who manages such and such. You want to use the correct name and title and request that they give you this information. This is true since you will be sending them something soon. And this approach usually gets you what you need. Say thank-you and call back in a day or so. Then ask for the manager by name and you will often get right through.

2. **Call when the secretary is out:** You are likely to get right through if you call when that secretary is out to lunch. Other good times are just before and after normal work hours. Less experienced staff members are likely to answer the phones and transfer your call to the boss. The boss might also be in early or working late.

Now that you're ready to actually start making calls, it might be helpful to review the examples in the following situations.

When Calling Someone by Referral

It is always best to be referred by someone else. If this is the case, immediately give the name of the person who suggested you call. For example, say:

"Hello, Mister Rhodes, Joan Bugsby suggested I give you a call."

If the receptionist asks why you are calling, say:

"A friend of Mister Rhodes' suggested I give him a call."

When a friend of the employer recommends that you call, you usually get right through. It's that simple.

When Calling Someone You Know

Sometimes using your telephone script just as it is written on your worksheet will not make sense. For example, if you are calling someone you know, you would normally begin with some friendly conversation before getting to the purpose of your call. Then, you could use your phone script by saying something like this:

"The reason I called is to let you know I am looking for a job, and I thought you might be able to help. Let me tell you a few things about myself. I am looking for a position as..." (Continue with the rest of your phone script here.)

When Calling Someone You Don't Know

While it is almost always best to call someone who you know or have been referred to, calling a prospective employer directly can be very effective. For example, let's say that you are calling organizations listed in the *Yellow Pages*, under a category of business or organization that needs people with your skills. This is a type of cold contact that many people have used to obtain interviews that would have been most difficult to obtain any other way. Here is how such a phone call might go:

"Hello, I'd like to speak to the manager."

Usually that will get you to who you want to talk to. In a larger organization you would ask for the person in charge of the department where you would most likely work. If the receptionist tries to screen your call by asking what it is you want, you might respond thusly:

"I'd like to ask a few questions related to that department," (Or the business, etc.)

If that doesn't work, then ask for the correct name and spelling of the person, saying that you need it in order to send them some correspondence (which is true). Then call back the next day and ask for that person by name. Once you get through, begin your normal phone script.

There are many other situations where you will need to adapt your basic script. Use your own judgment on this. With practice, it becomes easier.

The Phone Contact Goal — Get an Interview!

The primary goal of a phone contact is to get an interview. To succeed, you must be ready to get past the first and even the second rejection.

Ask three times: To increase your chances of getting an interview, you must practice asking three times for the interview. Here is an example:

1. **You:** When may I come in for an interview?

   Employer: I don't have any positions open now.

2. **You:** That's OK, I'd still like to come in to talk to you about the possibility of future openings.

   Employer: I really don't plan on hiring within the next six months or so.

3. **You:** Then I'd like to come in and learn more about what you do. I'm sure you know a lot about the industry, and I am looking for ideas on getting into your field and moving up.

Although this approach does not always work, asking the third time works more often than most people would believe. It is essential that you learn to keep asking after the first time you are told no. Of course, you should be sensitive to the person you are speaking to and not push too hard, but it is more often a question of not being persistent enough than being too aggressive.

Arrange for an Interview Time or Ask for Other Help

If the person agrees to an interview, arrange a specific time and date. If you are not sure of his or her complete name or address, you can always call back later and ask the receptionist. Sometimes you will decide not to ask for an interview. The person may not seem helpful or you may have caught them at a busy time. If so, there are alternative things you can do:

1. **Get a referral:** Ask for names of other people who might be able to help you. Find out how to contact them. Then add these new contacts to your job search network. When you call them, remember to tell them that you were referred by so and so.

2. **Ask to call back:** If your contact is busy when you call, ask if you can call back. Get a specific time and day to do this, and add the call to your to-do list for that day. When you do call back (and you must), the employer will likely be positively impressed. And may give you an interview for just that reason.

3. **Ask if it is OK to call back from time to time:** Maybe your contact will hear of an opening or have some other information for you. Many job seekers get their best leads from a person they have checked back with several times. Every two to three weeks seems like an interval that works well.

Send a Thank-You Note

Always follow up with anyone you contact via phone. Especially anyone who is helpful to you. This effort can make a big difference. The best way to follow up is with a thank-you note.

Send a thank-you note right after the phone call. If you arranged for an interview, send a note saying you look forward to your meeting. If they gave you a referral to someone else, send another note, later, telling how things turned out. Or send a thank-you note telling how you followed up on any suggestion they gave you. And notice how nicely a JIST Card fits into a thank-you note-sized envelope.

Phone Contacts Only Get You Interviews If You Use Them

Many people dread making phone contacts, so if you count yourself among them, begin with your friends. Role-play your phone contacts too, if at all possible. Have another person be the employer and see if you can overcome their resistance to seeing you by asking three times for an interview. But don't practice too long before making real phone contacts. Begin by calling people you know, then the people they refer you to. That will improve your confidence and give you practice in getting better. You might also contact the organizations in the phone book that you rated a "3" (indicating you were not at all interested in working there) as described in chapter 2. That way you just can't screw things up too badly.

Making phone calls is work and that is how you should approach it — as a job. It is easiest if you plan to make your calls at a certain time each day and continue this throughout your job search. With just two hours of making phone calls a day, most people learn to get at least two interviews. That's two interviews each day — 10 interviews a week — about twice what the average job seeker gets in a **month**. Which is a pretty good way to let your fingers do the walking.

Chapter Nine

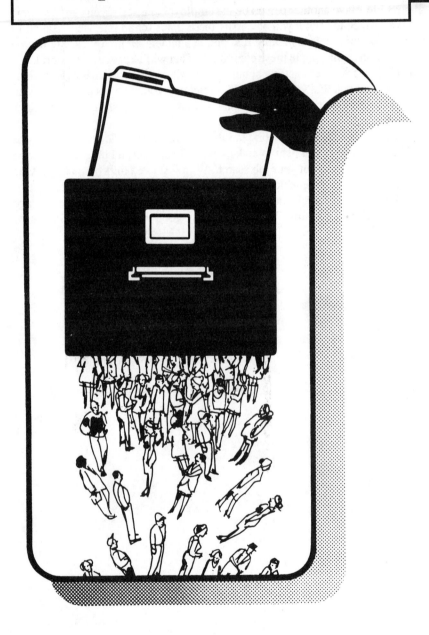

Discovering the Truth About Job Applications

Hardly anyone I know enjoys rejection. One way job seekers avoid it is by asking, at a place of possible employment, if they can fill out an application. Most employers will say "Yes," since it doesn't cost them much to do so. And they know exactly what to do after you're gone: file it.

Applications Are Designed to Screen You Out

Think about it. An "Application for Employment" creates a barrier between you and anyone who would actually hire or supervise you. In larger organizations there may be hundreds — sometimes thousands — of applications submitted for each job opening. The chance is slim that yours will jump out and be **THE** one. Let me tell you what the director of a large organization's personnel department recently told me.

"I've worked in personnel departments for over 15 years and am now in charge of the personnel functions of a Fortune 500 company. We get many thousands of applications per year. I would guess that most of them get less than 60 seconds of attention before getting filed. And we rarely go back and look through filed applications. If someone walks in today who meets the criteria of a job opening, they may be referred for an interview. The ones who came in yesterday probably won't. The truth is, most of our new employees are referred by our own employees. Maybe 15 percent or so are hired as the result of filling out an application. We accept applications because we are expected to — not because we need to."

More Reasons Applications Are Not an Effective Job Search Tool

Here are additional points to consider about their limited value.

Applications allow for limited information. Have you ever seen an application that asks you to list your strengths or why you think you would be a good employee? There are a few that do but 99 percent do not.

Applications encourage you to reveal your flaws. If you have limited work experience, gaps in your job history, want to change careers, are unemployed or underemployed, have ever been fired, or have anything other than a near-perfect work history, the application will encourage you to reveal it. It was designed to do just that.

Applications are usually used by personnel departments. The people who work in personnel departments are usually very nice. I even have a few as friends. But, unless you want to work in a personnel department, they can't hire you. They can only screen you out.

Lots of employers don't have personnel departments. About two-thirds of all workers are employed by small businesses with fewer than 250 employees. Many aren't big enough to have a personnel department and often don't even have applications. In spite of their size, small employers are an excellent source of jobs. Some big companies do not even accept applications. Some have decided that spending money to accept, file, and forget applications isn't worth it. Some others have completely shut down their personnel departments to job seekers. They now refer you to the local, state, or provincial employment office who will do their screening for them.

Some Good Words About Applications

There **are** some advantages in knowing how to complete applications. For one thing, you may be required to do so. Some employers may ask you to complete one before they interview you so they don't have to waste time with the details of your background. Larger companies sometimes have a policy requiring you to go through personnel before being considered. You may also be asked to complete an application after the job offer but before you begin. In all these cases, knowing what to do is important.

There's another good reason for learning how to complete applications — they force you to deal with your flaws. An application is designed to collect negative information. Learning how to deal with this gracefully is important preparation for handling tough interview questions and writing resumes.

Tips for Completing Your Application

Following are some basic tips for completing an application.

Read and follow directions. Read and follow the directions carefully. Don't write if it says print or put your year of birth where the month should have been. Employers notice this carelessness and assume that you will be similarly careless on the job. Work slowly and do it right.

Use an erasable pen. Black ink ballpoint pens have a professional appearance. Most stationery stores have special ones that can be erased as easily as a pencil. Always carry two such pens in case one stops working.

Be neat. Do you remember Employer's Expectation 1? Appearance counts. If your paperwork is messy, the negative impression will get you screened out. Fast.

Be positive. An application is designed to uncover negatives and anything negative you reveal to an employer can get you screened out. If your truthful answer to an application question would result in a negative impression, it is often best to leave that item blank. You can explain that item later in an interview or after being offered a job if it is important.

Be honest. I recommend honesty throughout your job search and do not advise you to falsify your application or anything else. If you would be screened out of a job by providing an honest response to an application question you may want to avoid using applications as a job search tool altogether. It can be done and often is. For less serious situations, such as being fired, the words you choose to explain what happened are very important. Always look for a way to express yourself that puts you in a positive light.

Be complete. Don't leave blank spaces. If the question does not apply to you, write "N/A," draw a line through it, or make some other response. However, in some cases it is better to write "will explain in interview" or leave it blank than to volunteer negative information.

Provide additional positive information. Since most applications don't ask you for your strengths and accomplishments, you should look for a place to mention them anyway. In the work experience section, mention that you were promoted, trained new staff or any other positives wherever you can fit them in. Mention any extracurricular school activities, volunteer work, or other accomplishments or proof that would support your ability to do the job.

Handling Application Problems

In the old days, applications often asked information that had nothing to do with your ability to do the job. Questions such as your age, your parents' occupations, and your marital status were common. With the change in laws, you are much less likely to find these sorts of questions today. Generally, issues that don't relate to your ability to perform the job should not be considered in the employment process.

Tips on Troublesome Questions

Here are some of the potentially troublesome questions you might get asked along with suggestions for handling each.

Position Desired: Applications often ask what sort of a job you want, what hours and days you want to work, the salary you expect, and other details. How you handle this can be very important. If you know of a specific job opening with this employer, you could use that job title. A safer approach would be to use the general career area or department that job is in. For example, if you were looking for a position as a warehouse manager, you might write "business or shipping/receiving management or related tasks." That approach would leave your options open to be considered for other jobs that might interest you. Saying "anything," however, indicates you don't know what you want to do and will not impress an employer.

Whatever job objective you do write down defines how and what you emphasize on the rest of your application. If you want to work as a general maintenance employee in a hospital, for example, you would emphasize experience working with your hands, training, military experience, and education that supports that job — even related hobbies. Consider every entry on your application and look for ways it can support your job objective.

Health Information: Health-related absences and accidents are expensive to an employer, so you will often be screened out if you've had a history of either. The issue here is whether or not your health will keep you from doing a good job and being a dependable worker. Unless you have a problem that will keep you from doing a good job, you should say your health is "excellent." Don't mark "fair" or even "good" without a good reason. Such responses will usually get you screened out.

Some applications have a checklist to screen for all sorts of specific medical problems. If the application doesn't ask, you may be asked in a pre-employment medical screening. If you do have a medical problem that limits your ability to do the job, is long-term and/or can get worse, you have a problem that is not easily resolved. If you lie on the application, you could be fired later for lying. Some conditions, such as chronic back pain, dizzy spells and seizures, or various physical and emotional disabilities, make it very difficult to find employment and the very nature of an application makes it even harder. One solution here is to get good career counseling in the preparation for and selection of a job objective. If the job does not require what you can't do, there is no longer a problem, is there? If your condition does not affect your ability to do the job, you could write "I have no limitations that affect my performance on this job." And that should be that.

Attendance: If you have a good attendance record, state it. Say "none" or "only two days absent out of the past year" if asked about your attendance record. If you have a good long-term record but were ill recently and have now recovered, you could say something like this:

"Over the past five years, I have had an excellent attendance record, missing fewer than three days a year for four of the five years."

If your attendance is rotten and you haven't a good explanation, consider leaving this blank and promise yourself to do better. If someone is forgiving enough to hire you.

Workers' Compensation: Workers' Compensation is pay you get for a job-related injury or illness that prevents you from working. Many employers do not want to hire someone who has received this pay in the past, since they assume they are accident-prone or unwilling to work. If you did receive this pay, consider leaving this section blank and discussing it in an interview if it comes up.

Unemployment Compensation: This is money you receive after leaving one job and before finding another. Employers pay for these expenses and do not like to take on as employees people who have misused these payments in the past. If you did receive it, say so and write in a good reason. For example, "company closed, am willing to relocate."

Education and Formal Training: Present any education and training that supports your job objective in as positive a way as possible. Since the spaces on an application are often small, you can't write much, so use whatever spaces you can to your advantage. If you received formal training in a setting other than a traditional school (the military is one good example), consider including it in the education section of the application. This would be particularly true if the training you received supports the job you now seek. Before completing the education section, first look over the rest of the application. If there are small or no sections for training you received in technical, trade, business, military or other programs, look for ways to squeeze it into the education section.

If you attended but did not complete high school, college, or some training program, do not emphasize that fact. Indicate that you "attended" and mention the job-related courses or major you took. If you went to three schools but graduated from only one, acknowledge just that school you graduated from if space is limited. Of course, mention anything you did while in school that might create a positive impression such as "kept grades in top half of class while working part-time to support myself," or "practiced in school band 10 to 20 hours a week in addition to class work."

Military Experience: Military experience is at least as important as any civilian job, schooling, or training. The military has the largest training and education budget of any single organization and the levels of responsibility held are often much higher than anything available to civilians of equal age and training. If the military section of an application does not let you present your training and experience well, use the education, work experience, and other sections of the application to present this. Present the information in civilian terms and emphasize those things that support your job objective.

Salary and Working Conditions: Do not state a specific salary. Write "open" or "salary negotiable," since you do not yet want to be screened out from consideration on this factor. If forced to, write in a very wide salary range, such as "mid-teens," "low to mid-thirties," or "$7 to $10 per hour."

Are you willing to work evenings if necessary? Weekends? The best response is to write (if asked) "will consider" or, if you do have a strong preference write something like "prefer daytime hours but will consider other shifts." The same approach applies to questions about relocation, travel, and other issues. While you don't have to take a job you don't want, you do not want to be screened out early either.

Previous Work Experience: Employers look at what you have done on previous jobs to support what you want to do now. This is a section that troubles many job seekers. It is unusual for anyone to have an "ideal" work history, yet you must learn to present yourself as a person who has a good chance of succeeding on the job you seek. Following are some common problems job seekers have and tips to help deal with them.

Gaps in Employment: If you have gaps between jobs, the odds are that you did something constructive during that time. If you went to school, did part-time jobs (self-employed), raised children, got career counseling, or did anything else, mention it. It provides a reason for the gap. If the gap was short, looking for a job is an acceptable reason. You can also avoid using specific employment dates if they display gaps in your history. For example, put "Spring 1990 to Spring 1991" for one job followed by "Spring 1991 to Present." For larger gaps, you can simply use the years, such as "1990 to 1991" or "1991 to Present."

Job Titles: If the job title you had does not accurately describe your responsibilities or duties, consider changing it. For example, if you were a "Customer Service Representative" but supervised a department of people, you could use the more generic and descriptive "Department Head, Customer

Service and Support." Use judgment on this and select new titles that would be helpful in communicating what you did but that do not misrepresent your actual responsibilities. Consider checking first with a previous employer to see if they would object to this.

Getting Fired: Most people get fired over what could be called a "personality conflict." Whatever the reason, **never** write "fired" on an application. Is there any way you could express, in a more positive way, your reason for leaving? If, after you left, you went to school or took a job paying more money, mention those things under "reason for leaving past jobs." If you are currently unemployed, think of some way to avoid saying you were fired. If all else fails and you did nothing criminal, what does the truth sound like? For example, "The job I left just did not work out the way I wanted. My boss wanted to do everything herself and I could not use my own ideas," could be re-worded on an application as "looking for a more responsible and demanding position."

Name of Supervisor: If you worry about what your ex-supervisor would say about you, there are two things you should do:

1. **Find out. Call up and/or go see your old boss.** Tell him or her you are looking for a new job and are concerned about what they would say to a prospective employer wanting a reference. You can usually negotiate what, exactly, the boss will say. Make sure both you and the boss are clear what will be said to reference inquiries, and say thanks. You could then follow up your visit with a letter reviewing what was discussed and enclose a draft letter of recommendation that they could modify to their satisfaction, sign, and return to you as a signed original.

2. **Get an alternate source.** If your ex-boss will say harmful things about you, consider giving the name of another responsible person in your old organization who will say good things about your performance.

Too Little or "No" Experience: If you have had no or limited paid work experience, you must fall back on what experience you do have. Look carefully at volunteer, education, training, hobbies, and other experiences. Some of these could count as jobs or provide the equivalent experience. Note something positive in the available space, even if it is not requested. For example, write "I worked in a variety of part-time jobs, while going to school," or "My studies allowed little free time and I concentrated my spare time on homework and family responsibilities," or "I am new to the job market but am now ready to put my complete energy into the career I have carefully chosen." or whatever else you might say that is positive.

If you have received job-related training, mention this again. For example, you could say "I have over 18 months of intensive job-related training, including over 150 hours of hands-on experience with equipment similar to yours."

Too Much Experience: If you feel you have too much experience, perhaps you should be looking for a more responsible job. The true issue is the employer's concern that you will not be satisfied with the job and the pay they have and you will leave. But if you have good reasons for seeking lower pay or responsibility levels, explain why. You could write, for example, "My children are grown and I now want a creative and challenging position that does not require relocation," or "I am very interested in positions paying from the mid-twenties (or whatever) and above."

If you have had many jobs, cluster the older ones under a heading like: "1982 to 1985 — A variety of increasingly responsible jobs in the sales and service areas." If you received any promotions on the job, say "Secretary, promoted to Office Manager" under job title or wherever it's appropriate.

Duties: Some applications provide a tiny space to describe your job. In these cases, select statements indicating your responsibility or achievements like: "supervised staff of seven in a three-state area," or "served over 3,000 people a month," or "opened and closed store, deposited $10,000 per week in bank." You don't have many words, so don't waste them.

More Tips on Completing an Application

A variety of questions may be asked on applications that don't clearly fit into major sections. Here are some of the most troublesome ones.

Arrest Record: Applications can ask if you have ever been convicted of a felony. The key word here is "convicted." Employers have a need to know of a convicted embezzler, for example, who is applying for a job as a bank teller. If you were charged but not convicted, our legal system defines you as innocent. Only you, of course, can know the truth, but if you were not convicted you don't have to say you are guilty of anything. The files of juveniles are usually closed and you do not have to reveal any arrest records from that time in your life.

If the application asks if you've ever been arrested, and you have, you might leave this section blank as you are not required to answer it in most situations. If the arrest was minor, you could write "minor traffic violations," or whatever is appropriate. If your arrest record is more serious, consider using job search techniques that do not let you get screened out based on an application. Also, depending on your offense, you should realistically avoid looking for certain jobs. People who were convicted of theft should not look for jobs handling money, for example. You may want to (and be qualified) to do such work but it is unwise to seek it.

Transportation: Some jobs require you to have your own car or have a valid driver's license. If you don't have what is requested, write "I will obtain a car if hired," or another appropriate comment.

Certification, Licenses, and Registration: If you have job-related credentials, mention them somewhere, even if the information is not requested.

Volunteer Activities: If asked, list those that support the job objective and mention specific skills used, responsibilities, or achievements that support your job objective. If these activities are an important part of your experience, consider putting them in the work experience section of an application.

Hobbies and Recreational Activities: List those that support your job objective in some way. If these activities made money or received recognition, mention that. For example, "I designed and developed prototype craft items now sold throughout the state," (which indicates good sales skills and self-motivation) or "I competed and coached an average of 20 hours a week on various gymnastics teams for over six years while maintaining a B average," (indicating you are a hard worker with good time management skills).

Future Plans: Emphasize your interest in doing a better job through specific education, training, career advancement, hard work, and superior performance.

References: The best references are those who know your work, who like you, and who are responsible people. Consider such people as your coach, teachers, managers from other departments you know from previous jobs, heads of organizations for which you do volunteer work, or professionals with whom you have worked on prior jobs. Friends and relatives won't be objective about you and employers don't usually contact them for that reason. Whomever you select, be sure to ask them if it is OK to list them and find out what they would say about you. You just can never be sure.

Often, previous employers will not give references over the phone due to company policy, or fears of legal action being brought against them. For this reason, it is often helpful to ask a previous employer to write you a letter of recommendation in advance. You can then make copies of it for prospective employers when asked. You may want to tell your previous employer the kinds of things you would appreciate being included in the letter such as your attendance record, hard work, certain skills or achievements, or other positives. The worst thing they can say is no.

Tell the Truth on Your Application

It is easy to lie on an application (or on a resume or in an interview, for that matter) but it is not a good idea. Many employers will fire you if they find out you lied about any important item on your application. A better approach is to leave a sensitive question blank. If you have a serious problem that an application would reveal, you'll be better off looking for job openings that don't require an application. The truth is, an application is more likely to do you harm than good. If you **do** fill one out, be sure that it is as good as you can make it and has nothing in it that could eliminate you from consideration.

Chapter Ten

Interviewing for Results
— *It All Comes Down to 60 Minutes*

Most interviews last about 60 minutes. One hour. It is the most important 60 minutes in your job search, and you should do everything in your power to see that it goes well. Even though you are likely to have many interviews, each one is hard to get and each one could be the one that gets you the job offer.

There is good research indicating that interviews are not a valid way to select good employees.[1] Most employers would agree. But while it is not always the best method, the fact is that how you do in an interview is very important in whether or not you will be considered for a job. Doing well in an interview is, more or less, a requirement for getting a job.

In order to have a successful interview you must do five things: make a positive impression; communicate your skills; answer problem questions; help the employer know why they should hire you; and follow up after the interview. These are interview essentials, and if you do them well, you can dramatically increase your chances of getting a job offer. This chapter will show you, step-by-step, how to do well in a job interview. By dividing the interview into sections and mastering one section at a time, those crucial 60 minutes won't seem so intimidating.

Tips to Overcome Your Fear of Interviews

Most job seekers **are** intimidated by job interviews. It's sort of like going to the dentist — there comes a time when you know you can no longer avoid it, but you don't look forward to it either. There are many reasons why interviews cause anxiety, but by understanding these reasons and responding appropriately, you can control your fear and trembling. Here's what you can do:

Reject Rejection

The word "interview" has two parts: "inter," which means "between" and "view," which surely means "look at." I do not claim to be an expert on root words, but it does seem that "interview" means, roughly, "two people looking at each other." In a job interview, that is precisely what should be going on. More often, however, there is the one-sided feeling that the powerful employer is giving the job seeker a thorough looking over. The job seeker conducting a conventional job search is likely to get rejected, which does not feel good.

One way to look at the interview is as a series of rejections, like this: No No No No No No No No No No No No No No No No No No No No No No No No No No No No No No No No *Yes*.

Finally, you meet someone who makes you a job offer. If you accept, that's a "Yes." Along the way, however, the rejection doesn't have to be one-sided. An interview should be, after all, a two-way communication. Employers are not the only ones who can say no.

The Importance of Interview "Chemistry"

Many employers claim they get a "feel" for a person during an interview. I have often heard interviewers say they did or did not hire someone based on a "gut reaction." This can be a very unnerving thought until you understand that what they feel can often be predicted. And if you know what might cause a negative reaction, you can try to change your behavior accordingly.

Most gut reactions are really responses to nonverbal behavior. Many of your most powerful signals can be nonverbal. As evidence of this, think about how a lie detector works. Your body gives off electro-chemical signals that can be measured, even if you try to stop them. Your voice, facial expressions, posture, and other subtle signals give you away too. Obviously, the only way to avoid this problem in a job interview is to be honest. If you overstate your abilities you often unconsciously communicate that you are hiding something, which many interviewers will notice.

Often, you may be completely unaware of how your nonverbal signals are creating a negative impression. Perhaps your grooming is inappropriate or out-of-date; maybe you play with your hair or slouch in your chair; or you may have a hard time expressing yourself without moving your hands too much.

Some time ago, I worked with a college graduate who had been chronically unemployed or underemployed for over 10 years. His credentials were great — a prestigious school, good grades, a desirable degree in business. Yet I immediately knew why he had such a hard time getting a decent job — his handshake was limp, he slouched terribly, his hair looked oily, and he looked like he slept under a bridge. While many of his problems were personality-related, his job search was bound to be unsuccessful simply based on his appearance. Any employer would react negatively to him.

The good news is that you can change many of your undesirable mannerisms. Ask a friend to role play interviews with you and provide constructive feedback on your nonverbal image. By becoming aware of negative signals, and by practicing to eliminate or change them, you can make intuition work for you.

Interviewers Are People Too

If you see interviewers as the enemy, you should reconsider. It might help to remind yourself that most bosses started out as job seekers and will very likely take on that role again. You should also realize that most employers are as nervous as you are in a job interview, and for some good reasons, like those that follow.

They probably have no training in interviewing. Just as most job seekers don't know how to find jobs, interviewers often don't know how to interview. How would they have learned? It is not at all unusual for a well-trained job seeker to be a better interviewer than the interviewer is. Really! I often hear job seekers say, "They didn't even ask me any hard questions! I had to tell them what I was good at because they never asked." Too true.

If they hire you, and you don't work out, they lose. If they make a mistake, their boss will know. Since it costs lots of money to train new staff, their decision is literally worth thousands of dollars. In small organizations or departments, if one person does not work out, everyone else feels the extra workload. The person who hired the new employee could lose their credibility and maybe even their job.

Everyone likes to be liked. I've known employers who hate to interview because they don't like to turn people down. You don't have to feel sorry for them, but it is something to think about.

So, you see, interviewers are not to be feared at all. Employers are just like us because they are us. Their roles are just a little different for now.

Three Types of Interviews

Do you remember "The Four Stages of a Job Opening" reviewed earlier in chapter 2 of this book? That process indicated that a job often opens up in stages and that many employers are willing to talk to job seekers before a job opening even exists. That process made a point that eludes most job seekers: if you define a job interview in a narrow, traditional sense, you can lose many good opportunities — often including the best jobs for you.

So how you define an interview is a critical part of a successful job search process. This section defines three types of interviews. They are:

1. The traditional job interview,

2. The information interview, and,

3. The JIST Job Search interview.

Much of this book works on the assumption that an interview can include something more than the "traditional" interview. All three types of interview share some characteristics, but there are significant differences too. If you know how to conduct yourself in each type of interview, you will have a distinct advantage over most job seekers. Let's take a closer look at each one.

First Interview Type: The Traditional Job Interview

This is what job seekers usually think of when the word "interview" is used. Essentially, it is a meeting with a person who has a job opening for which you might qualify, who is actively looking for someone to fill it and who has the authority to hire you. If you wait until then, however, the job is likely to be filled. It's an important lesson to learn.

This is not to say that traditional job interviews are not important. They are. But it would be irresponsible of me not to tell you that more than half of all jobs are filled in a different way. If you believe in your heart that an interview can happen only if you get a "Yes" to your question, "Do you have any job openings for me?" you will miss some of the very best opportunities.

Manipulation and Counter-Manipulation

In the traditional interview, your task is to present yourself well. The task of the interviewer is to find out what's wrong with you so you can be eliminated from consideration. This is not the friendliest of social situations. If the interviewer has any training on how to interview, you will face techniques intentionally designed to reveal your flaws. In a book considered by many to be required reading for interviewers, Richard Fear wrote:

> *"Since most applicants approach the interview with the objective of putting their best foot forward, the interviewer must be motivated from the very beginning to search for unfavorable information...We first concentrate on making a friend, then getting the information, and finally giving the information concerning the job."[2]*

In a traditional interview, any good interviewer will encourage you to be yourself and let your guard down. In an article by John and Merna Galassi titled "Preparing Individuals for Job Interviews: Suggestions From More Than 60 Years of Research," they conclude that the primary role of the interviewer is to weed out the "undesirables."[3] And they will manipulate you to reveal negative information, if at all possible. The very situation demands they behave this way.

A job seeker's reaction to all this manipulation is natural enough: you try to hide your faults and emphasize your strengths. Your objective, in these traditional interviews, is to get a second interview. If you leave the interview and that decision has not been made, go after a second interview in your follow-up efforts. I'll tell you more about follow-up later in the chapter.

The Major Types of Traditional Interviews

In addition to much manipulation, you are likely to encounter different interviewing styles. So that you will not be taken by surprise, let's take a look at some of the more common methods used in traditional interviews.

One-to-One: This is by far the most common preliminary interview, where you meet with a person whose role is to screen applicants and arrange follow-up interviews with the person who has the authority to hire. Other times, you may meet directly with the hiring authority. These one-to-one interviews are the focus of the techniques presented later in this chapter.

Group: While not as common, it's possible you could be asked to interview with two or more people involved in the selection process. I've even known of situations where a group of interviewers met with a group of applicants — all at the same time. Many of the techniques used in this book will work well in these settings too.

Nondirective: Some interviewers will ask few direct questions and, instead, encourage you to tell them whatever you want. For example, instead of asking "How did you do in your math classes?" they might ask "What did you like best about school?" If you are not prepared for such open-ended questions, you could quickly put your foot in your mouth.

Stress: Some interviewers intentionally try to get you upset. They want to see how you handle stress, whether you can accept criticism, or some other reaction. They hope to see how you are likely to act on the job in pressured situations. For example, they might try to get you angry by not accepting something you say as true. "I find it difficult to believe," they say, "that you were responsible for as large a program as you claim here on your resume. Why don't you just tell me what you really did." Another approach is to quickly fire questions at you but not give you time to completely answer or interrupt you mid-sentence with other questions. Not nice. But now you've been warned. I hope you don't run into this sort of interviewer but if so, be yourself and have a few laughs. The odds are the interview could turn out fine if you don't get hooked into throwing things around the room. If you do get a job offer following such an interview, you might want to ask yourself whether you would want to work for such a person. It might be fun to tell them what to do with their job.

Structured: This is becoming more common, particularly in larger organizations. The interviewer may have a list of things to ask all applicants and a form they fill out. Your experience and skills may be compared to specific job tasks or criteria. Even if highly structured, there is usually the opportunity for you to present what you feel is essential about yourself.

Disorganized: Let's face it, you will come across many interviewers who will not know how to interview you. They may talk about themselves too much or neglect to ask you any meaningful questions. Many people are competent managers but poor interviewers. I will show you how to help such lost souls learn the true you by providing some answers to questions they may not have asked.

Second Interview Type: The Information Interview

This is an interview that has become widely used (and often abused) since the mid-1970s. Richard Bolles popularized it in his book, *What Color Is Your Parachute?* In essence, it is to be used by job seekers who have not yet decided, exactly, what they want to do — or where. To correctly use the technique, you must first define your ideal job in terms of skills required, size and type of organization, salary level, interests, what sort of co-workers, and other preferences (like you did in chapter 5). The next step is to gather information on just where a job of this sort might exist and what it might be called.

If you do your homework before using this method and if you are truly honest and sincere about seeking information but not a job, then the technique is both effective and fun. Unfortunately, this technique has been misused and abused. People who really want to get a job have used the technique as a trick to get in to see someone. ("I'm not looking for a job but am conducting a survey . . . ") Well, that is dishonest and most employers resent the misrepresentation. Many employers are now wary about anyone, even the sincere ones, asking to see them for any reason. Bolles laments this and points out that some trainers and others who should know better have encouraged this dishonesty. He does point out, however, that the technique is still useful, particularly outside of larger cities and with smaller organizations.

"Profit" Interviews Can Create Jobs

Years before information interviewing, Bernard Haldane developed a technique for those seeking managerial and professional positions. He articulated his approach in a book that I consider a classic, titled *How to Make a Habit of Success,* published in 1960.[4] In it, you identify an employer that is of particular interest. That organization meets most of the criteria set by the job seeker **and** the job seeker clearly sees how that organization could benefit from employing him or her. Once that happens, the job seeker carefully puts together a written business proposal to be presented to the person or persons within that organization who make decisions. The plan would address what you propose to do; how it would be done; how much money (or other benefits) the project or activity will generate; how much it will cost (including your salary and benefits), and why you are the one person most uniquely qualified to successfully complete the tasks.

The key word in all this is "profit," since if you propose other benefits, but not more profit, your case is surely weakened. If all goes well, you have a job created for you where none existed before. It **does** happen! In fact, Haldane and Associates, the career counseling firm founded by Bernard Haldane, provides data indicating that almost two-thirds of the people they work with have jobs created just for them by using this technique.

Third Interview Type: The JIST Job Search Interview

This interview type refers to a variety of situations where a job opening may or may not now exist, but where it still makes sense to go in and speak with someone about the possibility of present or future employment. For example, if you seek an interview for a job that is now open (a traditional job opening) you would ask "Do you have any job openings?" And very often, the answer would be "No." If, on the other hand, you had said "I would like to speak with the person in charge of (this or that)," you would probably get to talk to them. That would be an interview in the way I define it, even if there is no job opening yet. If you got a "Yes" after asking if there are any openings, that would be an interview too.

This definition of an interview is quite broad and makes it much easier to obtain. But not every conversation is an interview. Here are the criteria:

1. You must know what sort of job you want and;
2. You must be able to communicate clearly why someone should hire you for that job and;
3. The interviewer must know something about the sort of job you are looking for, or at the very least, know other people who may know.

This type of interview provides a tremendous advantage to you. Now you can interview with employers before they have a job opening and avoid the competition from others completely. And since the employer won't be trying to eliminate you from other applicants, the interview can be much more relaxed.

The Seven Phases of an Interview

The objective of an interview is to get a job offer. In order to accomplish that you must first get to the person who has the authority to hire you and present yourself well. A certain amount of judgment is required for you to know how to act in various sorts of interviews. If there **is** a job opening and you want it, you would behave differently from an interview where no opening existed. But just what do you do? To find out, let's turn our attention to the practical, how-to issues of our newly redefined interview. To help you, I've divided the JIST Job Search Interview into seven major phases:

Phase I: **Before You Go In.** Before you even meet the interviewer, you will create an impression. If it's bad, nothing good can come of it.

Phase II: **Opening Moves.** An interview isn't a game, exactly, but how you begin it will affect whether you win or lose.

Phase III: **The Interview Itself.** This is the longest and most complete part of an interview. It's here that you are asked problem questions and have the opportunity to present your skills. The impression you make here will be a lasting one and is highly dependent on your ability to communicate.

Phase IV: **Closing the Interview.** There is more to ending an interview than simply saying good-bye.

Phase V: **Following Up.** The interview is not over until you send a thank-you note, plus other necessities. People who follow up get jobs over those who do not. It's that simple.

Phase VI: **Negotiating.** This could happen in your first interview and knowing what to do, and how, can be worth many, many dollars.

Phase VII: **Making a Final Decision.** Sometimes, saying no to a job offer you've worked hard to get is the nicest thing you can do for yourself. Among other things, I'll provide you with a simple decision-making process to help you evaluate an important life decision on its own merits.

Now let's get started with some specific techniques to help you present yourself well in each of the seven phases of an interview.

Phase I: Before You Go In

While often overlooked, what happens before the interview begins is very, very important. Before you actually meet the interviewer you often have indirect contact that creates an impression. This contact can be with others who know the interviewer, or directly, as with a phone call or correspondence. When you first meet the interviewer, you will also create an impression by your appearance and manner. Let's look at the issues here and see what you can do to prepare for them.

Preliminary Contacts

There are three ways an interviewer may form an impression of you before meeting you face-to-face. Let's take these one at a time.

1. **The Interviewer Already Knows You:** There are many situations where an interviewer may know you from previous contacts or from someone else telling them of you. When this is so, your best approach is to acknowledge that relationship but treat the interview in all other respects as a business meeting. Even if you are the best of friends, remember that a decision to hire you involves hard cash. It will not be done lightly.

2. **Previous Phone Contacts:** The phone is an important job search tool. How you handle yourself on the phone will create an impression, even though the contacts are brief. You created an impression when you set up the interview. Consider another call to verify the interview the day before, or even the day of the interview itself. Say something like: "Hi, I want to make sure our interview for two o'clock tomorrow is still on." Get any directions you need. It is just another way of demonstrating your attention to details and helps communicate the sense of importance you are giving this interview.

3. **Previous Paperwork:** Prior to most interviews, you will provide the employer with some sort of paperwork that will create an impression. Sending a note or letter prior to the interview often creates the impression that you are well-organized. Copies of applications, resumes, and JIST Cards seen in advance help the interviewer know more about you. If they are well done, as they must be, they will help create a positive impression. For these reasons, all the paperwork you present to an employer must be as professional and well done as possible.

Researching the Organization

Knowing something about the organization and the interviewer will pay off. This is not practical in situations where you call or drop in unexpectedly as when making a cold contact, but it does make sense in other situations. For example, let's say you have targeted a particular organization as one of the few that seem able to provide you with the kind of job you want. Because of that interview's importance to you, it would be wise to be well prepared for it. Briefly, there are three ways of researching for an interview.

The library is a good place to start. Ask the librarian for sources of information on the organization that interests you. There are often national, state, and local directories listing businesses and other organizations that provide some information. Newspapers might contain articles and news releases regarding the organization, and back issues are often available at the library. Major newspapers are indexed and articles are cross-referenced to help you find what you are looking for.

The organization itself is a good source of information. Call the receptionist or even the interviewer and ask them to suggest materials you might read. Annual reports or catalogs are sometimes available but anything you get will help. It won't hurt for your interviewer to know how thorough you are, either.

Ask others who might know about the organization or the interviewer. This is one of the best sources of information. An hour on the telephone can give you information you could not obtain otherwise. Use the networking technique by contacting someone who seems likely to know what you want—or knows someone who would. Find out what you can, then ask for the name of someone else who would know more.

Here are some things you might want to find out about **before** you go to a job interview:

The Organization: Size, number of employees; major products or services; competitors and the competitive environment; major changes in policies or status; reputation, values, and major weaknesses or opportunities.

The Interviewer: Level and area of responsibility; special work-related projects, interests, or accomplishments; personal information (family, hobbies, etc.), and management style.

The Position: If an opening exists or if similar jobs now exist; what happened to others in similar positions; salary range and benefits; duties and responsibilities, and what the last person did wrong (to avoid it) or right (to emphasize it).

The more you can find out before you begin, the better you are likely to do in the interview. Employers appreciate someone who does their homework. You will be better prepared for any questions that may come up and can more readily direct the interview to concentrate on presenting your skills well.

Getting to and Waiting for the Interview

There are several details that may be helpful to consider before the interview itself.

Get There on Time: Try to schedule several interviews within the same area and time frame to avoid excessive travel. If you are driving, get directions from the receptionist and be sure you know how to get there and how long it takes. Allow plenty of time for parking and plan on being there five to 10 minutes early. If you are using public transportation make sure you know what to do to get there on time.

Final Grooming: Arrive early enough to slip into a restroom and correct any grooming problems your travel may have caused (wind-blown hair, etc.).

The Receptionist: Many organizations have a receptionist and this person is important to you. Assume that everything you say or do will get back to the interviewer. It will. A friendly chat with the receptionist can also be a productive way to find out more about the organization. For example, if it seems appropriate, ask them what it is like to work there, what they do in their job, or even what sort of a person the boss is. They are often happy to share these things with you in a helpful way. A thank-you note to them following your interview will surely create a positive impression. Treat them with respect and they will help you by saying nice things about you to the boss; mistreat them and you will not get a job there.

Waiting Room Behavior: It is important to relax and to look relaxed. Occupy yourself with something businesslike. For example, this could be a good time to review your notes on questions you might like to ask in the interview, key skills you want to present, or other interview details. Or bring a work-related magazine to read or pick one up in the reception room. They may also have publications from the organization itself that you may not have seen yet. During the entire interviewing process, I advise you not to smoke since a non-smoker is often seen as a more desirable worker. You may have other mannerisms that may create negative impressions, too. Don't slouch in your seat. Don't create a mess by spreading out your coat and papers across the next seat.

If the Interviewer Is Late: Hope that it happens. If you arrive promptly but had to wait past the appointed time, that puts the interviewer in a "gee, I'm sorry, I owe you one" frame of mind. If they are 15 minutes late, approach the receptionist and say something like this: "I have an appointment to keep yet today. Do you think it will be much longer before (insert interviewer's name) will be free?" Be nice, but don't act like you can sit around all day either. If you have to wait more than 25 minutes beyond the scheduled time, ask to reschedule at a better time. Say it is no problem for you and you understand things do come up. Besides, you say, you want to be sure Mr. or Ms. So-and-So doesn't feel rushed when they see you. Set up the new time, accept any apology with a smile, and be on your way. When you do come back for your interview, the odds are that the interviewer will treat you very well indeed.

Phase II: Opening Moves

You've gotten to the right office, on time, and the interviewer now walks into the room. What is the first thing that will happen? They will **see** you!

In a monumental and thorough work by Steven Mangum titled *Job Search, A Review of the Literature*, he found that "appearance, communication skills, and attitudes dominate the research. Attire and physical attractiveness visibly influence the hiring process."[5] I cannot stress enough the importance of your appearance in the job search. It is a major factor in getting eliminated.

Appearance Counts

The importance of this issue is highlighted by the results of a study which evaluated the effect of nonverbal communication style.[6] Two actors, one male, one female, were videotaped while role playing an interview. Two tapes were made of each, using precisely the same responses to the same questions. In one tape they made good eye contact while speaking, spoke clearly, presented good posture. In the other, they did not. They dressed the same for each and, I emphasize, used the same words in responding to the same questions.

These tapes were then randomly shown to 52 professional interviewers who were asked to score the interviews in various categories. No interviewer saw the same actor in both roles. What do you suppose happened? It would be no surprise to guess which job seeker role was rated more positively. Naturally, the "good" interview was chosen over the "bad" one. What was astonishing was that, of all the interviewers, not one would have invited back the person who had poor nonverbal skills. The same people using the same responses but who had good nonverbal communication skills would have been invited back by 88 percent of the interviewers. The results of this study show that your various personality traits (adaptive skills) are observed by interviewers. Let's look at some of the other appearance-related issues employers use to define your personality and make hiring decisions.

Dress and Grooming: This gets complex, what with various styles, color, preferences, and other factors. Entire books have been written on the subject and there are many differences of opinion on just what is right for various people for various occasions. To avoid the controversy, I present this simple rule:

Mike Farr's Interview Dress and Grooming Rule

Dress and groom like the interviewer is likely to dress — but cleaner.

My rule means that a bank teller would dress, when going to an interview, like their boss would dress. An auto mechanic, on the other hand, would look inappropriate going to an interview dressed like the manager of a bank. If there is any doubt about just how to dress or groom, guess conservative. Pay attention to details. Are your shoes shined? Are your clothes clean and pressed? Is your hair neat? Are you absolutely clean? Have you looked closely at yourself in the mirror? It is best to get someone else's opinion on the impression you make. A better clothing store can help you select a coordinated job-search outfit. Plan to invest some money in at least one set of good quality interviewing clothes. Notice, when you are all spruced up, how good you feel. That can affect your whole performance in the interview.

A Firm Handshake and Good Eye Contact: Shaking hands is a common custom and, while it seems a small detail, do be aware of yours. If the employer offers their hand, give them a firm but not too firm handshake as you smile. As ridiculous as it sounds, a little practice helps. Avoid staring but do look at the interviewer when either of you is speaking. It will help you concentrate on what is being said as well as indicate to the employer that you are listening closely and have good social skills.

Posture and More: The very best way to see yourself as others see you is to role play an interview while it is videotaped. Looking at and listening to the playback is sometimes shocking to people. If this equipment is not available to you, all is not lost. Pay close attention to your own posture, mannerisms, and other body language. Ask yourself how an employer might evaluate you if they saw that behavior. Look at other people and copy the posture and behavior of ones you think would look good in an interview situation. Let's look at some problem areas to watch for and improve.

When you are sitting, lean slightly forward in your chair and keep your head up, looking directly at the interviewer. This helps you look interested and alert. Try to notice any distracting movements or mannerisms. A woman in one of my workshops saw herself in a videotape playing with her hair over and over. It was only then that she even realized she did it at all and how distracting it was. Seek out and eliminate similar behavior from the interview.

Pay attention to your voice. If you are naturally soft spoken, work on increasing your voice volume slightly. Listen to news announcers and other professional speakers. They don't say "aaahhh" every 10 seconds, or say "You know what I mean?" or other repetitive words or phrases. You may hardly be aware of doing this, but do watch for it. Professional speakers are also good models to copy for good volume, speed, and voice tone. I, for example, have a fairly deep voice. I have learned to raise it up and down while doing presentations, so everyone doesn't go to sleep. If you work on improving your voice delivery, you will improve as you gain experience and conduct more interviews.

Establishing the Relationship

Open the interview with an approach intended to establish a relaxed, social tone. Here are some ideas of what to say in the first few minutes.

Use the interviewer's name. Address the interviewer by name as often as possible, particularly in the early part of the interview and again when you are ending it. Be formal, using a Mr. Jones or Ms. Smith or some other approach unless they suggest otherwise.

Play the chit-chat game for awhile. The interviewer will often comment on the weather, ask if you had trouble getting there, or some other common opening. Be friendly and make a few appropriate comments. Do not push your way into the business of your visit too early since these informal openings are standard measures of your socialization skills.

Smile. It's nonverbal and people will respond more favorably to you if you smile often.

Comment on something personal in the interviewer's office. "I love your office! Who helped decorate it?" Or, "I noticed the sailboat. Do you sail?" Or, "Is that a Phantom II computer terminal I noticed downstairs? How do you like it?" Or, "Your receptionist is great! How long has he been here?" The idea here is to express interest in something they are interested in and encourage them to speak about it. It is a compliment if your enthusiasm shows. It also often provides you the opportunity to share something you have in common, so try to pick a topic you know something about.

Ask some opening questions. As soon as you have both completed the necessary and pleasant chit-chat, be prepared to ask a few light questions to get the interview off in a useful direction. This can happen within a minute of your first greeting, but is more likely to take up to five minutes. Some of the transitional questions that follow could be used in a traditional interview setting, while others assume that you are interviewing before a job is actually open.

"How did you get started in this type of career?" (Or business or whatever.)

"I'd like to know more about what your organization does. Would you mind telling me?"

"I have a background in _____ and am interested in how I might be considered to work in an organization such as yours."

"I have three years experience plus two years of training in the field of _____. I am actively looking for a job and know that you probably do not have openings now but would be interested in future openings. Perhaps if I told you a few things about myself, you could give me some ideas of whether you would be interested in me."

Some questions are more assertive than others, but a busy employer will prefer this over a "gee, I'm not really sure why I'm here" approach. Whatever questions you ask, the objective is to make a smooth transition from the opening moments to the heart of the interview where you present your skills and they evaluate you as a person.

Phase III: The Interview Itself

If you have created a reasonably positive image of yourself so far, an interviewer will now be interested in the specifics of why they should consider hiring you. This back-and-forth conversation usually lasts from 15 to 45 minutes and many consider it to be the most important — and most difficult — task in the entire job search. But you will have several advantages over the normal job seeker: you know what sort of job you want and; you know what skills are required to do well in that job, and you have those very skills. The only thing that remains to be done is to communicate this. This is best done in answering the questions an employer will ask you.

Handling Problem Questions

According to one employer survey, about 90 percent of all job seekers they interview cannot provide a good answer to a problem question.[7] **Everyone has a problem of some sort and the employer will try to find yours. Expect it.** Let's say, for example, that you have been out of work for three months. That could be seen as a problem, unless you can provide a good reason for it.

Relate to what an employer is looking for. Research indicates that most employers will react to three issues during the interview. If any of these "employer's expectations" are not met, it is unlikely that you will get a job offer. They are:

1. **Appearance:** Do you look like the type of person who will succeed on the job?

2. **Dependability:** Can you be depended on to be reliable and to do a good job for a reasonable length of time?

3. **Credentials:** Do you have the necessary training, experience, skills and credentials to indicate that you are able to do the job well?

Most problem questions have to do with either the second or third expectations.

See every question as an opportunity. Your interview will be short, so you must make the most of it. Each question provides an opportunity for you to present your skills, the skills you have that are needed by the employer. Remember that the interviewer is a person just like you. You must be honest and be able to support, with proof, anything you say about yourself. If you have carefully selected your job objective and know your own skills, you will find it easy to present reasons why they should hire you.

Ask some questions early on. Some interviewers are happy to discuss details of the position you seek. If possible, find out as much as you can about the position early in the interview. Ask about the type of person they look for to fill this sort of position, what sort of people have done well in those jobs before, or what sorts of responsibilities the job has. Once you know more about what the interviewer is looking for, you can "fit" your later responses to what you now know they want. Let's say that you found out that the position requires someone who is good at meeting people and who is organized. Assuming you have those skills, you could later emphasize how good you are at meeting people. The examples you use to support that could also provide evidence of how organized you can be.

The Three-Step Process for Answering Interview Questions

There are hundreds of questions that could be asked of you in an interview. There is no way you can memorize a "correct" response for each possible question. Interviews just aren't like that. They are often conversational and informal. The unexpected often happens. For these reasons, it is far more important to develop an **approach** to answering any interview question rather than memorizing a correct response for each. As you practice using a standard approach, it becomes easier to provide a good response to almost any question that is asked. Following is a simple method for answering most interview questions in a natural, honest, and positive way.

The Three-Step Process for Answering Interview Questions

Step 1: **Understand What Is Really Being Asked.**

It usually relates to Employer's Expectation 2, regarding your adaptive skills and personality: Can we depend on you? Are you easy to get along with? and Are you a good worker? The question may also relate to Employer's Expectation 3, namely, Do you have the experience and training to do the job if we hire you?

Step 2: **Answer the Question Briefly, In a Non-Damaging Way.**

Acknowledge the facts, but present them as an advantage, not a disadvantage.

Step 3: **Answer the Real Question by Presenting Your Related Skills.**

Once you understand the employer's real concern, you can get around to answering the often hidden question by presenting the skills you have related to the job. Let me give you an example of how this works:

Example Problem Question: "We were looking for someone with more experience in this field. Why should we consider you over others with better credentials?"

Step 1: This question is difficult but it is asked often. To prepare for it, you must remember that employers often hire people who present themselves well over those with better credentials. Your best shot is to emphasize whatever personal strengths you have that could offer an advantage to an employer. They want to know whether you have anything going for you that can help you overcome a more experienced worker. Well, do you? (If you answer "No," go back to chapter 1 and begin again!) Refer to your JIST Card. Are you a hard worker? Do you learn fast? Have you had intensive training or hands-on experience? Do you have skills from other activities that can transfer to this job?

Step 2: Here is an example of how one person might answer the question without damage: "I'm sure there are people who have more years of experience or better credentials. I do, though, have four years of combined training and hands-on experience using the latest methods and techniques. Because my training is recent, I am open to new ideas and have gotten used to working hard and learning quickly."

Step 3: The response begun above can continue: "As you know, I held down a full-time job and family responsibilities while going to school. During those two years, I had an excellent attendance record both at work and school, missing only one day in two years. I also received two merit increases in salary and my grades were in the top 25 percent. To do all this, I learned to organize my time and set priorities. I worked hard to prepare myself in this new career area and am willing to keep working to establish myself. The position you have available is what I am prepared to do. I am willing to work harder than the next person because I have the desire to keep learning and to do a good job. With my education complete, I can now turn my full attention to my next job."

The response did take the opportunity to present the skills necessary to do well in any job. This job seeker sounds dependable, which meets Employer's Expectation 2. And he gave examples of situations where he had used the skills needed by the job in other settings, thus meeting Employer's Expectation 3. It was a good response.

More on Answering Problem Questions

Now that you have seen how to construct a good response to difficult interview questions, it is time to move on to the other phases of the interview process. Because of the importance of answering interview questions, the next chapter will provide specific answers to the 10 most frequently asked problem questions as well as more information on a process that will help you answer most interview questions.

Phase IV: Closing the Interview

There are a few things to remember as the interview is coming to an end. Let's review them briefly.

Don't let the interview last too long. Most interviews last 30 to 60 minutes. Unless the employer asks otherwise, plan on staying no longer than one hour. After the interview begins, watch for hints from the interviewer (looking at a watch, rustling papers, etc.). Exceptions to the one hour rule should be made only at the interviewer's request.

Summarize the key points of the interview. Use your judgment here and keep it short! Review the major issues that came up in the interview. This is an optional step and can be skipped if time is short.

If a problem came up, repeat your resolution of it. Whatever you think that particular interviewer may see as a reason not to hire you, bring it up again and present your reasons why you don't see it as a problem. If you are not sure, be direct and ask "Is there anything about me that concerns you or might keep you from hiring me?" Whatever comes up, do as well as you can in responding to it.

Review your strengths for this job. This is another chance for you to present your skills that relate to this particular job. Emphasize your key strengths only and keep it brief. Your JIST Card will help you do this.

Use the "Call-Back Close." This is an approach that is quite strong. You may not be comfortable with it at first but role play and practice in your early interviews will help you get more comfortable. It does work. Here it is:

The Call-Back Close

1. **Thank the interviewer by name.** While shaking their hand, say: "Thank you (Mr., Mrs. or Ms. _____) for your time today."

2. **Express interest.** Depending on the situation, express your interest in the job, organization, service, product, or person interviewed:

   "I'm very interested in the ideas we went over today." or;

   "I'm very interested in your organization. It seems to be an exciting place to work." or;

   "I enjoyed the visit with you and am impressed by all you have accomplished." or, if a job opening exists and you want it, definitely say,

   "I am definitely interested in this position."

3. **Mention your busy schedule.** Say "I'm busy for the next week, but..."

4. **Arrange a reason and a time to call back.** Your objective is to leave a reason for you to get back in touch and to arrange for a specific day and time to do so. For example, say "I'm sure I'll have questions. When would be the best time for me to get back with you?"

   Notice that I said "When can I..." rather than "Is it OK to..." The first way does not easily allow a "no" response. Get a specific day (Monday) and a best time to call (between 9 and 10 a.m.).

5. **Say "thank you" and "good- bye."**

Phase V: Following Up

The interview has ended, you made it home, and now it's all over, right? Not right. You need to follow-up. As I've said throughout this book, following up can make the difference between being unemployed and getting a good job fast. Here is what you should do when you get home.

Make notes on the interview. While it is fresh in your mind, jot down key points. A week later, you may not remember something essential.

Schedule your follow-up. If you agreed to call back next Monday between 9 and 10 a.m., you are likely to forget unless you put it on your schedule. Tips for developing a system for following up will be covered in chapter 14.

Send your thank-you note. Send the note the very same day if possible. Enclose a JIST Card if it seems appropriate.

Call when you said you would! If you call when you said you would, you will create the impression of being organized and wanting the job. If you do have a specific question, ask it. If a job opening exists and you do want it, say that you want it and why. If no job opening exists, just say how you enjoyed the visit and would like to stay in touch during your job search. This would also be a good time to ask, if you had not done it before, for the names of anyone else with whom you might speak about a position for a person with your skills and experience.

Schedule for more follow-up. The last thing to do is to schedule the next time you want to follow-up with this person. That, too, is explained in chapter 14.

Phase VI: **Negotiating**

I'll cover tips for negotiating salary in the next chapter, but there are other negotiable areas which are often overlooked.

Title: Some job titles look better on a resume and sound better in an interview. Just by changing the wording, you can position yourself for more responsibility ("office manager" vs. "secretary," for example).

Hours: I once accepted a job that paid a bit less than I wanted, but it let me take one afternoon off per week. I still worked over 40 hours but those afternoons sailing sure felt good.

Salary Review: Ask to have your salary reviewed for an increase after three to six months. Negotiate a specific increase to be given then, if your performance is good.

Advancement: Discuss the next level of responsibility toward which you might work. Find out how you might get there and how long it might take.

Education and Training: Some organizations pay for course work, seminars, or other training. This can be a tremendous benefit, if you can get it.

Vacations: Smaller organizations are more flexible on this. Ask for more and you just might get it.

Fringe Benefits: "Fringes" are often standard for everyone in the same organization, but sometimes there is flexibility. For example, negotiation for special insurance benefits (by showing that you are more valuable than some other employees), could be worth real money to you.

Working Conditions: Perhaps you like to do some work from home, come in at 8:15 a.m. instead of 8:00, prefer to have your own office (with a window), or some other special request. The time to negotiate these things is before you start working there.

Money Isn't Everything

Let's assume that you get a job offer that is close to, but not quite in the pay range you wanted. Before you turn it down, think about what other things you might ask for that would make the job acceptable. Then ask for them.

A Word About Timing

The time to negotiate is **after** you've been offered the job. Do not discuss your preferred salary or any other related negotiable subject in an interview until after a job offer has clearly been given. Many, many job seekers have been eliminated from consideration over this very issue.

Saying No

NEVER EVER turn down a job offer in an interview! Let's say that you get an offer at half the salary you expected. Avoid the temptation to turn the offer down there and then. Instead say: "Thank you for your offer. I am flattered that you think I can do the job. Because my decision is so important to me, I would like to consider your offer and get back with you within two days."

Leave, and see if you change your mind. If not, call back and say, in effect: "I've given your offer considerable thought and feel that I just can't take it at the salary you've offered. Is there any way that I could be paid more, in the range of _____?" If the employer cannot meet your salary needs, say thank you again, and let them know you are interested in future openings within your salary range. Then stay in touch. You never know...

Saying Yes

As with saying no too quickly, take time to think about accepting a job too. If you **do** want it, do not jeopardize obtaining it with unreasonable demands. Ask for 24 hours to consider your decision and, when calling back, consider negotiating for something reasonable. A bit more money, every other Tuesday afternoon off, or whatever would be nice if you can get it easily. If there is a problem with your requests, make it very clear that you want the job anyway. When can you start?

Phase VII: Making a Final Decision

It is rare to find the perfect job. There are usually compromises to be made. But, too often, a job is accepted without thorough knowledge of just what it would be like to actually work there. At the time, it **seems** to be a good idea. Unfortunately, what seemed good then doesn't always turn out that way later. The major problem is that many people never make a careful decision at all. They don't take the time to weigh the pros and the cons. One job leads to another and careers develop by accident. But there is an alternative.

In a book titled, *Decision Making,* Irving Janis and Leon Mann present research and theory on the process — and consequences — of making important decisions.[8] They found that various groups who used this process were more likely to stick to their decision and have fewer regrets afterwards then those who did not. To make any important decision they suggest that you consider the alternatives in a systematic way.

I've adapted their decision-making approach a bit for use in the job search. Look over the Career Choice Balance Sheet to see how it works. The form won't tell you what to do, but it will help you to see more clearly the advantages and disadvantages involved. Based on these, go ahead and make your own decision — it is sure to be the right one for you at the time.

The Career Choice Balance Sheet		
Option Considered: *sales director*		
	Positives	Negatives
Tangible Things for Me	good pay advancement good use of my skills	long hours stressful high - turnover
Tangible Things for Others	more $ for recreational activities and new house down payment	less time for recreation longer commute

The Career Choice Balance Sheet

Option Considered: *sales director*

	Positives	Negatives
Self-Approval— Disapproval	*firm has good reputation* *more responsibility*	*conform more to Company policy*
Social Approval— Disapproval	*impressive title* *spouse is supportive*	*success may change relationship with my friends*

Chapter Ten Endnotes

1. There is lots of research out there to support the limited validity of interviewing in the selection process. One good article is by M.D. Dunnette and W.C. Borman titled "Personal Selection and Classification Systems," *Annual Review of Psychology*, vol. 30, 1979, pp. 477-525.

2. Richard Fear's book, titled *The Evaluation Interview*, published by McGraw Hill, is considered a classic text for interviewers but is of great value for a job seeker as well.

3. This article appeared in the *Personnel and Guidance Journal*, vol. 12, 1978, pp. 188-191.

4. Haldane is considered by some the "father" of the Life/Work Planning Movement later popularized so well by Richard Bolles. A 1975 revision of Haldane's book was published by Warner Books and may still be available in libraries.

5. Mangum's book, *Job Search: A Review of the Literature,* was published by Olympus Research Center, Salt Lake City, Utah, in 1982. While it is a wonderful source of research, the book is out of print and will be hard to find.

6. Thomas McGovern and Howard Tinsley, "Interviewer Evaluations of Interviewee Nonverbal Behavior," *Journal of Vocational Behavior,* vol. 13, pp. 163-171.

7. While there is much research to support this assertion, one source is the "Northwestern Endicott Report," from The Placement Center, Northwestern University, Wisconsin.

8. Irving Janis and Leon Mann, *Decision Making,* published by the Free Press, 1977. Janis and Dan Wheeler wrote a good article on this topic titled "Thinking Clearly About Career Choices," in *Psychology Today,* vol. 5, 1978.

Chapter Eleven

Answering Problem Interview Questions

In the previous chapter you learned how to handle each of the seven phases of an interview. This chapter builds upon that knowledge by providing specific techniques for answering problem interview questions. This is a very important issue since, according to one survey of employers, 80 percent of the job seekers they interviewed were unable to adequately answer one or more interview question.[1] And it is clear that if you leave the interviewer with a negative or uncertain impression of your ability or interest in the doing the job, you won't get a job offer.

The Most Frequently Asked Interview Questions

Knowing and practicing answers to a relatively small but important cluster of difficult questions will prepare you to answer many others. Some questions seem to be asked more than others. Others are seldom asked directly but are the basis for the question that is asked instead. For example, a conversational question about your family relationships may really be an attempt to discover whether or not you will be a reliable worker.

From the thousands of questions that could be asked, I have constructed 10 questions that represent the types of issues employers are most likely to be concerned with. It is partly based on research on the questions employers actually ask and partly on my sense of which questions provide the best patterns for teaching you the principles of constructing a good response to other questions.[2] Here is my list of the most important ones for you to know how to answer.

The Top 10 Problem Interview Questions
1. Why don't you tell me about yourself?
2. Why should I hire you?
3. What are your major strengths?
4. What are your major weaknesses?
5. What sort of pay do you expect to receive?
6. How does your previous experience relate to the jobs we have here?
7. What are your plans for the future?
8. What will your former employers (or teachers, if you are a recent student) say about you?
9. Why are you looking for this sort of position and why here?
10. Why don't you tell me about your personal situation?

The Three-Step Process to Answering Interviewing Questions

Because each of you is different, there can be no one correct way to answer these and other questions. For this reason, it is important for you to learn a strategy for answering any interview question. One important strategy presented in the previous chapter is the Three-Step Process reviewed below.

The Three-Step Process to Answering Interview Questions
Step 1: **Understand What Is Really Being Asked.** It usually relates to Employer's Expectation 2, regarding your adaptive skills and personality: Can we depend on you? Are you easy to get along with? and Are you a good worker?
Step 2: **Answer The Question Briefly, In A Non-Damaging Way.** Acknowledge the facts, but present them as an advantage, not a disadvantage.
Step 3: **Answer The Real Question By Presenting Your Related Skills.** Once you understand the employer's real concern, you can get around to answering the often hidden question by presenting your skills and experiences related to the job.

The Three-Step Process is important for understanding that the interview question being asked often is looking for underlying information. The technique that follows will help you provide that information in an effective way.

The "Prove-It" Technique

In the third step of the Three-Step Process you are to provide an answer to the real question being asked. In doing so I have found it important to structure your response to include the following elements:

Present a Concrete Example: People relate to and remember stories. Saying you have a skill is not nearly as powerful as describing a situation where you used that skill. The story should include enough details to make sense of the who, what, where, when, and why.

Quantify: Whenever possible, numbers should be used to provide a basis for what was done. For example, the number of customers served or the amount of cash handled.

Results: It is important to provide some data regarding the positive results you obtained. For example, sales increased by 3 percent over the previous year or profits went up 50 percent. Use numbers to quantify your results.

Link It Up: While the connection between your story and doing the job well may seem obvious to you, make sure it is clear to the employer. A simple statement is often enough to accomplish this.

Because of all the work you have done in earlier sections of this book, it should be fairly easy to provide proof to support the skills you discuss in an interview. The technique of providing proof of your ability to handle a job from examples of your previous experience is the basic interview strategy to use. I will refer to it in sections that follow and it is most important that you remember the basic steps.

Answers to the Top 10 Problem Interview Questions

Following are sample answers to the problem questions I listed earlier. For each one I provide an analysis of what is really being asked followed by a strategy for answering it and one or more sample responses. In each case I will use the Three-Step Process, including the Prove-It approach for constructing a response. These techniques will allow you to construct your own response to most interview questions, so learn to use them to evaluate your own answers to similar questions.

Question 1: "Why Don't You Tell Me About Yourself?"

Analysis: This is an open-ended question. You could start anywhere, but telling your life's history in two hours or less is not what is really being asked. Instead, such a question is a test of your ability to select what is important and communicate it clearly and quickly. Obviously, the questioner expects you to relate your background to the position being considered.

Strategy: There are several basic approaches that could be used. One would be to go ahead and provide a brief response to the question as it is asked and the other is to request a clarification of the question before answering it. In both cases, you would quickly turn your response to focus on your skills, experience, and training that prepared you for the sort of job you now want.

Example 1: If you answered the question as it were asked you might say something like this: "I grew up in the Southwest and have one brother and one sister. My parents both worked and I had a happy childhood. I always did well in school and by the time I graduated from high school I had taken a year's worth of business courses. I knew then that I wanted to work in a business setting and had several part-time office jobs while still in high school. After high school I worked in a variety of business settings and learned a great deal about how various businesses ran. For example, I was given complete responsibility for the daily operations of a wholesale distribution company that grossed over 2 million dollars a year. That was only three years after I graduated from high school. There I learned to supervise other people and solve problems under pressure. I also got more interested in the financial end of running a business and decided, after three years and three promotions, to go after a position where I could have more involvement in key strategies and long-term management decisions."

Comments: Notice how this job seeker provided a few bits of personal history then quickly turned to mention skills and experiences directly related to the job now sought.

Example 2: You could ask the interviewer to help you narrow down things they really want to know with a response such as this: "There's so much to tell! Would you like me to emphasize my personal history, the special training and education I have that prepared me for this sort of position, or the skills and job-related experiences I have to support my objective?"

Comments: If you do this well, most employers will tell you what sorts of things they are most interested in and you can then concentrate on giving them what they want.

Question 2: "Why Should I Hire You?"

Analysis: This is a direct and fair question. Though it is rarely asked this clearly, it is THE question behind any other question that will be asked. It has no hidden meaning.

Strategy: A direct question deserves a direct response. Why should they hire you? The best response provides advantages to them, not to you. This often involves providing proof that you can help them make more money by improving efficiency, reducing costs, increasing sales, or solving problems (by coming to work on time, improving customer services, organizing one or more operations, or a variety of other things).

Example: Here is an example of a response from a person with considerable prior experience: "You should hire me because I don't need to be trained and have a proven track record. I have over 15 years of education and experience related to this position. Over six of those years have been in management positions similar to the one available here. In my last position, I was promoted three times in the six years I was there. I most recently had responsibility for 15 staff and a warehousing operation that processed over 30 million dollars worth of materials a year. In the last two years, I managed a 40 percent increase in volume processed with only a six percent increase in expenses. I am hard working and have earned a reputation as a dependable and creative problem solver. The opportunities here excite me. My substantial experience will help me know how to approach the similar situations here. I am also willing to ask questions and accept advice from others. This will be an important factor in taking advantage of what has already been accomplished here."

Comments: This job seeker's response emphasized the Prove-It technique. While they presented their skills and experience in a direct and confident way, they avoided a know-it-all attitude by being open to others' suggestions.

The Reasons Why Someone Should Hire You

In the spaces below, list the major advantages you offer an employer over someone else. Emphasize your strengths. These could be personality (or good worker) traits, transferable skills, special training, prior experience, or anything else you think is important. These are the things to emphasize in your interview.

1. _____

2. _____

3. _____

Question 3: "What Are Your Major Strengths?"

Analysis: Like the previous question, this one has little hidden meaning.

Strategy: Your response should first emphasize your adaptive or self-management skills. The decision to hire you is very much based on these skills and you can deal with the details of your specific, job-related skills later. Your JIST Card should contain the key skills to emphasize in your response. Remember that here, as elsewhere, your response must be brief.

Example: Here is a response from a person who has little prior work experience related to the job they seek: "One of my major strengths is my ability to work hard towards a goal. Once I decide to do something, it will probably get done. For example, I graduated from high school four years ago. Many of my friends started working and others went on to school. At the time I didn't know what I wanted to do, so going on to school did not make sense. The jobs I could get at the time didn't excite me either, so I looked into joining the Navy. I took the test and discovered a few things about myself that surprised me. For one thing, I was much better at understanding complex problems than my grades in high school would suggest. Well, I signed up for a three year hitch that included intensive training in electronics. I worked hard and graduated in the top 20 percent of my class. As an electronics technician, I was assigned to monitor, diagnose, and repair an advanced electronics system that was worth about 20 million dollars. I was promoted several times to the rank of petty officer and received an honorable discharge after my tour of duty. I now know what I want to do and am prepared to spend extra time learning whatever is needed to do well here."

Comments: Once you begin speaking about one of your strengths, the others often fall into place naturally. Remember to provide some proof.

Question 4: "What Are Your Major Weaknesses?"

Analysis: This is a trick question. If you answer the question as it is asked, you could easily damage your ability to get the job. By trying to throw you off guard, the employer can see how you might react in similar tough situations on the job. I have often asked this question to groups of job seekers and usually get one of two types of responses. The first goes like this: "I really don't have any major weaknesses." That response is obviously untrue and evasive. The other type of response I usually get is an honest one like this: "Well, I am really disorganized. I suppose I should do better at that, but my life has just been too hectic, what with the bankruptcy and embezzlement charges and all." While this type of response might get an "A" for honesty, it gets an "F" for interview technique.

Strategy: What's needed here is an honest, undamaging response followed by a brief, positive presentation to counter the negative.

Example 1: "Well, I have been accused by co-workers of being too involved in my work. I usually come in a little early to organize my day and stay late to get a project done on time."

Example 2: "I need to learn to be more patient. I often do things myself just because I know I can do them faster and better than someone else. This has not let me be as good at delegating as I want to be. But I am working on it. I'm now spending more time showing others how to do the things I want done and that has helped. They often do better than I expected if I am clear enough with what I want done — and how.

Comments: These responses could both be expanded with some Prove-It content but they successfully use the three basic steps in answering a problem question outlined earlier in this chapter.

Question 5: "What Sort of Pay Do You Expect to Receive?"

Analysis: If you are unprepared for this question, it is highly probable that any response will damage your ability to get a job offer. The employer wants you to name a number which can then be compared to a figure they have in mind. For example, suppose that the employer is looking to pay someone $18,000 a year. If you say you were hoping for $20,000, you will probably be eliminated from consideration. They will be afraid that, if you took the job, you may not stay. If you say you would take $16,000 one of two things could happen.

1. You could get hired at $16,000 a year, making that response the most expensive two seconds in your entire life or,[3]

2. The employer may keep looking for someone else, since you must only be worth $16,000 and they were looking for someone, well, worth more.

This question is designed to help the employer either eliminate you from consideration or save money at your expense. You could get lucky and name the salary they had in mind but the stakes are too high for me to recommend that approach. Which brings me to...

Farr's Salary Negotiation Rule #1
Never talk money until after they decide they want you.

Your objective in an initial interview is to create a positive impression. It is unlikely you will get a firm job offer in a first interview. If salary comes up, avoid getting nailed down. Here are some things you could say:

"Are you making me a job offer?" (A bit corny, yes, but you just might be surprised at the result.) or;

"What salary range do you pay for positions with similar requirements?" or;

"I'm very interested in the position and my salary would be negotiable." or,

"Tell me what you have in mind for the salary range."

In most situations, these responses will either get the employer to say what salary range they were thinking of or put the subject to rest until the proper time. But let's suppose you run into a clever, demanding interviewer who insists you disclose your salary expectations before telling you what they are willing to pay. Here is what I suggest:

Farr's Salary Negotiation Rule #2

Know, in advance, the probable salary range
for similar jobs in similar organizations.

To find out, phone around and ask questions. You should know what similar jobs in your area are paying. The trick here is to think in terms of a wide range in salary.

Let's say that you figure their range, in the example above, is somewhere between $16,000 and $22,000. That is a wide range, I admit, but you could then say this: "I was looking for a salary in the mid-teens to low twenties."

That covers a lot of territory! It would include from $14,000 to $24,000 a year or so. You can use the same strategy for any salary bracket you may be considering. For example, if you wanted $28,000 a year and their range might be $23,000 to $33,000, you could say "A salary in the mid-twenties to low-thirties," etcetera, wherever your salary fits. This technique is called "bracketing" and is the third salary negotiation rule or,

---

Farr's Salary Negotiation Rule #3

Always bracket your stated salary range to begin within their probable
salary range and end a bit above what you expect to settle for.

If you are offered the job, you are likely to get offered more than they (or you) may have originally been willing to consider. Which brings me to my last rule:

Farr's Salary Negotiation Rule #4

Never say no to a job offer either before it is made or
within 24 hours afterwards.

Perhaps you think it impossible to say no before an offer is made but I have seen it done many times. In a first interview, let's say that salary does come up. If you were hoping to get a minimum salary of $22,000 a year and they told you they were hoping to pay $20,000, you just might show some disappointment. You might even say something like, "Oh no, I couldn't consider that!" and if you did, that would be the end. Before you were even offered the job, you turned it down.

But suppose that particular job turned out to be (if you had only hung around to find out more) the perfect job for you in all respects but the salary. You may have been delighted to take it. But it would rarely, now, be seriously offered. Suppose also that the employer (if only they had gotten to know the delightful person you are) found you to be the kind of person to hire even if it took a few extra dollars — say $2,000 more — to get you. In either case, you would strike a bargain.

For this reason, NEVER give a hint that the salary they discuss is not acceptable to you. Say, instead, "That is somewhat lower than I had hoped but this position does sound very interesting. If I were to consider this, what sorts of things could I do to quickly become more valuable to this organization?"

Remember that a discussion of salary is not necessarily a job offer. Do not let them eliminate you from consideration unless and until you get a firm job offer. If you are not sure, ask "Is this a job offer?" If it is, and if the figure they give you is low, say something like "Thank you for the offer. The position is very much what I wanted in many ways and I am delighted at your interest. This is an important decision for me and I would like some time to consider your offer."

Even if their offer is an insult, do not break their office furniture and stamp out. Be nice (any job offer is good for your ego when you get to turn it down). At worst, you can call them tomorrow and say "I am flattered by your job offer but feel that it would not be fair of me to accept. The salary is lower than I would like and that is the one reason I cannot accept it. Perhaps you could reconsider your offer or keep me in mind for future openings that might allow me to be worth more to you?" Even as you say no, leave the door open to keep negotiating. If the employer wants you, they may be willing to meet your terms. It happens more than you might imagine.

Comments: Do not use the above as a technique to get a higher wage. Understand that once you say no to their offer, the deal is off. You must be willing to lose that job forever.

Question 6: "How Does Your Previous Experience Relate to the Jobs We Have Here?"

Analysis: This is another direct question that requires a direct response. It relates to Employer's Expectation 3 (credentials) and your response will be very important if you have created a good impression up to this point.This question does require you to overcome any weaknesses your background might present when you are compared to other job seekers.

Here are some common typical stumbling blocks: you are just out of school and have limited experience in this career; this is your first job or you have not worked for a period of time; your prior work experience was not the same as the tasks required in this job; your previous level of responsibility was lower or higher than this job; you have had lots of jobs but no clear career direction; you do not have the educational or other credentials many others might have in similar jobs.

Strategy: Lead with your strengths. If it is obvious that other job seekers might have more education, more years of experience or whatever, acknowledge that, then present your strengths. Use the standard three-step approach to answering a problem question. And, again, your JIST Card often provides starting content.

Example 1: "As you know, I have just completed an intensive program in the area of computer programming (or whatever). In addition, I have over three years of work experience in a variety of business settings. That work experience included managing a small business during the absence of the owner. I learned to handle money there and a variety of basic bookkeeping tasks. I also inventoried and organized products worth over $300,000. These experiences helped me understand the consequences of computer programming in a business setting. While I am new to the career of programming, I am familiar with the language used by your equipment. My educational experience was very thorough and I have over three hundred hours of interactive computer time as part of my course work. Because I am new, I plan to work harder and will spend personal time as needed to meet any necessary deadlines required on the job."

Comments: This response emphasizes transferable skills (knowledge of accounting procedures) and adaptive skills (meeting deadlines and working hard). This is necessary to counter a lack of previous work experience as a programmer. In this situation, what was learned in school is also very important and should be emphasized as the equivalent of "real" work.

Example 2: "In my previous position I used many of the same skills needed to do this job well. Even though it was in a different industry, managing a business requires the types of organizational and supervisory skills that I possess. Over the past seven years I guided my region to become one of the most profitable in our company. Sales expanded at an average of 30 percent per year during the years I was responsible and profits rose at a similar rate. Since this was a mature company, such performance was highly unusual. I received two promotions during those seven years and rose to the executive level at a pace, I was later told, no one had previously achieved. I am now seeking a challenge in a smaller, growth-oriented company such as yours. I feel my experience and contacts have prepared me for this step in my career."

Comments: This response acknowledged that the previous career field differed from the one now being considered, but emphasized achievements and prior success. To accomplish this, all sorts of executive skills would have had to be used. The response also included the motivation to move on to the challenge of a smaller organization.

Question 7: "What Are Your Plans for the Future?"

Analysis: This question really explores your motives for working. It is very much asking whether you can be depended on to stay on this job and work hard at it.

Strategy: Your best approach is an honest one, as it always is. I'm not encouraging you to reveal negative information but you should be prepared to answer the employer's concern in a direct and positive way. Which issues of concern to an employer will depend on the details of your background? Some examples: Will you be happy with the salary? (If not, might you leave?); Will you leave to raise a family?; Do you have a history of leaving jobs after a short period of time?; Have you just moved to the area and appear a temporary or transient resident?; Are you overqualified?; Do you have the energy and commitment to advance in this job? (In some cases, an employer may find this a negative!), and Might you appear to have some other reason to eventually become dissatisfied?

Any of these reasons, and others, can be of concern to an employer. If your situation presents an obvious problem, use the standard three-step approach to answering problem questions. If you feel you do not have any problem to defend, use steps 2 and steps 3 of the three-step approach to assure the employer that, in effect, this is the precise organization you want to stay with and do well for — at least the rest of your adult life. (Just kidding...)

Example 1: For a younger person or one just entering a new career: "I realize I need to establish myself in this field and am very willing to get started. I've thought about what I want to do and am very sure my skills are the right ones to do well in this career. For example, I am good at dealing with people. In one position, I provided services to over 1,000 different people a week. During the 18 months I was there, I served well over 72 customers and not once did I get a formal complaint. In fact, I was often complimented on the attention I gave them. I learned there that I enjoy public contact and am delighted at the idea of this position for that reason. I want to learn more about the business and grow with it. As my contributions and value to the organization increase, I hope to be considered for more responsible positions."

Comments: The employer wants to know that you will stay on the job and work hard for your pay. This response helps the employer feel more comfortable with that concern. Note that this response could be based on work experiences gained in a fast-food job!

Example 2: For a person with work history gaps or various short jobs: "I've had a number of jobs (or one, or have been unemployed) and I have learned to value a good, stable position. My variety of experiences are an asset since I have learned so many things I can now apply to this position. I am looking for a position where I can settle in, work hard, and stay put."

Comments: This would be an acceptable response, except it is too short and no proof was offered. The ideal place to introduce a story would have been right before the last sentence. Some positions, such as sales-oriented ones, require you to be ambitious and perhaps aggressive. Other jobs have requirements particular to the career field or specific organization. You can't always predict what an employer might want but you should have a good idea based on the work you did earlier in the book. If you did it correctly, you have what the position requires. Say so.

Question 8: "What Will Your Former Employers (or teachers, references, warden, or keeper, depending on the situation) Say About You?"

Analysis: This question again goes after Employer's Expectation 2. They want to know about your adaptive skills — are you easy to get along with, are you a good worker, etc. Your former employers may tell them of any problems you had — or they may not. As you know, many employers will check your references before they hire you, so anything you say here may not match what a former employer says. That could be bad news for you.

Strategy: Be certain to discuss your job-search plans with former employers. Do the same with anyone else who may be contacted for a reference. Clearly tell them the type of job you now seek and why you are prepared to do well in it. (Remember, also, that these folks can be part of your network too.) If a previous employer may say something negative, discuss this openly with them and find out what they will say in advance. If you were fired or resigned under pressure, still negotiate what would be said to a prospective employer. Lots of successful people have had personality conflicts with their employers. It may also be wise to get a written letter of reference, particularly from a not-too-enthusiastic employer. They will rarely be brave enough to write you a negative letter. And the letter may be enough to satisfy a potential employer. Larger organizations often don't allow references to be given and this may be a great relief to you. Check it out.

If possible, use references who will say nice things about you. If your boss won't, find someone who will. Often, an interviewer appreciates an honest response. If you failed in a job, telling the truth is sometimes the best policy. Tell it like it was but DO NOT be too critical of your old boss. Doing that will make you sound like a person who blames others and does not accept responsibility. Besides, you were partly at fault. Admit it but quickly take the opportunity to say what you learned from the experience.

Example: "My three former employers will all say I work hard, am very reliable and loyal. The reason I left my previous job, however, is the result of what I can only call a personality conflict. I was deeply upset by this but decided that it was time I parted with my former employer. You can call and get a positive reference, but I thought it only fair to tell you. I still respect that old hog and hardly ever call her names in my sleep now. While there, I received several promotions and as my authority increased there were more conflicts. Our styles were just not the same. I had no idea the problem was so serious because I was so involved in my work. That was my error and I have since learned to pay more attention to interpersonal matters."

Comments: There is one sentence in the above that doesn't belong. Can you guess which one? Also, this response could be strengthened by some introduction of positive skills with a story to support it.

Question 9: "Why Are You Looking for This Sort of Position and Why Here?"

Analysis: The employer wants to know if you are the sort of person who is looking for any job, anywhere. If you are, they will not be impressed. Employers look for people who want to do what needs to be done. They rightly assume that such a person will work harder and be more productive than one who simply sees it as a job. People who have a good reason to seek a particular sort of position will be seen as more committed and more likely to stay on the job longer. The same is true for people who want to work in a particular organization.

Strategy: Since you already know why you are a good match for the type of job you want, it should be simple enough to explain. In responding to the question, mention your motivations for selecting this career objective, the special skills you have that the position requires, and any special training or credentials you have that relate to the position.

The question actually has two parts. The first is why this position and the second is why here? If you have a reason for selecting the type of organization you are considering or have even selected this particular organization as highly desirable, be prepared to explain why. If at all possible, learn as much as you can about the organizations you interview with. Call other people to get details, use the library, ask for an annual report, or whatever else it takes to become informed.

Example: "I've spent a lot of time considering various careers and think that this is the best area for me. The reason is that this career requires many of my strongest skills. For example, my abilities in analyzing and solving problems are two of the skills I enjoy most. In a previous position, I would often become aware of a problem no one had noticed and develop a solution. In one situation, I suggested a plan that resulted in reducing customer returns of leased equipment by 15 percent. That may not sound like much, but the result was an increase in retained leases of over $250,000 a year. The plan cost about $100 to implement. This particular organization seems to be the type that would let me develop my problem-solving skills. It is well-run, growing rapidly, and open to new ideas. Your sales went up 30 percent last year and you are getting ready to introduce several major new products. If I work hard and prove my value here, I feel I would have the opportunity to stay with the business as it grows — and grow with it."

Comments: This response uses Prove-It nicely. It could have been said by an experienced manager or a good secretary.

Question 10: "Why Don't You Tell Me About Your Personal Situation?"

Analysis: A good interviewer will rarely ask this question so directly to find out what they want to know. Casual, friendly conversation will often provide them with the information they need. In most cases, they seek information that would indicate you are unstable or undependable. For instance:

The Issue	The Reason
Do you have marital or family troubles?	Missed work, poor performance, poor interpersonal skills
Do you handle money and personal responsibilities poorly?	Theft of property, irresponsible job-related decisions
Do you live in a good, stable home?	Socio-economic bias, renters less stable than owners
How do you use leisure time?	Drinking, socially unacceptable behavior
Do you have young children?	Days off and child care problems
Marital status?	If single, will you stay? If married, will you devote the necessary time?

Strategy: There are other issues that may be of concern to them. Often, these are based on assumptions a particular employer has about persons with certain characteristics. These beliefs are often irrelevant, but if the employer wonders whether they can depend on you, it is in your own best interest to deal with their doubts. Be aware that even your casual conversation should avoid reference to a potential problem area unless you can present it in a positive way. In responding to a question about your personal situation, be friendly and briefly let the employer know that your personal situation is not a problem.

Examples:

1. **Young children at home:** "I have two children, both in school. Childcare is no problem since they stay with a good friend."

2. **Single head of household:** "I'm not married and have two children at home. It is very important to me to have a steady income and so childcare is no problem."

3. **Young and single:** "I'm not married and if I should, that would not change my plans for a full-time career. For now, I can devote my full attention to my career."

4. **Just moved here:** "I've decided to settle here in Depression Gulch permanently. I've rented an apartment and the six moving vans are unloading there now."

5. **Relatives, upbringing:** "I had a good childhood. Both of my parents still live within an hour's flight from here and I see them several times a year."

6. **Leisure time:** "My time is family-centered when I'm not working. I'm also active in several community organizations and spend at least some time each week in church activities."

   Comments: While all of these responses could be expanded, they should give you an idea of the sorts of approaches you can take with your own answers. The message you want to give is that your personal situation will not hurt your ability to work and, indeed, could help it. If your personal life does disrupt your work, expect most employers to lose patience quickly. It is not their problem, nor should it be.

Handling Obvious and Not-So-Obvious "Problems"

Most job seekers have at least one problem which they fear will cause an employer to respond negatively. Some of these are obvious, that is, they can be seen by an employer during an interview; others are not so obvious but are the sort of things an employer might not be enthusiastic about. How you handle these or similar problems differ depending on the situation. Many employers will not react in the way you expect and will give you a fair chance. They will be interested in your ability to do the job you seek. Your task is to convince them that your problem will not be an issue. Here are some considerations:

Does the problem affect your ability to do the work you seek? If it is a serious limitation or safety hazard, you should consider this in your selection of a position and consider changing your objectives. This does not necessarily mean you need to change careers but it does mean that you should look for a position where the limitation is not serious. For example, a person with a prison record should not seek a job as a bank teller. A person with seizures should not paint tall houses. A person with back problems should not dig ditches.

Avoid being screened out early. Assuming your job objective is reasonable, but you still are concerned that you won't be seriously considered because of your problem, use job-search techniques that don't require you to reveal it too early. For example, I worked with a man who used a wheelchair. He wanted to work as a dispatcher. This position used his voice and his mind but not his legs and was a good job objective for him. Yet employers were often unwilling to hire him. The wheelchair probably was an issue. I helped him learn to get interviews by using the phone rather than filling out applications. Employers had no idea he was in a wheelchair until he came for the interview. He was direct about the problem and said he got there and would do the same every day. He then presented his skills and abilities rather than getting stuck on his disability. He got a job as a dispatcher and was still there three years later. His legs didn't affect his job performance.

If the problem is obvious or comes up in the interview, deal with it. Use the standard "Three Steps to Answering a Problem Question."

If the problem is not obvious and won't seriously affect your ability to do the job, don't bring it up. Do not discuss your problem unless you fear you will eventually lose your job if it is found out, and you have received or are negotiating to accept a job offer. Too many job seekers reveal a problem on an application when they could have simply left the space blank. Too many bring up a problem that is not a problem at all in a preliminary interview. ("I want you to know, Madam, that a great aunt, once removed, had some odd habits.") Save your secret until after they like you and want to hire you.

"Turtling" a Negative into a Positive

Like a turtle on its back, a problem is a problem only if you leave it that way. By turning it over ("turtling" is what I have come to call this), you can often turn a perceived disadvantage into an advantage. Examples follow:

Too Old: "I am a very stable worker requiring very little training. I have been dependable all my life and I am at a point in my career where I don't plan on changing jobs. I still have 10 years of working until I plan on retiring. How long has the average young person stayed here?"

Too Young: "I don't have any bad work habits to break, so I can be quickly trained to do things the way you want. I plan on working hard to get established. I'll also work for less money than a more experienced worker."

Prison (or Arrest) Record: "You need to know that I've spent time in jail. I learned my lesson and paid any debt to society for a mistake I have not repeated. While there, I studied hard and earned a certificate in this trade. I was in the top one-third of my class . . ."

Physical Limitations: "Thank you for the job offer. Before I accept, you should know that I have a minor physical limitation but it will not affect my performance on the job . . . "

Unemployed: "I've been between jobs now for three months. During that time, I've carefully researched what I want to do and now I'm certain. Let me explain . . . "

Overweight: "You may have noticed that I am a tad overweight. Some people think that overweight people are slow, won't work hard, or will be absent frequently. Let me tell you about myself . . ."

Gender: "Not many women (or men) are interested in these kinds of positions, so let me tell you why I am . . . "

Race: The best approach here is to assume there is no problem with your race. There often is not and if there is, there shouldn't be. Present your skills, rest your case, send a thank-you note, and go on to set up the next interview.

Physical Disability: Don't be defensive or clinical. People will want to know that your disability will not be a problem, so explain why it won't be. Then emphasize why you can do the job better than the next job seeker.

While your particular upside-down turtle may not be in the above examples, I hope you get the point. If it comes up, kick it over. Find a way to present it in a positive way. You should also realize that you may or may not assume that your particular situation may be seen as a problem by some employers. If you feel that it might negatively affect an employer's opinion of you, you may want to bring it up just to be sure. You often don't have to, of course, but if you have nothing to hide, let the employer know that your "problem" is not a problem at all.

Handling Illegal Questions

Technically, this is a free country and interviewers can ask whatever they wish. Dumb questions, questions in poor taste, and personal questions can all be asked. It's what employers do that can get them in trouble with the law. It is illegal to hire or not hire someone based on certain criteria. It is also very difficult to prove that someone actually does that.

As a job seeker, the more important issue might be whether or not you want the job. If you want to insist you do not have to answer a certain question, fine. But also realize the question was probably intended to find out whether you will be a good employee. That is a legitimate concern for an employer and you have the responsibility, if you want the job, to let them know you will be a good choice.

There are situations (thankfully, very rare) where an interviewer's questions are offensive, either in the way they are asked or in the types of questions asked. If that is the case, you could fairly conclude you would not consider working for such a person. Ever. You might reach over the desk, crumple up your resume, toss it in the trash, and walk out. Or you might report them to the authorities. Yes, this would be a situation where a thank-you note would not be required.

94 Interview Questions

The following list of questions came from a survey of companies who interviewed college students for jobs.[4] While some of the questions relate to a new graduate, most could be posed to any job seeker. There are too many questions to memorize responses in advance. And even if you had a response for each of these, you could easily be asked others. I've included the list as proof of the need to develop a systematic way to respond to interview questions — such as the Three-Step Process and Prove-It techniques covered earlier in this chapter.

94 Interview Questions
1. What are your future vocational plans?
2. In what school activities have you participated? Why? Which did you enjoy the most?
3. How do you spend your spare time? What are your hobbies?
4. In what type of position are you most interested?
5. Why do you think you might like to work for our company?
6. What jobs have you held? How were they obtained?
7. What courses did you like best? Least? Why?
8. Why did you choose your particular field of work?
9. What percentage of your school expenses did you earn? How?
10. How did you spend your vacations while in school?
11. What do you know about our company?
12. Do you feel that you have received a good general training?
13. What qualifications do you have that make you feel that you will be successful in your field?
14. What extracurricular offices have you held?
15. What are your ideas on salary?
16. How do you feel about your family?
17. How interested are you in sports?
18. If you were starting school all over again... ?
19. Can you forget your education and start from scratch?
20. Do you prefer any specific geographic location? Why?
21. Do you have a girl (boy) friend? Is it serious?
22. How much money do you hope to earn at age _____?

94 Interview Questions

23. Why did you decide to go to the school you attended?
24. How did you rank in your graduating class in high school? Other schools?
25. Do you think that your extracurricular activities were worth the time you devoted to them? Why?
26. What do you think determines a person's progress in a good company?
27. What personal characteristics are necessary for success in your chosen field?
28. Why do you think you would like this particular type of job?
29. What is your father's occupation?
30. Tell me about your home life during the time you were growing up.
31. Are you looking for a permanent or temporary job?
32. Do you prefer working with others or by yourself?
33. Who are your best friends?
34. What kind of boss do you prefer?
35. Are you primarily interested in making money?
36. Can you take instructions without feeling upset?
37. Tell me a story!
38. Do you live with your parents? Which of your parents has had the most profound influence on you?
39. How did previous employers treat you?
40. What have you learned from some of the jobs you have held?
41. Can you get recommendations from previous employers?
42. What interests you about our product or service?
43. What was your record in military service?
44. Have you ever changed your major field of interest? Why?
45. When did you choose your major?
46. How did your grades after military service compare with those previously earned?
47. Do you feel you have done the best work of which you are capable?
48. How did you happen to go to post secondary school?
49. What do you know about opportunities in the field in which you are trained?
50. How long do you expect to work?
51. Have you ever had any difficulty getting along with fellow students and faculty? Fellow workers?
52. Which of your school years was most difficult?
53. What is the source of your spending money?
54. Do you own any life insurance?
55. Have you saved any money?

94 Interview Questions

56. Do you have any debts?
57. How old were you when you became self-supporting?
58. Do you attend church?
59. Did you enjoy school?
60. Do you like routine work?
61. Do you like regular work?
62. What size city do you prefer?
63. When did you first contribute to family income?
64. What is your major weakness?
65. Define cooperation.
66. Will you fight to get ahead?
67. Do you demand attention?
68. Do you have an analytical mind?
69. Are you eager to please?
70. What do you do to keep in good physical condition?
71. How do you usually spend Sunday?
72. Have you had any serious illness or injury?
73. Are you willing to go where the company sends you?
74. What job in our company would you choose if you were entirely free to do so?
75. Is it an effort for you to be tolerant of persons with a background and interests different from your own?
76. What types of books have you read?
77. Have you plans for further education?
78. What types of people seem to rub you the wrong way?
79. Do you enjoy sports as a participant? As an observer?
80. Have you ever tutored another student?
81. What jobs have you enjoyed the most? The least? Why?
82. What are your own special abilities?
83. What job in our company do you want to work toward?
84. Would you prefer a large or a small company? Why?
85. What is your idea of how industry operates today?
86. Do you like to travel?
87. How about overtime work?
88. What kind of work interests you?
89. What are the disadvantages of your chosen field?
90. Do you think that grades should be considered by employers? Why or why not?

94 Interview Questions

91. Are you interested in research?

92. If married, how often do you entertain at home?

93. To what extent do you use liquor?

94. What have you done that shows initiative and willingness to work?

Some Final Interview Tips

You can't prepare for everything that might happen in an interview. But you will find that interviewing for jobs before they are advertised will be a much more comfortable exchange than the traditional interview setting. But whatever interview you find yourself in, remember to be yourself and tell them why they should hire you. You are better prepared to do well in the interview now than most job seekers. Much better.

Chapter Eleven Endnotes

1. From the "Northwestern Endicott Report," The Placement Center, Northwestern University, Wisconsin.

2. Over the years, many lists of interview questions have been developed. One excellent source based on thorough research into the topic is from the article by John and Merna Galassi titled "Preparing Individuals for Job Interviews: Suggestions from More Than 60 Years of Research," *Personnel and Guidance Journal,* vol. 12, 1978. Among other things, the article provides a list of 20 frequently asked questions.

3. This error is even more expensive than it at first seems since you would be losing $2,000 the first year alone. If you stayed in that job for five years and got a 10 percent increase each year, you would have earned over $12,000 more by starting at $18,000 a year rather than at $16,000. I'd like to think that this one suggestion alone will make the price of this book worth it, with the rest thrown in for free. If the salary negotiation ideas work for you, consider sending a donation for my yacht and party fund as a small token of your appreciation.

4. Ibid., John and Merna Galassi.

Chapter Twelve

Producing Superior Resumes

You should already know that there are a few problems with resumes. Along with the application form, the resume is the tool employers use most to screen out job seekers. There have been many, many books written on resumes and any respectable job search book ought to cover them. But most job search experts give bad advice on how to use your resume. They often tell you that the best way to get a job is to send out lots of resumes. That is bad advice since the best way to get a job is to get interviews. And a resume is not a particularly good tool to help you get interviews.

A resume is also one of those things about which almost everyone seems to have an opinion. If you were to show your resume to any three people, you would get three different suggestions on how to improve it. So, one of the problems with resumes is that everyone is an expert but that few agree. My own opinion is that you will probably want or need one at some time during your job search, so you might as well get one done. I have provided enough information in this chapter to meet the needs of most job seekers but there are some additional resume books mentioned in the appendix should you want more information.

Do You Really Need a Resume at All?

For a variety of reasons, some career professionals suggest that resumes aren't needed at all. Some of these reasons make a lot of sense.

Resumes aren't good job search tools. Although I've said it before in this book, it's worth repeating. Resumes will often be used to screen you out, not in. Trying to get an interview by sending out dozens of resumes is usually a waste of stamps. There are far more effective methods to get in to see people than sending them a resume.

Some jobs don't require resumes. Employers of office, managerial, professional, and technical workers often want the details provided in a resume. But for many jobs, particularly entry-level or unskilled positions, resumes often aren't required.

Some job search methods don't use resumes. Many people get jobs without ever needing a resume. This is as true for professional and managerial positions as it is for other jobs. If you have read the material in this book, you should realize that it is easy enough to get an interview without a resume at all.

Some Good Reasons You Should Have a Resume

In my opinion, all things considered, there are more good reasons to have a resume than not. For instance:

Resumes help structure your communications. A good resume requires you to clarify your job objective, select related skills and experiences, and get it all down in a short format. Those are all very worthwhile activities that will improve your ability to handle the interview — where the real action is.

If used properly, a resume can be an effective job search tool. A good resume is a tool to communicate your skills. It can help you meet an employer's expectations or provide details in an efficient way to an employer who may not otherwise ask for them during a preliminary interview.

Employers often ask for resumes. This alone is reason enough to have a resume. If an employer asks for one, why have excuses for not having one?

Four Tips for Using a Resume Effectively

At best, a resume will help you get an interview. However, there are better ways of getting one — as you've learned in earlier chapters of this book. Here is a quick review of how to use your resume to its best effect:

1. **Get the interview first.** Don't send an unsolicited resume. It is almost always better to directly contact the employer by phone or in person. Then send your resume after you schedule an interview, so the employer can read about you before your meeting.

2. **Send your resume after an interview.** Send a thank-you note after an interview and enclose a JIST Card (my preference) or resume. Or both.

3. **Send copies to people you know.** Give copies of your resume (and JIST Card) to everyone in your growing job-search network. They can pass them along to others who might be interested.

4. **If all else fails use traditional techniques.** If you can't make direct contact with a prospective employer, send your resume in the traditional way. An example would be answering a want ad with only a box number for an address. But if that's all you do, don't expect much to happen.

The Two Types of Resumes

Resume styles vary. The two most common types are the **chronological** and the **skills** resume. Each has its advantages. This chapter shows you how to develop both of these types along with examples of each. There are also samples of a third type, the combination resume. This resume combines parts of both the chronological and the skills resumes.

The Chronological Resume

The word "chronology" refers to time and a chronological resume begins with your most recent work experiences and moves back in time. This type of format is the traditional one that has been used for many years. It is a good format if you have had several years of experience in the same field and at a similar level of responsibility to what you want in your next job. A major advantage to a simple chronological resume is that it can be completed in about an hour. Most employers will find such a resume perfectly acceptable, if not exciting, providing it is neat and has no errors.

Two sample chronological resumes follow for Judith Jones. The first is a simple one that provides only the basics while the "improved" example adds some features. While the first example could be improved upon, it does present a job objective and other facts and would be an acceptable resume for many employers. The improved chronological resume is for the same person but has additional content along with other improvements. Because it is easy to create, I suggest that you write a simple chronological resume before making a "better" one. You can use it early in your job search while you work on a more sophisticated resume. The important point here is to get an acceptable resume together quickly so you won't be sitting at home worrying about your resume instead of going out and looking for a job.

Simple Chronological Resume

Judith J. Jones   (317) 653-9217 (home)
115 South Hawthorne Avenue   (317) 272-7608 (message)
Chicago, Illinois 46204

JOB OBJECTIVE

Desire a position in the office management, secretarial, or clerical area. Prefer a position requiring responsibility and a variety of tasks.

EDUCATION AND TRAINING

Acme Business College, Indianapolis, Indiana — Graduate of a one-year business/secretarial program, 1989.

John Adams High School, South Bend, Indiana — Diploma, business education.

U.S. Army — Financial procedures, accounting functions.

Other: Continuing education classes and workshops in Business Communication, Scheduling Systems, and Customer Relations.

EXPERIENCE

1986-1989 — Returned to school to complete and update my business skills. Learned word processing and other new office techniques.

1985-1986 — Claims Processor, Blue Spear Insurance Co., Indianapolis, Indiana. Handled customer medical claims, used a CRT, filed, miscellaneous clerical duties.

1984-1985 — Sales Clerk, Judy's Boutique, Indianapolis, Indiana. Responsible for counter sales, display design, and selected tasks.

1982-1984 — E4, U.S. Army. Assigned to various stations as a specialist in finance operations. Promoted prior to honorable discharge.

Previous jobs — Held part-time and summer jobs throughout high school.

PERSONAL

I am reliable, hardworking, and good with people.

Improved Chronological Resume

Judith J. Jones   (317) 653-9217   (home)
115 South Hawthorne Avenue   (317) 272-7608 (message)
Chicago, Illinois 46204

JOB OBJECTIVE

Seeking position requiring excellent management and secretarial skills in office environment. Position should require a variety of tasks including typing, word processing, accounting/bookkeeping functions, and customer contact.

EDUCATION AND TRAINING

Acme Business College, Indianapolis, Indiana. Completed one-year program in Professional Secretarial and Office Management. Grades in top 30 percent of my class. Courses: word processing, accounting theory and systems, time management, basic supervision, and others.

John Adams High School, South Bend, Indiana. Graduated with emphasis on business and secretarial courses. Won shorthand contest.

Other: Continuing education at my own expense (Business Communications, Customer Relations, Computer Applications, other courses).

EXPERIENCE

1986-1989 — Returned to business school to update skills. Advanced coursework in accounting and office management. Learned to operate word processing and PC based accounting and spreadsheet software. Gained operating knowledge of computers.

1985-1986 — Claims Processor, Blue Spear Insurance Company, Indianapolis, Indiana. Handled 50 complex medical insurance claims per day — 18 percent above department average. Received two merit raises for performance.

1984-1985 — Assistant Manager, Judy's Boutique, Indianapolis, Indiana. Managed sales, financial records, inventory, purchasing, correspondence, and related tasks during owner's absence. Supervised four employees. Sales increased 15 percent during my tenure.

1982-1984 — Finance Specialist (E4), U.S. Army. Responsible for the systematic processing of 500 invoices per day from commercial vendors. Trained and supervised eight employees. Devised internal system allowing 15 percent increase in invoices processed with a decrease in personnel.

1978-1982 — Various part-time and summer jobs through high school. Learned to deal with customers, meet deadlines, and other skills.

SPECIAL SKILLS AND ABILITIES

Type 80 words per minute on electric typewriter, more on word processor; can operate most office equipment. Good math skills. Accept supervision, able to supervise others. Excellent attendance record.

PERSONAL

I have excellent references, learn quickly, and am willing to relocate.

Some Tips for Completing a Simple Chronological Resume

Many of these tips will help you construct other resume types as well but are presented here to relate to the major sections of a chronological resume. Additional resume samples at the end of this section give you ideas regarding format and other issues.

The Header: There is no need to put the word "resume" on your resume since it will be obvious what it is.

Name and Address: This should be simple enough. Use your formal name if possible and include an address where you can be reached for some time. If it is an out-of-town address, this will need to be explained in a cover letter.

Phone Numbers: If an employer does try to reach you, it will probably be by phone. You could try to be home at all times but that is hardly a good way to get a job. Instead, include a second phone number where messages can be left if you are not at home. Type "home" for your home number and "message" for the other one. That way, an employer will know you probably won't be there, but to leave a message. If you can use your business phone number for your job search, put it on the resume and identify it simply as "business" but still provide one or more alternate numbers. You might also consider using a telephone answering machine. While they are not universally loved, they are far better than missing a call. And don't forget to include your area code as you never know who will be calling you — or from where.

Job Objective: While resumes don't include a job objective, yours should unless you have some good reason not to. If possible, avoid using a narrow job title, but don't try to include everything either. Use an active verb and avoid a self-centered approach as employers are far more interested in what you can do for them than what you want from them. Here are some examples of simple but useful job objectives.

Sample Job Objectives

- A responsible, general office position in a busy, medium-sized organization.
- Management position in the warehousing industry. Position should require supervisory, problem-solving, and organizational skills.
- Computer programming and/or systems analysis. Prefer an accounting-oriented emphasis and a solutions-oriented organization.
- General labor in the building trades or factory assembly areas.
- Medical assistant or secretary in a physician's office, hospital, or other health services environment.
- Responsible position requiring skills in public relations, writing, and reporting.

- A challenging position as a computer programmer or analyst incorporating skills in business, accounting, and supervision of others.

- An aggressive and success-oriented professional, seeking a sales position offering both challenge and growth.

- Desire a position in the office management, secretarial, or clerical area. Position should require flexibility, good organizational skills, and ability to handle people.

Education and Training: This section could be moved to the bottom of your resume or even dropped if it doesn't help support your job objective. Your educational credentials become less important as you gain more work experience. Usually, though, you should emphasize the most recent or highest level of education or training that relates to the job. Drop details that don't support your objective. If you are a recent graduate and if your education or training was job-related (or if you have limited paid work experience in your career area), this may be the most important part of your resume and should go at the beginning.

Work and Volunteer History: This section provides the details of your work history, starting with your most recent job. Military experience is handled in the same way as work experience. If you don't have a lot of paid work experience, you can also include any unpaid work in this section as if it were a job, which it was.

Job Title: If your actual job title did not accurately reflect your responsibilities, consider changing it so that it does. You may need to explain this in an interview and you should definitely not misrepresent yourself.

Employer: Provide the organization's name, city and state or province where it is located. The state or province is optional if your work experience and job search are local.

Employment Dates: Use the techniques presented in chapter 9 covering applications to avoid displaying any gaps in your job history. If you do have a significant period of time where you did not work, did you do anything else during that time that could explain it in a positive way? School? Travel? Raise a family? Self-employment? Even if you mowed lawns and painted houses for money while you were unemployed, that could count as self-employment. It's much better than saying you were unemployed.

In writing about your work experience, be sure to use action words and emphasize what you accomplished. Quantify what you did and provide evidence you did it well. Take particular care to mention skills that would directly relate to doing well in the job you want. If you've had little paid work experience related to the job you want, emphasize your transferable skills that relate to that job and stress non-work experiences as needed to fill out your resume.

Professional Organizations: Consider mentioning any job-related professional groups, particularly if you were an officer or were active in some other way.

Recognition and Awards: If you have received any formal recognition or awards, consider mentioning them. Use a separate section or list them under the skills, education, or personal sections.

Personal Information: The older tradition is that somewhere on a resume you put things like height, weight, marital status, hobbies, leisure activities, and other trivia. What for? Earlier I advised you to make every word count — if it does not support your job objective, delete it. Same here. There are situations where these characteristics or activities might help you and, if so, you can go ahead and use them. But in most situations this information is irrelevant and should be cut. I do, however, like to end a resume on a personal note. Some of the sample resumes provide a touch of playfulness as well as selected positives from outside their school and work lives. This is also a good place to list significant community involvements, a willingness to relocate, or personal characteristics an employer might like.

References: It is not necessary to include the names of your references on a resume. There are better things to do with that precious space. It's not even necessary to state "references available upon request" at the bottom of your resume. If an employer wants them, they know they can ask you for them. However, it would be helpful to line up your references in advance. Pick people who know your work as an employee, volunteer, or student. Ask them if they would say anything negative about you to a prospective employer. Nobody is perfect. This could also give you the opportunity to negotiate what they will say and a chance to get them off your list before they do you any damage. Once you know who to include, type up a clean reference list on a separate sheet. Include their name, address, phone number, and other pertinent details.

Be aware that some employers are not allowed by their organizations to give references. I have refused to hire people who probably had good references but about whom I could not get information. If this is the case with a previous employer, ask them to write a letter of reference for you to photocopy as needed. Do not provide reference information unless you are asked to do so.

Including Useful Words and Phrases

While it is important to use your own language and style in communicating your skills in a resume, you should be aware that using action words creates a more positive impression than other approaches. For this reason, I've put together a list of words and phrases that should help you in writing your resume. Some you have seen from earlier chapters and some are new. Go through the list and consider using those that are particularly strong for the job you want **and** that you can do well.

Action Words		
• Administered	• Expanded	• Planned
• Analyzed	• Implemented	• Presented
• Controlled	• Improved	• Promoted
• Coordinated	• Increased productivity	• Reduced expenses
• Created	• Increased profits	• Researched
• Designed	• Initiated	• Scheduled
• Developed	• Innovated	• Solved
• Diagnosed	• Instructed	• Supervised
• Directed	• Modified	• Trained
• Established policy	• Negotiated	
• Established priorities	• Organized	

You now have enough information to put together a simple resume. What follows, having to do with skills resumes, is really optional for most people. The important thing is to have an acceptable resume and go about the task of finding a job.

The Skills Resume

A skills resume is sometimes called a functional resume. In this resume, your experience is organized under key skills instead of by jobs you have had. In a well-done skills resume, these same skills are the ones you need to succeed in the job you want. They should also be skills that you are good at and like to use. Look at the sample skills resume that follows to see how this works.

A Skills Resume

Lisa M. Rhodes
813 Evergreen Drive

Home: (413) 643-2173   Littleton, Colorado 81613   Message: (413) 442-1659

Position

Sales oriented position in a retail sales or distribution business.

Skills and Abilities

Communications:	Good written and verbal presentations skills. Use proper grammar and have a good speaking voice.
Interpersonal:	Am able to accept supervision and get along well with co-workers. Received positive evaluations from previous supervisors.
Flexible:	Willing to try new things and am interested in improving efficiency on assigned tasks.
Attention to Detail:	Like to see assigned areas of responsibility completed correctly. Am concerned with quality and my work is typically orderly and attractive.
Hardworking:	Have previously worked long hours in strenuous activities while attending school full-time. During this time, maintained above average grades. At times, I was handling as many as 65 hours a week in school and other structured activities.
Customer Contacts:	Have had as many as 5,000 customer contacts a month in a busy retail outlet. Averaged lower than a .001% rate of complaints and was given the new "Employee of the Month" award in my second month of employment.
Cash Sales:	Handled over $2,000 a day in cash sales. Balanced register and prepared daily sales summary and deposits.

Education

Graduate, Franklin Township High School. Took advanced English and other classes. Member of award winning band. Excellent attendance record.

Other

Active gymnastics competitor for 4 years taught me discipline, teamwork, and following instructions. I am ambitious, outgoing, and willing to work!

Comments on Lisa's Resume: Lisa is a recent high-school graduate whose only work experience has been at a hamburger place. A skills resume is a good approach for her since it allows her to emphasize strengths. While the format is simple, the resume presents her in a positive way. Since her employment will be at the entry-level in a nontechnical area, an employer will be more interested in her basic transferable and adaptive skills than in job-content ones. Her work experience is a plus. Notice how she presented her gymnastics experience under "hard-working."

Use a Skills Resume to Highlight Your Strengths and Avoid Displaying Your Weaknesses

In its simplest form, a chronological resume is little more than a list of job titles that displays what you **have done** rather than what you **can or want** to do. If you want to change your career or increase your level of responsibility, a chronological resume can often be an obituary. Employers look for a successful record in a similar position. By using a skills resume, you can present accomplishments from all your life experiences. It is a good format when you need to "hide" problems that a chronological resume might show. Examples include limited paid work experience, weak credentials, gaps in your job history, or a lack of work experience in the field you want to get into now.

A well-written skills resume presents your strengths and avoids showing your weaknesses. It does this by highlighting what you have done under the heading of your specific skills rather than jobs you have held. Some employers don't like skills resumes for this reason and they are also harder to write. Still, a skills resume is worthwhile for many people and may be exactly what you need. Even if you don't have anything to hide, a skills resume can let you emphasize key skills and experiences more clearly. In the "Fine Tuning" section of this chapter, there are tips for incorporating a chronological listing of jobs too, so a skills resume should be considered by anyone. If you have a good work history, you can combine the best elements of both resume types into a combination resume. Some of the examples at the end of this chapter have done just that.

Constructing a Skills Resume

The skills resume uses a number of sections that are similar to those in a chronological one. Here I will discuss only those sections that are substantially different — the job objective and skills sections. Don't be afraid to use a little creativity in writing your own skills resume, since there are no rules that have not been successfully broken by someone. The samples at the end of this section will give you ideas on resume language, organization, layout, and how to handle special problems.

The Job Objective

While a simple chronological resume does not absolutely require a career objective, a skills resume does. Without a reasonably clear objective, it is not possible to select and organize the key skills you have to support it. It may be that the job objective you wrote for the chronological resume is good just as it is, but for a skills resume, your job objective statement should answer the following questions.

1. **What sort of position, title, and area of specialization do you seek?** By now, you should know how to present what sort of job you are seeking. Is it too narrow and specific? Is it so broad or vague as to be meaningless? Earlier chapters on clarifying your job objective, JIST Cards, and other topics can be reviewed as needed to more clearly identify the sort of job you want and how to communicate this.

2. **What level of responsibility interests you?** Job objectives often indicate a level of responsibility, particularly for supervisory or management roles. If in doubt, always try to keep open the possibility of getting a job with a higher level of responsibility (and salary) than your previous one. Avoid a job title that will limit you.

3. **What are your most important skills?** What are the two or three most important skills or personal characteristics needed to succeed on the job you've targeted? You should consider including one or more of these in your job objective. Review the "Sample Job Objectives" earlier in this chapter and look over the sample resumes at the end of the chapter. Notice that they use professional-sounding headings such as "position desired" or "career objective" to introduce the job objective section.

The Skills Section

This section could also be titled "Areas of Accomplishment," "Summary of Qualifications," "Areas of Expertise and Ability," and other terms. Whatever you choose to call it, this section is what makes a skills resume. To construct it, you must carefully consider which skills you want to emphasize. You should feature those skills which are essential to success on the job you want **and** those skills which are your particular strengths. You probably have a good idea of which skills meet both criteria but you may find it helpful to review earlier chapters, particularly chapters 3 through 5.

Identifying Your Key Skills

If you have done a good job in selecting a job objective, the skills you have and want to use will be similar to those needed in the job you seek. You can use the *Occupational Outlook Handbook* to identify the key skills required for many jobs and compare them to the skills you identified in chapters 3 through 5.

After some research, list below the key skills that you have **and** are most likely required in the job you are seeking. Write at least three, but no more than six, of your key skills for this job.

1. _____   4. _____

2. _____   5. _____

3. _____   6. _____

Keep revising this list until you are comfortable that these skills are the ones you want to use as key skills in your skills section of your resume.

Proving Your Key Skills

Once you decide which skills to emphasize, write down each skill on a separate piece of paper. Below it, note examples of when you used that skill. Whenever possible, quantify the example and emphasize results. It is best to use proofs that come from previous work experience but it's not essential. There are several examples of how this works in earlier chapters and I've provided one more sample below. This example uses a non-work experience so that you can see how this might be included in a resume.

Sample Key Skill Proof
Key Skill: Meeting Deadlines
Proof: I volunteered to help my social organization raise money. I found out about special government funds available but the proposal deadline was only 24 hours away. I stayed up all night writing a proposal and submitted it on time. We were one of only three whose proposal was approved and awarded over $100,000.

Editing Your Key Skills Proofs

Writing thorough proofs for each skill you selected will take about an hour. When you are done, select those proofs that you feel are particularly valuable in supporting your job objective. You should have at least two proofs for each skill area. Once you have selected your proofs, rewrite them using action words and short sentences and delete anything that is not essential. For example, here is a rewrite of the proof I provided earlier. Do a similar editing job on each of your own proofs until they are clear, short, and powerful.

Key Skill Rewrite
Key Skill: Meeting Deadlines
Proof: On 24-hour notice, I submitted a complex proposal that successfully obtained over $100,000 in funding.

These proof statements will form the basis for your resume narrative in the skills section. Notice that a statement such as the one above indicates that a variety of skills were required in order to do what is described, not just meeting deadlines. In this example, it required writing skills, the ability to organize thoughts, make quick decisions, deal with budgets, and persuasive ability. The fact that this particular proof comes from a non-work experience is not that important now and is not obvious to the reader (unless you want it to be).

Editing and Production Tips

Before you make a final draft of your skills resume, look over the sample resumes in this chapter for ideas on content and format. Several of them use interesting techniques that may be useful for your particular situation.

For example, if you have a good work history, including a very brief chronological listing of jobs on your resume can be a helpful addition to your skills resume. If you have substantial work history, beginning the resume with a summary of total experience can provide the basis for details that follow. A narrative approach sometimes works better than a more conventional listing of, say, your educational or military experience. Remember that this is **your** resume, so do with it what you think is best. Trust your own good judgment. Here are some additional tips.

Write It Yourself: While I expect you to use ideas and even words or phrases you like from sample resumes, it is important that your resume is your own. Use your own skills and support them with your own accomplishments. If you do not have good written communication skills, it is perfectly OK to get help from someone who does. Just make sure your resume ends up sounding like you wrote it.

Length: Opinions differ on this, but one or two pages is a good range, not three. If you are seeking a managerial, professional, or technical position where most people have prior training or experience, two pages is the norm.

Don't Be Humble! Like an interview, this is no place to be too humble. Stress your accomplishments. If you don't communicate what you can do, who will?

Be Specific: Give facts and numbers. Instead of saying you are good with people, say "I supervised and trained six people in the accounting department and increased their productivity by 30 percent."

Keep It Lively: Use action verbs and short sentences. Avoid negatives of any kind. Emphasize accomplishments and results.

Tell the Truth: A significant percentage of resumes include false information. Don't even consider it. If you lie now you deserve to lose your job later if you are caught. That does not mean that you should reveal any negatives that you have or think you have. Nothing said is better than telling an untruth. The interview is the place to explain any problems that you have to deal with, not the resume.

Make Every Word Count: Write a long rough draft and then edit, edit, edit. If a word or phrase does not support your job objective, consider dropping it. Rewrite and edit until it communicates what you really want to say about yourself, and it looks the way you want it to. Type (or have typed) a draft copy on which you can make any final changes. After all this, have your final copy typed. Once more, very carefully, review it for typographical and other errors.

Make It Error-Free: Ask someone else to look for grammar and spelling errors. Check each word again before you have it printed and send it to an employer. It is amazing how many errors can get into the final version.

Appearance: You surely know that your resume's overall appearance will effect an employer's opinion of you. Is it well-organized? Is it "crisp" and professional looking?

Typing or Typesetting: It is perfectly acceptable to type your resume if you use a good quality business typewriter with a new ribbon, or word processor using a letter quality printer. Dot matrix printer output or sloppy type from an old typewriter is not acceptable. Typesetting or desktop publishing is another alternative that some people prefer. This book is typeset, not typed. Most print shops can typeset your resume. The result can be very attractive since you can use bold and different sizes and styles of type. You can also get two or more typed pages on one typeset page. Some employers don't like typeset resumes because they're not tailored to their specific job opening, but you can't please everyone.

Getting Copies Made: Most print shops can make good quality photocopies but make sure that the copy quality is excellent rather than just good. Photocopying is economical for smaller numbers of resumes or if you have several more targeted resumes produced in smaller quantities. Print shops can also offset print your resume and this makes sense if you want a hundred or more. Ask the print shop for advice and insist on top quality appearance.

Paper: A good quality paper is important. Most print shops have a selection of papers and you can often get matching envelopes. While most resumes are on white paper, I prefer an off-white (ivory) or very light tan-colored paper. You could use other light pastel colors, but I do not recommend red, purple, or green tints.

Now, Use It!

Many job seekers say they are still improving their resume when they should be out looking for a job. A better approach is to do a simple, error-free resume at first. Then actively look for a job. You can always work on a better version at night and on weekends. You may just get a job offer before you get the "improved" resume completed. It happens quite often.

A Few Final Words on Resume Experts

If you ask 10 people for advice on your resume, they will all be willing to give it. And no two of them will agree. You will have to make up your own mind about your resume. Feel free to break any "rules" if you have a good reason for doing so. Some resumes in the examples break rules and none are perfect. However, they are all based on real resumes used by people who wrote them themselves and who got good jobs. So look them over, then write your own.

Resume Examples

Note: Sample resumes have been squeezed to fit on these pages. Actual resumes would be arranged somewhat differently.

Before: Too disorganized and with little emphasis on accomplishments, this is a poor resume. Delete the "personal" section!

Robin Lee

5413 Armstrong Drive	Soc.Sec. No. 103 23 2987
Phoenix, AZ 85001	Phone No. (512) 648-6643

Personal

Marital Status-Single	Height - 5'6"
DOB 1/9/65	Health-Good

Career Objective

I would like to further my education in the fields of finance, marketing, and business administration.

Education

Duncan Business College	Graduated May 1990
876 Applegate, Phoenix, AZ 85008	
Phone: (512) 336-2222	
Graduated from: the Legal	
Technology Course	
Batesville High School	Graduated June 1988
899 School Road, Phoenix, AZ 85889	
Phone: (512) 335-1122	

Business and College Courses

Typing I, II, III and IV	Accounting	Business English
Data Processing Concepts	Shorthand	Communications Skills
Legal Procedures	Business Math	Math and Machines
Secretarial Administration	Word Processing	Business Law

Skills and Equipment

Typing: 60 wpm, Shorthand: 90 wpm, 10 key punch: 160 strokes perminute. IBM Selectric III, Word Perfect on PC, Wang Word Processor, assorted calculators and photography machines.

Work Experience

Administrative Secretary
January 1, 1990 thru Present
Alpha Consulting, Inc.
32 East Bends, Phoenix, AZ 85001
Phone: (512) 278-5401
I process all papers that come through the office. I handle sending out bills, receiving escrow monies, checkbook balancing, and all records management.
Receptionist
October 1988 - December 1990
Quick Trucking, Inc
12 Trucking Rd., Phoenix, AZ 85032
Phone: (512) 885-1143
I answered phones and gave out information to customers.

Personal References

Mr. & Mrs. Soandso	Dr. I. Docare
857 Suburban Avenue	56 Somewhere Street
Suburbia, AZ 85111	Anotherplace, AZ 85422
Phone (512) 888-0099	Phone: (512) 333-2245

Others available upon request

After: This version uses chronological and skills resume elements. The configuration and format is much improved over the original. It is for a recent technical school graduate with some related work experience.

Robin Lee

5413 Armstrong Drive
Phoenix, AZ 85001

Home: (512) 648-6643
Answering Service: (512) 272-7608

Career Objective

Office Manager, Executive or Legal Secretary. Will consider responsible positions requiring advanced business adminstration, office, and organizational skills.

Education and Training

Advanced	Duncan Business College, Phoenix, AZ. Graduate of Executive and Legal Office Technology program, top 30% of class. Emphasis on business procedures, accounting, automated systems, business law, administration and legal terminology.
High School	Batesville High School, Phoenix, AZ. Active in Arizona's Business Leaders of America, won Business English Award. Maintained a B+ average with courses in typing, word processing, and accounting. Advanced English composition and language, and office procedures.

Skills

Organizational	Have managed all business office responsibilities for a staff of five, with gross revenues of over $350,000/yr. Independently composed most customer correspondence. Set up a word processing and client tracking system that increased staff customer contact time by 20% and revenues 30% by accurate accounting records of the business. Work well under pressure and can handle a variety of tasks at once.
Office	Take shorthand at 90wpm and type, accurately and steadily, 60 wpm. Familiar with various word processing systems including Word Perfect, Mac, Wordstar, and others. Knowledgeable of several manual and automated accounting and data entry systems. Excellent spelling and language skills.

Experience

Office Manager: Alpha Consulting, Inc., Phoenix, AZ. January 1990 through present. Responsible for all office functions of a busy office: accounting, correspondence, customer referrals, and other activities. Perfect attendance record, two salary increases, excellent references. Report to the President.

Receptionist: Quick Trucking, Inc., Phoenix, AZ., October 1988 to December 1989. Began part-time while in high school. Promoted to receptionist position and responsible for over 4,000 incoming phone calls per month, greeting visitors, processing mail and maintaining good customer relations. Received many letters from customers regarding my services, no complaints in over 40,000 phone transactions. Received several merit raises and excellent performance ratings.

THOMAS P. MARRIN
80 Harrison Avenue
Baldwin, Long Island., New York 11563
Answering Service: (716) 223-4705

Objective:
A middle/upper level management position with responsibilities including problem solving, planning, organizing, and budget management.

Education:
University of Notre Dame, BS in Business Administration. Course emphasis on accounting, supervision, and marketing. Upper 25% of class.

Military:
US Army — 2nd Infantry Division, 1982-1986. 1st Lieutenant and platoon leader — stationed in Korea and Ft. Knox, Kentucky. Supervised an annual budget of nearly $2 million and equipment valued at over $80 million. Responsible for training, scheduling, and activities of as many as 40 people. Received several commendations. Honorable discharge.

Business Experience:
Wills Express Transit Co.,Inc., Mineola, New York
Vice President Corporate Equipment — 1990 to Present
Controlled purchase, maintenance, and disposal of 1,100 trailers and 65 company cars with $2.7 million operating and $3 million capital expense responsibilities.
- Scheduled trailer purchases, 6 divisions.
- Operated under planned maintenance budget in company's second best profit year while operating revenues declined 2.5%.
- Originated schedule to correlate drivers' needs with available trailers.
- Developed systematic purchase and disposal plan for company car fleet.

Asst. Vice President Corporate Operations — 1988-1990
Coordinated activities of six sections of corporate operations with an operating budget over $10 million.
- Directed implementation of zero base budgeting.
- Developed and prepared executive officer analyses detailing achievable cost reduction measures. Resulted in cost reduction of over $600,000 in first two years.
- Designed policy and procedure for special equipment leasing program during peak seasons. Cut capital purchases by over $1 million.

Manager of Communications — 1987-1988
- Directed and Managed $1.4 million communication network involving 650 phones, 150 WATS lines, 3 switchboards, 1 teletype machine, 5 employees.
- Installed computerized WATS Control System. Optimized utilization of WATS lines and pinpointed personal abuse. Achieved payback earlier than originally projected.
- Devised procedures that allowed simultaneous 20% increase in WATS calls and a $75,000/year savings. Hayfield Publishing Company, Hempstead, New York.

Communications Administrator — 1986-1987
- Managed daily operations of a large communications center. Reduced costs and improved services.

Although this is a chronological resume, there is an adequate presentation of skills. Notice how several positions with the same company are handled separately, showing his promotions to higher levels of responsibility and allowing each position to be given adequate attention. His military experience is presented as any other paid position supporting his job objective by using budget figures and numbers of people supervised. He should provide an alternative phone number.

Darrel T. Craig	2306 Cincinnati Street, Kingsford, PA 15171
Message: (412) 464-1273	Home: (412) 437-6217

Career Objective
Challenging position in programming or related areas which would best use my expertise in the business environment. This position should have many opportunities for an aggressive, dedicated individual with leadership abilities to advance.

Programming Skills
Work included functional program design to relate to the business world in payroll, inventory and data base management, and sales and loan amortization reports. In conjunction with design would be coding, implementation, debugging, and file maintenance. Working knowledge of Ansi COBOL on DEC PDP 11/70 and Prime 750 computers, data base management using COBOL as host language on Prime 750, RPGII, Basic Plus, and prior instruction in Fortran. Operations included tape and disk file organization, access, and maintenance.

Areas of Specific Expertise
Interpersonal communication strengths, public relations capabilities, innovative problem solving, and analytical talents.

Sales
Extremely successful in sales and sales management. A total of nine years experience in sales. Sold burglar alarm products to distributors and burglar alarm dealers. Increased company's sales from $16,000 to over $70,000 per month.
Creatively organized sales programs and marketing concepts. Trained sales personnel in prospecting techniques while also training service personnel in proper installation of burglar alarms. Result: 90% of all new business was generated through referrals from existing customers.

Management
Managed burglar alarm company for four years while increasing profits yearly.
Supervised office, sales, and installation personnel. Supervised and delegated work to assistants in accounting functions and inventory control. Worked as assistant credit manager, responsible for over $2 million per month in charge sales. Handled semi-annual inventory of 5 branch stores totaling millions of dollars and supervised 120 people.

Accounting
Balanced all books and prepared tax forms for burglar alarm company. Eight years experience in credit and collections, with emphasis on collections. Was able to collect a "bad debt" deemed "uncollectable" by company in excess of $250,000.
Over $150,000 in bad checks were retured to the company yearly; collected approximately 98% each year.

Education
School of Computer Technology, Philadelphia, PA
Diploma, Business Application Programming/TECH EXEC
On a 4 point scale, I averaged 3.97
Robert Morris College, Pittsburgh, PA
Associate Degree in Accounting, Minor in Management

This is a resume of a career changer. His prior work history is mentioned, but there is no chronological listing.While some employers will object to the lack of dates, Darrel does a good job of quantifying his previous experience, but connection between his present job objective as a programmer and how his experience supports this could be improved. For example, managing collections requires discipline, persistence, and attention to detail. These are the same skills required in programming. The skills he emphasizes do not directly support his objective. While he is good in sales, how does that relate to programming? He should consider either modifying his job objective to include sales or select another skill to emphasize.

Deborah Levy

4141 Beachway Road   (213) 432-8064
Redondo Beach, California 90277   (213) 888-7365

Objective: Management Position in a Major Hotel
Summary of Experience: Four years experience in sales, catering, banquet
                           services, and guest relations in 300-room hotel.
                           Doubled sales revenues from conferences and meetings.
                           Increased dining room and bar revenues by 44%. Won
                           prestigious national and local awards for increased
                           productivity and services.
Experience: Park Regency Hotel, Los Angeles, California
                           Assistant Manager, 1989 to Present
                           • Oversee a staff of 36, including dining room and bar,
                             housekeeping, and public relations operations.
                           • Introduced new menus and increased dining room
                             revenues by 44%. Gourmet America awarded us their
                             Hotel Haute Cuisine first place award in both 1989
                             and 1990.
                           • Attracted 28% more diners with the first revival of
                             Big Band Cocktail Dances in the Los Angeles area.
                           Kingsmont Hotel, Redondo Beach, California
                           Sales and Public Relations 1987 to 1989
                           • Doubled revenues per month from conferences and
                             meetings.
                           • Redecorated meeting rooms and updated sound and
                             visual media equipment. Trained staff to operate and
                             maintain equipment.
                           • Instituted Outstanding Employee Courtesy awards,
                             which resulted in an upgrade from B to AAA Plus in
                             the Car and Travel Handbook.
Education: Associate's Degree in Hotel Management from
                           Henfield College of San Francisco. One year with the
                           Boileau Culinary Institute, where I won the 1987 Grand
                           Prize Scholarship. Bachelor of Arts in English
                           Literature, University of Virginia.

This is a simple but very acceptable chronological resume. She put her education on
the bottom of this resume to emphasize her related work experience and closed the
resume with her additional strength of related education. Notice that while this
resume is short, she finds room to present some key accomplishments and skills.
Her job objective is broad enough for her to be considered for many positions and
does not eliminate many at all.

Tricia List   Home: (219) 637-2184
613 Seaview Road   Message: (219) 637-6182
Seattle, Washington 81614

Career Objective

I seek a challenging, responsible position in video production. Ideally, this position would require creative as well as technical skills.

Production Experience

My experience in video production has been derived from various studio and location projects, for broadcast on both commerical and public television. While working for WTVC-TV, I worked on their high interest news program, P.M. Magazine. Initially, my major duties included transcribing and logging video interviews, maintaining public information files, scouting and coordinating locations, and composing the weekly program synopsis for publication in *TV Guide*. Later I progressed to the position of production assistant for segments such as "At the Ballet" and a variety of others.

I was also the sole producer/director of THE HUMANE SOCIETY. This video program was acquired by Goodman Communications, Inc., Channel 19 in Ft. Lauderdale, Florida, for broadcast on Cable Television and later syndicated nationally.

More recently, I worked on several productions for a program series entitled Art Institute Magazine, a regularly scheduled program broadcast on Cable Television. My responsibilities included such positions as script writer, lighting technician, set designer, videographer, editor, and assistant producer/director. Program titles included "American Artist: Paul Mandole," "Airbrush Techniques," and "The Pin-Hole Camera."

Proven Production Skills

Pre-Production: Work well with others. Understanding and amiable when consulting clients. A natural problem-solver. Experienced in detailed research and analytical functions. (Former positions include Abstractor and Legal Assistant.) Excellent writing skills. Efficient organizer.

Production: Strong visual acuity, with emphasis on form as well as creativity. Videography with sharp focus and smooth movement. Experienced photographer (stills, slide inserts, copy work). Versed in audio recording and editing techniques. Accomplished in lighting and set design. Potential for on-camera talent. Hardworking with or without supervision.

Post Production: Can finish projects within time allotted. Proven skills in maintaining records, files and cross-references. Capable of follow-up consultation and further project development. Approach editing process with both logic and intuition. Dependable, career-oriented, eager to learn more.

Education

A.S. Degree; Washington Academy of Fine Arts
Course work emphasized video media and included: •Video production •Audio-visual production • Public relations • Subject research • Photography • Business managment • Marketing

---

With no employment or other dates, this is clearly a skills resume. Tricia uses a narrative approach in reviewing her production experience. This works reasonably well, although I would like to see more emphasis on her results. For example, if one of her programs was broadcast, how many people saw it? Did it receive any recognition or awards? Was it repeated? How much was it sold for? Most of Tricia's video experience was while she was a student and, later, as a part-time employee for a small TV station. She also has long periods of underemployment and unemployment she does not want to display. While the resume could be improved, it presents her well and will help support her request for an interview.

Long Hue
4431 Old Mill Road
Kansas City, Kansas 66301

(614) 886-4040   (614) 634-5151

CAREER OBJECTIVE: Supervisor of Building Maintenance

SUMMARY: Four years experience in maintaining a $24,000,000 scientific
facility that requires exceptionally high standards of security and
cleanliness. Two years experience hiring, supervising, and
training 24 employees. Reorganized workload to save
$22,000/year in salaries and wages.

EMPLOYMENT HISTORY:

The Hadley Research Center, Kansas City, Kansas
Maintenance Supervisor, November 1990 to Present

- Hire, supervise, and train staff.

- Saved $22,000/year by replacing four retiring full-time
  employees with part-time staff.

- Conduct regular training and refresher courses to keep staff
  current on equipment and procedures.

- Maintain stringent oversight of safety procedures and
  hazardous waste disposal.

August 1982 to October 1990
Electronic Specialist

- Maintained complex scientific equipment valued at $1.5
  million.

- Cleaned, calibrated, adjusted, rewired, and repaired as needed.

- Conduct periodic fire and accident drills. Filed evaluations of
  each drill with the Hadley Center Director and State
  Environmental Agency.

This is another simple chronological resume that does a good job of presenting skills
that support his job objective. Long does not mention his education or training since
he is a high school graduate who has learned his skills on the job. Yet this certainly
does not come across as a weakness.

BILL WILLIAMS
632 East 23rd Street
Manchester, New Hampshire 26142
(114) 743-7209 • (114) 747-3207

JOB OBJECTIVE
Position should require organizational and persuasive ability in motivating others toward common objectives. Prefer active responsibilities in managing job sites for an active, growing, and service-oriented profit organization.

ORGANIZATION
Developed a wallcovering distributorship which grossed $875,000 within its first year of operation and made a net profit of $87,000. Restructured and supervised operations and personnel of retail outlet employing staff of 35. Founded a community leadership organization for youth, which expanded to over 200 members and a national affiliation within two years.

SUPERVISION/MANAGEMENT
In various capacities directly supervised as many as 35 staff. Experienced in selection, recruitment and training of management, office, retail, and labor personnel. With 30% fewer staff and lower expenses, successfully competed with established businesses, and virtually captured their market within one year. Had lowest staff turnover and absenteeism rate in the company, as the result of improved managment/personnel programs.

COMMUNICATION SKILLS
Developed and conducted training seminars for groups as large as 20. Facilitated numerous small groups to solve problems. Demonstrated persuasive skills in relating to organizations and individuals. For example, packaged a service program that resulted in an $85,000 sale.

PEOPLE SKILLS
Coordinated and directed over 150 people during a political election. Received an award for work in human rights for the City of Manchester. Promoted, coordinated, and directed a recreational facility for 300 people. Presented research papers to members of a study group.

EDUCATION
Boston University, B.S. Business; University of New Hampshire, Graduate Work

PERSONAL
Married 16 years, three children, and eager to use skills.

SUMMARY OF EXPERIENCE
Sales Representative, Beeler's Coatings, Easten New Hampshire. Sold paint to dealers for a manufacturer. Increased sales first year 5% while company was having a 5% decrease in sales. Won the company's "tight fisted award," for keeping the expenses in the territory more under budget than any other salesman.

Manager, Berghoff-Smith, Inc., Manchester. Organized and managed the local branch of a wallcovering distributor.

Sales Representative, New Deco Wall Covering, Inc., New England. Sold wallcoverings to dealers, contractors, mass merchandisers, and decorators. Increased sales almost $100,000 in one year. Opened over 100 dealers.

Assistant General Manager, and Sales Representative, Price & Andrews, Inc. Functioned in many capacities from direct customer contact to managerial functions. Mainly sold paint and wallcoverings to dealers and contractors. Increased sales from $300,000 to around $800,000 while adding over 200 new dealers.

Bill used a modified skills resume because he was unemployed for some time and did not want to make it obvious. He also had several gaps in prior employment so he left all employment dates off the resume. He quantified the results of his efforts with dollars and percentages. This resume took effort but is absolutely accurate. Bill had survived for nearly a year doing odd jobs, and when he organized his history and began communicating more clearly, he suddenly did better in getting interviews. He was employed in a good job in less than four weeks after this resume was finished. The people who hired him, by the way, never asked for his resume.

JOHN H. SHEADY

6415 Lava Court   Home: (303) 379-8276
Laurel, California 99643   Message: (303) 786-6780

JOB OBJECTIVE:

An effective and articulate problem solver, seeking a responsible position in a sales or service oriented organization

AREAS OF EXPERTISE:

Communications:
Relate in a friendly, yet personal style with people of diverse backgrounds. Have considerable experience in formal and informal sales presentations to groups as large as 300 persons. Able to express self clearly in a variety of written formats. Desire to please others facilitates relaxed, one-to-one communications.

Sales:
Over a period of years, have consistently demonstrated superior achievement in representing products and services in many different settings. In the competitive food service industry, "converted" over $1,000,000 revenue annually from competing accounts. As an account representative with the Great Widget Company, personally handled sales contracts as large as $150,000. Not simple "order taking," these sales required complex, technical presentations; detailed report writing; considerable pre-sales planning; and group presentations. Required extensive travel over a fourteen state region.

People Skills:
Able to quickly gain trust and confidence. As a sales representative for a major corporation, accumulated over eighty unsolicited complimentary letters from customers. In various positions in supervision and management, have consistently demonstrated the ability to increase the productivity of people at all levels. Have supervised staffs as large as 15 people.

Problem Solver/Analyzer:
Able to approach large and complex systems and resolve problems to maximize efficiency. In many cases, a product or service was involved as a tool in the problem resolution process. Successful implementation of the proposed improvements required the purchase of the service. One example involved the use of data processing techniques which resulted in a savings to one customer of over $200,000.

Persistence/Energy:
In virtually all tasks undertaken, have used a natural and spontaneous personal energy to perform beyond expectations. A desire to successfully complete projects provides the motivation to achieve excellence. Example: As sales representative, was assigned half the medical facilities in Illinois. During allotted time, visited ALL facilities in area — many of whom had not been visited in over three years. Results were a 110% increase in annual sales from this region.

EDUCATION:

Northwest Community College — Computer Science/Math; Argyle Business College — Business Degree. One week or longer courses in: Sales, Supervision, Management, Customer Service, Public Speaking, and related topics.

PERSONAL:

Married seven years; enjoy challenges; active in community affairs; a participant rather than an observer in life.

REFERENCES AVAILABLE UPON REQUEST

John looked up the skills required for sales and service jobs in the *Occupational Outlook Handbook*, then listed those skills in this resume with examples of when he used them. He uses action words and provides good examples but leaves off employment dates to avoid showing that he is unemployed or had a series of relatively short-term jobs in the past. He circulated this resume to his friends and acquaintenances and got a lead that resulted in a job paying $6,000 more than his previous job.

Before: A simple resume that is improved upon in the next example.

DAVID ROBERT HAMLIN JUNIOR

Present Address: Permanent Address:
1693 Lori Terrace   1432 Walnut Street
Eaglewood, FL 47293   Port Charlotte, FL 47297
Phone 243-7692   Phone 267-5391

CAREER OBJECTIVE

I am eager to obtain an electronics-oriented position and advance within the company after proving my abilities and skills. In the future, I plan to continue my education part-time.

EDUCATION

Florida Technical Institute
7459 Pyramid Blvd.
Fort Myers, FL
Phone (717) 543-7430

Course of Study: Electronics Engineering Technology

Graduation Date: June, 1991

Degree: Associate of Applied Science in Electronics Engineering Technology

Subjects Studied: Basic Electronics, Solid State Fundamentals, Communications Electronics, Pulse Techniques, Technical Communication, Electronic Circuit Analysis, Digital Fundamentals, TV Systems, Microprocessors and Special Devices, Industrial Electronics, Radio Communications, Microwave Communications.

Warren Central High School
5762 Hannible Way
Port Charlotte, FL 47297

WORK EXPERIENCE
6/90 - present

Terminal Repair Corp
615 West Jefferson
Port Charlotte, FL 47297
Phone# (717) 444-5555
Supervisor: Ima Hardcase
Title: Field Service Technican
Duties: Traveling to various stores using the company van to repair or replace defective terminals, printers, and telephones.

6/88 - 3/90

Bradley's TV Sales and Service
3206 East Avenue
Port Charlotte, FL 47297
(717) 632-3321
Supervisor: Ross Reed
Title: Helper, Repair person
Duties: Helped owner run business. Repaired consumer electronics and appliances.

HOBBIES AND INTERESTS

Computer programming, photography, trumpet playing, bowling, listening to music, leader/member of a private gaming club.

REFERENCES

Character References available upon request.

After: This example shows a change from a cluttered chronological resume to a combination resume that includes his skills and a listing of jobs held. Because he is a recent graduate, he emphasized his education and training as a major issue and provides lots of details of his accomplishments there.

DAVID ROBERT HAMLIN

1693 Lori Terrace   home: (717) 243-7692
Eaglewood, FL 47293   message: (717) 267-5391

CAREER OBJECTIVE

Field service position requiring advanced diagnostics and repair of electronics and computer equipment. Position should require skills in customer contact, problem solving and technical assistance.

EDUCATION & TRAINING

Florida Technical Institute, Fort Myers, FL: Graduate of an advanced two year degree program in Electronics Engineering Technology. Top 20% of class while working part-time and maintaining a perfect attendance record. Extensive course work and over 1,000 hours hands-on experience in solid state, digital and analog systems; communication, TV, radio and industrial electronics; computer, pulse, microwave and optical systems; circuit analysis and trouble shooting; mechanical systems and special devices repair. Am particularly strong in the diagnosis and repair of electro-mechanical and computerized office equipment.

On The Job: Specific knowledge of field diagnostics and repair of a variety of electronic equipment. Familiar with standard hand tools and diagnostic equipment. Substantial experience with customer contact, training, and support needs.

High School: Warren Central H.S., Port Charlotte, FL. In advanced program, graduated in top 5% of class, with Honors. Elective courses in advanced algebra, calculus, trigonometry, geometry, physics, and computer programming. Won numerous awards including Who's Who in American High Schools. Active in computer and electronics oriented extra-curricular activities throughout these years and have extensive informal experience and training in these areas.

EXPERIENCE

Terminal Repair Co., Port Charlotte, FL: Field Service Technician, mid-1986 to present. Responsible for statewide on-site maintenance of computer terminals, printers and telephone systems of several large retail accounts. Annual billings for these accounts were over $200,000. Increased customer satisfaction and reduced breakdowns by preventive maintenance and informal training of key operators throughout the system. Won maintenance contract renewal against larger competitor who bid a lower price.

Bradley's TV Sales & Service, Port Charlotte, FL: 1983 - 1986. Worked part-time and summers repairing TV's, VCR's and related equipment. Took over the work of a full-time repair person and handled a 30% increase in repair business during this time. Purchased own diagnostic equipment, improved parts inventory and reduced turnaround time of broken equipment by over 50%.

Miscellaneous: Held a variety of jobs during high school and prior to advanced training, equivalent to over two years of full-time experience. Am familiar with a variety of business environments as a result and am equally comfortable with professional, clerical and unskilled staff. Received several promotions and routinely volunteered to maintain a variety of electronic equipment. Excellent references are available from previous employers.

OTHER SKILLS & STRENGTHS

Require little supervision, good interpersonal and communciation skills, attention to detail, accept responsiblity, meet deadlines and learn quicky.

Peter M. Neely
203 Evergreen Road
Houston, Texas 39127
(237) 649-1234 or (237) 643-2917
Position Desired: Truck Driver

Summary of Work Experience:	Over twenty years of stable work history, including substantial experience with diesel engines, electrical systems, and all types of mechanical equipment. Good record keeping and attention to details. Excellent driving record.

SKILLS

Driving Record/ Licenses:	Chauffeur's license, qualified and able to drive anything that rolls. No traffic citations for over 20 years. Accident free record.
Vehicle Maintenance:	Am very careful in adhering to correct preventive maintenance schedules and avoid most breakdowns as a result. Substantial mechanical and electrical systems training and experience permits many breakdowns to be repaired immediately and avoid towing.
Record Keeping:	Excellent attention to detail. Familiar with recording procedures and submit required records on a timely basis.
Routing:	Knowledge of many states. Good map reading and route planning skills.
Other:	Not afraid of hard work, flexible, get along well with others, meet deadlines, responsible.

Work Experience:

1989 - Present:	CAPITAL TRUCK CENTER, Houston, Texas Pick up and deliver all types of commerical vehicles from across the United States. Carry large sums of money and entrusted with handling complex truck purchasing transactions.
1985 - 1989	QUALITY PLATING CO., Houston, Texas Promoted from production to Production and Quality Control. Developed numerous work simplification and production improvements resulting in substantial cost savings.
1983 - 1985	BLUE CROSS MANUFACTURING, Houston, Texas Received several increases in salary and responsibility before leaving for a more challenging position.
1980 - 1983	Truck delivery of food products to destinations throughout the South. Supervised up to 12 men in the operations and maintenance of a variety of heavy equipment.

MILITARY
United States Air Force — Operated power plants, training in diesel engines and electrical systems. Stationed in Alaska, California, Wyoming and other states. Honorable discharge.

EDUCATION
Cleveland Township High School, South Warren, Texas

PERSONAL
C.B. radio communications, volunteer fireman, camping.
Married, excellent health.

Peter lost his job when the plant closed in the late-1980s. He picked up a survival job as a truck driver and now wanted to make this his career. Notice how he presents those skills and experiences essential for the success of a truck driver. He also listed some positive personal characteristics under "personal." Because he has a stable work history, he includes employment dates and companies in this combined format. The miscellaneous jobs he had before 1983 are simply clustered together since they are less important, as a group, than his more recent experience. He has also tied in his military experience to support his job objective in a direct way!

FRANK E. PERKINS
9272 Kessler Boulevard
Indianapolis, Indiana 46235
(317) 555-0119 or (317) 555-9761

CAREER OBJECTIVE

Challenging purchasing position with progressive opportunities where proven talents and skills in . . .

Negotiation
Problem Solving
Supervision & Organization
. . . can be effectively utilized to our mutual benefit.

TYPICAL ACCOMPLISHMENTS

Throughout twenty years of work experience, a variety of skills and capabilities have been demonstrated. Among them:

COST ANALYSIS
- Analyzed cost data on $650,000 inventory.
- Purchased raw materials for processing in the area of $4,000,000 annually.

COST EFFECTIVENESS
- Interviewed vendors to obtain information on products, prices, quality, and delivery.
- Developed over 200 new vendors, increased competitive bidding 300%, thereby realizing lower prices.
- Suceeded in getting vendors to go on a cost plus 10% basis.

SUPERVISION AND ORGANIZATION
- Supervised, directed, and trained 8-10 people in taking physical inventory.
- Designed inventory tags and four-part shop order ticket using NCR paper, saving company 750 hours annually.

POSITION HELD

1985 to 1992
- Service Supply Company, Indianapolis, Indiana Buyer and Accountant

EDUCATION

- Indiana University, Major — Accounting

PERSONAL QUALITIES

- Ability to plan and make decisions rapidly.

Independent, self-motivated, adaptable, and reliable.

Frank presents his experiences positively, in a clean and simple format using lots of white space. Sentences are short with good use of action words and he includes numbers to document his effectiveness and responsibilities. He handles his lack of a college degree well by simply listing, at the end, that he did attend a major university. He can explain this in an inverview should it come up.

Cecil Robbins
517 No. Haines Street
Chattanooga, Tennessee 71317
(761) 473-1276 Home
(761) 473-7153 Message

Job Objective: Custodian

Capabilities
- Experienced in the use of most heavy duty cleaning tools such as wet and dry vacuum, buffer, and scrubber.
- Can use cleaning solvents and chemicals safely and properly to avoid both personal injury and damage to property.
- Capable of performing several tasks in succession using personal judgment under minimal or no supervision.
- Instructed several employees in the correct working procedures and in setting proper standards for work quality.
- Experienced salesman capable of communicating well with public and representing company products.

Recognition
Received an award from employer for the cleanest work area. Work was used to set the standard for other employees in their work performance.

Work Summary

1989 to Present	Holiday Inn, Chattanooga
	Night janitor, promoted to day custodian. Supervise three janitorial staff, order supplies, schedule services for a busy 260 bed, 12 meeting room and restaurant facility.
1987 to 1989	Applegate Transit, Chattanooga
	Janitor. Received two merit raises. Loss of job due to a severe business downturn at Applegate.

Other
Get along well with others, efficient worker that gets things done, very reliable, have own transportation.

This is a simple resume that combines some elements both of the chronological and skills resumes. Cecil does not have a high school diploma (yet!), so his education is not mentioned. In his work history, he mentions several positive factors rather than simply listing his titles and duties. For the position desired, this is a good resume. It provides enough detail to arouse interest, and it presents a positive image, exactly what a resume should do.

Chapter Thirteen

Writing Cover Letters and Thank-You Notes

This is a brief chapter covering two short but important job search tools — cover letters and thank-you notes. Let's begin with cover letters.

Unless you personally hand a resume to a prospective employer, some sort of letter will usually accompany it. Depending on the situation, you may feel comfortable sending your resume along with a simple note but more formal situations require a typed cover letter. These letters fall into two major categories:

1. Cover letters to someone you know
2. Cover letters to someone you don't know

Cover Letters Addressed to Someone You Know

If you have read other chapters in this book, you should know that "someone you know" could include almost anyone. It is far more desirable to call someone who has advertised in the paper than simply send a letter and resume. There are also the *Yellow Pages*, personal referrals, and so many other ways of coming to know someone. So here I'll assume you have made some sort of personal contact before sending your resume. Within this assumption there are hundreds of variations, but I will discuss the most important ones and let you adapt them to your own situation. Once you have had initial prior contact with someone, you might send them a resume and cover letter under the following conditions:

1. An interview is scheduled, but no specific job is available.
2. An interview is scheduled and there is a specific job opening that may interest you.
3. After an interview takes place.
4. No interview is scheduled.

Tips for Superior Cover Letters

Here is a standard approach to cover letters that can be adapted as needed for each of these situations. Virtually every good cover letter follows these guidelines:

Present a Good Appearance: Your contacts with prospective employers should always be professional. Buy good quality stationery and matching envelopes. The standard 8 1/2-by- 11-inch paper size is usually used and I prefer a white, ivory, or light beige-colored paper. A typewriter with excellent type quality or a word processor with letter quality output (not dot-matrix) is a must.

Use an Appropriate Format: Any standard business correspondence format is acceptable. Look at the examples for ideas.

Provide a Friendly Review: Begin your letter with a reminder of any prior contacts and the reason for your correspondence now.

Target Your Skills and Experiences: To do this well, you must know something about the organization or person with whom you are dealing. Present any relevant background that may be of particular interest to the person you are writing.

Define the Next Step: Don't close your letter without clearly identifying what you will do next!

Sample Cover Letters Addressed to People You Know

I've included several examples of cover letters that incorporate these guidelines and address a variety of situations.

Sample Cover Letter: John Furn

(Pre-interview, no specific job opening)

John Furn
616 Kings Way
Minneapolis, MN 54312

February 10, 19XX

Mrs. Francine Cook
Park-Halsey Corporation
5413 Armstrong Drive
Minneapolis, Minnesota 54317

Dear Mrs. Cook:

When Steve Marks suggested I call you, I had no idea you would be so helpful. I've already followed up with several of the suggestions you made and am now looking forward to meeting with you next Tuesday. The resume I've enclosed is to give you a better sense of my qualifications. Perhaps it will help you think of other organizations who may be interested in my background.

The resume does not say why I've moved to Minneapolis and you may find that of interest. My spouse and I visited the city several years ago and thought it a good place to live. She has obtained a very good position here and, based on that, we decided it was time to commit ourselves to a move. As you can see from my work experience, I tend to stay-on and move-up in jobs, so I now want to more carefully research the job opportunities here before making a commitment. Your help in this task is greatly appreciated.

Feel free to contact me if you have any questions, otherwise, I look forward to meeting you in person next Tuesday.

Sincerely,

John Furn

Sample Cover Letter: **Richard Swanson**

    (Pre-interview, for a specific job opening)

                          Richard Swanson
                          113 So. Meridian Street
                          Greenwich, Connecticut 11721

March 10, 19XX

Mr. William Hines
New England Power and Light Company
604 Waterway Blvd.
Parien, Connecticut 11716

Mr. Hines:

    I am following up on the brief chat we had today by phone. After getting the details on the position you have open, I am certain that it is the kind of job I have been looking for. A copy of my resume is enclosed providing more details of my background. I hope you have a chance to review it before we meet next week.

    My special interest has long been in the large-volume order processing systems that your organization has developed so well. While in school I researched the flow of order processing work for a large corporation as part of a class assignment. With some simple and inexpensive changes I recommended in their manual system, check-processing time was reduced by an average of three days. For the number of checks and dollars involved, this one change resulted in an estimated increase in interest revenues of over $350,000 per year. Details do count!

    While I have recently graduated from business school, I do have considerable experience for a person of my age. I have worked in a variety of jobs dealing with large numbers of people and deadline pressure. My studies have also been far more "hands-on" and practical than those of most schools, so I have a good working knowledge of current business systems and procedures. This includes a basic understanding of random analysis and systems design, including automation. I am also a hard worker and realize I will need to apply myself to get established in my career.

    I am most interested in the position you have available and am excited about the potential it offers. I look forward to seeing you next week.

Sincerely,

Richard Swanson

Sample Cover Letter: Sandra Kijeh

(Following an interview)

Sandra A. Kijeh
115 So. Hawthorn Drive
Port Charlotte, Florida 81641

April 10, 19XX

Christine Massey
Import Distributors, Inc.
417 East Main Street
Atlanta, Georgia 21649

Dear Ms. Massey:

I know you have a busy schedule so I was pleasantly surprised when you extended the interview. While you don't have a position open now, your organization is just the sort of place I would like to work in. As we discussed, I like to be busy with a variety of duties and the active pace I saw at your company is what I seek.

Your ideas on increasing business sound creative enough to work. I've thought about the customer service problem and would like to discuss with you a possible solution. It would involve the use of a simple system of color-coded files that would prioritize older correspondence. The handling of complaints could also be speeded up through the use of simple form letters similar to those you mentioned. I have some thoughts on how this might be done too, and will work out a draft of procedures and sample letters if you are interested.

Whether or not you have a position for me in the future, I appreciate the time you have given me. An extra copy of my resume is enclosed for your files — or to pass on to someone else.

Let me know if you want to discuss the ideas I presented earlier in the letter. I will call you next week as you suggested to keep you informed of my progress.

Sincerely,

Sandra Kijeh

Cover Letters Addressed to Someone You Don't Know

If it is not practical to directly contact a prospective employer via phone or some other method, it is acceptable to send a resume and cover letter. This approach makes sense if you are moving to a distant location or if you are responding to a "blind" ad offering only a post office box number.

The approach of sending out "To Whom It May Concern" letters by the basketful has been discussed elsewhere in this book. I do not recommend it. However, there are ways to modify this "shotgun" approach to be more effective. Try to find something you have in common with the person you are contacting. By mentioning this link, your letter then becomes a very personal request for assistance. Look at the two letters that follow for ideas.

Sample Cover Letter: **John Andrews**

(In response to a want ad)

John Andrews
12 Lake Street
Chicago, Illinois 60631

January 17, 19XX

The Morning Sun
Box N4317
2 Early Drive
Toronto, Ontario R5C 1S3

RE: Receptionist/Bookkeeper Job Opening

As I plan on relocating to Toronto, your advertisement for a Receptionist/Bookkeeper caught my attention. Your ad stated yours is a small office and that is precisely what I am looking for. I like dealing with people and in a previous position had over 5,000 customer contacts a month. With that experience, I have learned to handle things quickly and pleasantly.

The varied activities in a position combining bookkeeping and reception sound very interesting. I have received formal training in accounting methods and am familiar with accounts receivable, accounts payable, and general ledger posting. I also have some experience with computerized accounting if your plans include that.

My resume is enclosed for your consideration. Note that I went to school in Toronto and I plan on returning there soon to establish my career. Several of my family also live there and I have provided their local phone number should you wish to contact me. Please contact that number soon, since I plan on being in Toronto in the near future and would like to speak with you about this or future positions with your company.

Sincerely,

John Andrews

Sample Cover Letter: John B. Goode

("Shotgun" Approach)

John B. Goode
321 Smokie Way
Nashville, Tennessee 31201

July 10, 19XX

Paul Resley
Operations Manager
Rollem Trucking Co.
I-70 Freeway Drive
Kansas City, Missouri 78401

Mr. Resley:

I obtained your name from the membership directory of the Affiliated Trucking Association. I have been a member for over 10 years and I am very active in the Southeast Region. The reason I am writing is to ask for your help. The firm I had been employed with has been bought by a larger corporation. The operations here have been disbanded, leaving me unemployed.

While I like where I live, I know that finding a position at the level of responsibility I seek may require a move. As a center of the transportation business, your city is one of those I have targeted for special attention. A copy of my resume is enclosed for your use.

I'd like you to review it and consider where a person with my background would get a good reception in Kansas City. Perhaps you could think of a specific person for me to contact?

I have specialized in fast-growing organizations or ones that have experienced rapid change. My particular strength is in bringing things under control, then increasing profits. While my resume does not state this, I have excellent references from my former employer and would have stayed if a similar position existed at their new location.

As a member of the association, I hoped that you would provide some special attention to my request for assistance. Please call my answering service collect if you have any immediate leads. I plan on coming to Kansas City on a job-hunting trip within the next six weeks. Prior to then I will call you for advice on who I might contact for interviews. Even if they have no jobs open for me now, perhaps they will know of someone else who might! Thanks in advance for your help on this.

Sincerely,

John B. Goode
Treasurer, Southeast Region
Affiliated Trucking Association

Tips for Writing Thank-You Notes

I have mentioned the importance of sending thank-you notes many times in this book. Here are some additional tips on their preparation and use.

Paper and Envelope: Use a good quality note paper with matching envelope. Most stationery stores have them. Avoid "cute" covers. A simple "Thank You" on the front will do. I suggest off-white and buff colors.

Typed vs. Handwritten: Handwritten notes are fine unless your handwriting is illegible or sloppy. If so, type them.

Salutation: Unless you already know the person you are thanking, don't use their first name. Write "Dear Mrs. Pam Smith" or "Dear Mrs. Smith" rather than "Dear Pam." Include the date.

The Note Itself: Keep it short and friendly. This is not the place to write "The reason you should hire me is . . ." Remember, the note is a thank-you for what **they** did, not a hard-sell pitch for what **you** want. As appropriate, be specific about when you will next contact them. If you plan to meet with them soon, still send a note saying you look forward to the meeting and thanking them for the appointment.

Your Signature: Use your first and last name. Avoid initials and make your signature legible.

When to Send It: Write and send your note no later than 24 hours after you make your contact. Ideally, you should write it immediately after the contact while the details are still fresh in your mind. Always send a note after an interview, even if things did not go well. It can't hurt.

Enclose a JIST Card: Depending on the situation, a JIST Card is often the ideal enclosure to include with a thank-you note. It's small, soft-sell, and provides your phone number, should they wish to reach you. It will remind them of you should any jobs open up or give them a tool to pass along to someone else. Make sure your thank-you notes and envelopes are big enough to enclose an unfolded JIST Card.

Here are two sample thank-you notes:

April 1, 1991

Dear Mr. O'Beel,

Thank you for the brief phone conversation we had this morning. I plan on following up with the names of the people you gave me as soon as possible and will let you know how things work out. Since I caught you right before your vacation, I'll follow your suggestion to call again in three weeks. Have a great time! Sincerely, Sara Hall

October 31, 1999

Debbie Childs
2234 Riverwood Avenue
Philadelphia, PA 17963

Ms. Helen A. Colcord
Henderson and Associates, Inc.
1801 Washington Blvd., Suite 1201
Philadelpha, PA 17963

Dear Ms. Colcord,

Thank you for sharing your time with me so generously yesterday. I really
appreciated talking to you about your career field.
The information you shared with me increased my desire to work in such an area.
Your advice has already proven helpful as I have an apppointment to meet with
Robert Hopper on Friday.
In case you think of someone else who might need a person like me, I'm enclosing
another JIST Card.

Sincerely,

Debbie Childs

Chapter Fourteen

Organizing Your Time to Get Results

You now know more about finding a job than most people in North America. In some ways, this may be the most important chapter in this book. The reason is that the methods you have learned will work only if you use them. This chapter will help you decide on a job search schedule designed to turn getting a job into a job itself.

Your Objective Is Two Interviews Per Day

The more interviews you get, the sooner you will get a job offer. If you spend six hours a day looking for a job, you are likely to get more interviews than if you spent only two hours. The average job seeker gets about two interviews per week and spends fewer than 15 hours a week on their job search. At that rate, it takes an average of three to four months to find a job. For most people, that is much longer than it needs to be.

As an alternative, I suggest that you set out to get at least two interviews each day throughout your job search. With the new definition of an interview I am using in this book, that is now quite possible. Remember, an interview can now be any face-to-face contact with a person who hires or supervises people with your skills, whether or not they have a job opening now. Here is the arithmetic for getting two interviews a day:

The Arithmetic of Getting Two Interviews a Day
2 Interviews a Day × 5 Days a Week = 10 Interviews a Week
10 Interviews a Week × 4 Weeks = 40 Interviews a Month

Contrast this with the fact that the average job seeker gets two interviews a week and takes three to four months to get a job. At that pace, it takes 24 interviews or so to get a job. With 40 interviews in just one month it's easy to understand how people using JIST's approach cut their job search time in half. So part of the secret of job search success is to devote as much time and energy to *getting* a job as you will to keeping it once you have found it. In a sense, getting a job *is* a job.

Below are some tips for setting up your job search campaign in an organized and efficient manner.

Setting Up Your Job Search Office

To organize your job search as if it were a job, you need a place where you can work. Usually, this will be a place in your home set aside as your job search office. Following are some essentials you'll need to help you set up this office.

A Telephone: It is very important that you have access to a telephone throughout your job search. If you don't have one, set up your office in the home of a friend or relative who does.

Basic Furniture: You will need a table or desk to write on, a chair, and enough space to store your materials.

A Quiet Place: Just as on a job, you must have a place where you can concentrate. If you have children or other at-home responsibilities, arrange for someone else to care for them during your "office hours." Ask for cooperation from all family members to avoid interference during your job search time. It is best to select a place where you can safely leave your materials. Then you won't have to set up your work space every day.

Some Materials You Will Need

- A good ink pen (erasable black ink if possible)
- Several pencils with erasers
- Lined paper for notes, contact lists, and other uses
- 3-by-5-inch cards for use as job lead cards
- 3-by-5-inch card file box with dividers

- Thank-you notes and envelopes
- Resumes and JIST Cards
- Business-sized envelopes
- Stamps
- *Yellow Pages* phone book
- Calendars and planning schedules
- Access to a good print quality typewriter or word-processor (optional)
- A copy of this book, of course

Creating Special Forms and Systems

By using the job search methods you have learned in this book, you can develop hundreds of contacts. Keeping track of all this is more than your memory can handle. Look at the following 3-by-5-inch card. It shows the kinds of information you can keep about each person who helps you in your job search.

```
Organization: Mutual Health Insurance
Contact Person: Anna Koch      Phone: 701-355-0216
Source of Lead: Uncle Bob
Notes: 4/10 Called. Anna on vacation. Call back
4/15. 4/15 interview set 4/20 at 1:30. 4/20
Anna showed me around. (Friendly people)
Sent thank you note and JIST card. Call back
5/1. 5/1 Second interview 5/8 at 9 a.m.!
```

Although the card used in this example is specially printed, you can keep the same kind of information on blank 3-by-5-inch cards available at most department and stationery stores. Plan on using at least a hundred of these cards. Create one card for each person who gave you a referral or is a possible employer. Keep brief notes each time you talk with them to help you remember important details for your next contact.

Develop a Follow-Up Card Box

Most department and stationery stores have small boxes made to hold 3-by-5-inch cards. They also have tabbed dividers for these boxes. Buy an inexpensive card file box and enough dividers to set up a box as described here.

Set up a divider for each day of the month, numbering them 1 through 31. Once this has been done, file each completed Job Lead Card under the date you want to follow up on it. See the following examples of how this box might then be used.

Example 1: You get the name of a referral to call, but you can't get to them right away. You create a Job Lead Card and file it under tomorrow's date.

Example 2: You call someone from a *Yellow Pages* listing, but they are busy this week. They tell you to call back in two weeks. You file their Job Lead Card under the date exactly two weeks in the future.

Example 3: You get an interview with a person who doesn't have any jobs now, but they give you a name of someone else who might. After you send a thank-you note, you file this Job Lead Card under a date a few weeks in the future.

As you contact more and more people in your job search, the number of people you file away for future follow-up will keep increasing. You will find more and more "new" leads as you follow up with people you've already contacted one or more times in the past. This is one of the most effective ways of getting a job.

At the beginning of each week, you simply review all the Job Lead Cards you filed for this week. On your weekly schedule, list any interviews or follow-up calls you promised for a particular time and date. At the beginning of each day, pull the Job Lead Cards filed under that date. List them on your Daily Contact Sheet (described in the following section) for that day.

Use a Daily Contact Sheet

This is a simple form you can make on regular lined sheets of paper. The sheet has four columns as in the example below:

Daily Contact Sheet			
Contact Name/ Organization	**Referral Source**	**Job Lead Card**	**Phone Number**
1. _____			
2. _____			
3. _____			
4. _____			
5. _____			

Complete one of these forms each day. I suggest that you list at least 20 people or organizations to contact before you begin any phone calls that day. Use any source to get these leads — referrals, *Yellow Pages*, want ads, and so on.

Creating a Weekly Job Search Schedule

The steps that follow will help you organize each week of your job search to get the most from your time.

Step 1: Decide How Many Hours Per Week to Look

How many hours per week do you plan to spend looking for a job?

In most cases, I recommend about 25 hours per week for a person who is looking for full-time work. An active job search is difficult work, and 40 hours per week is too much for many people. Since the average job seeker spends about five hours per week actively looking for work, this is much more than the average. Whatever you decide is fine. You should realize that the less time you spend, the longer you are likely to be unemployed. Record here the number of hours per week you plan to spend looking for a job:_____.

Step 2: Decide Which Days to Look

Decide what days each week you will use to look for work. Since most businesses are open Monday through Friday, these are often the best days to look. In the first column of the following form check the days you plan to use for your job search. Don't mark in the other columns yet.

Weekly Planning Worksheet		
Check Day	**Number of Hours**	**Time**
___ Monday		
___ Tuesday		
___ Wednesday		
___ Thursday		
___ Friday		
___ Saturday		
___ Sunday		
Total No. Hours/Week		

Step 3: Decide How Many Hours Per Day to Look

Using the form you've already started, decide how many hours you will spend looking for work on each of the days you selected. For example, if you selected Mondays, you may decide to spend five hours each Monday looking for work. You would then write "5" in the "Number of Hours" column on the form. Do this with all the days you checked until the total equals the number of hours per week you listed in Step 1.

Step 4: Decide What Times on Each Day to Look

Using the same form, use the remaining time column to list the times you will use each day to look for work. For example, if you decided to spend six hours each Monday looking for work, you might decide to begin at 8 a.m. and work till noon (4 hours), take an hour off for lunch, then work from 1 to 3 p.m. (2 hours).

Step 5: Create a Weekly Job Search Schedule

Use a monthly calendar to mark off the days and times you've scheduled each week to look for a job. A regular calendar sheet will do for this, allowing you to see your basic schedule for an entire month at a glance.

Creating a Daily Job Search Schedule

You have decided what days and what hours to spend on your job search. But what will you do each day? You still need a daily plan to get the most out of each hour. Look at the following sample daily plan. Yours may look different, but you should use many of the same ideas on your own daily schedule.

A Sample Daily Schedule	
7:00 a.m.	Get up, shower, dress, and eat breakfast
8:00-8:15	Organize my work space, review schedule for interviews or promised follow-ups, update schedule as needed
8:15-9:00	Review old leads for follow-up (from follow-up box), develop new leads (want ads, *Yellow Pages*, warm contact lists, and so on), complete daily contact list
9:00-10:00	Make phone calls
10:00-10:15	Take a break!
10:15-11:00	Make phone calls
11:00-Noon	Send follow-up notes as needed
12:00 p.m.	Lunch break
1:00- 3:00	Go on interviews, cold contacts in the field, research for interviews at library

Some Tips for Your Job Search Schedule

Set Daily Objectives for Interviews: Remember that we have redefined an interview. An interview now includes seeing people who hire people like you but don't necessarily have a job opening. Don't stop calling until you have met your daily objective. Your goal should be to get at least two interviews per day. Remember that since we redefined what an interview is, they are now easy to get. Many people get more that two interviews per day if they use the techniques I suggest.

Expect to Get Rejected: You will need to make 10 to 15 phone calls to get one interview. Most people can make that many calls in an hour, so two hours of calls can result in two interviews. The calls that don't get you an interview are often friendly. So the rejection you experience is really no big deal.

Make Phone Calls, Be Active: You won't get a job by reading job search books or working on your resume. Save those activities for other times. During the day, concentrate on active job search methods.

Stick to Your Schedule: Arrange interviews at times other than those you planned to spend in your job search office. Plan to take care of your personal business after your office hours, too.

Don't Get Discouraged: Looking for a job is hard work, so take time for breaks. And take time to take care of yourself. If you follow these recommendations, you will soon have the job you want.

In Conclusion

The final lessons I can offer are these:

- **Trust Yourself.** No one can know you better than you.
- **Decide To Do Something Worthwhile.** Whether it is raising a family or saving the whales, believe in something you do as special, as lasting, as valuable.
- **Work Well.** All work is worth doing, so put your energy into it and do it as well as you are able.
- **Enjoy Life.** There is always something to marvel at if you look for it.
- **Send Thank-You Notes.** Many people will help you throughout your life, in large and small ways. Let them know you appreciate them. The more you give, the more you seem to get in return.

Thank you for reading this book. I wish you good fortune in your job search and your life.

Appendix

A Somewhat Annotated and Admittedly Biased List of Resource and Reference Materials for the Job Search and Related Topics

There are thousands of resource books and other materials that might be mentioned here but I am selecting for mention only those that I know about and think are good enough to mention. Although some of the books I mention are rather obscure, a good library will have most of them. You will also find many of the books in a bookstore or would be able to order them through one, if you prefer to own your own.

You should also know that I have my biases. Over the past 10 years I have browsed through hundreds of job search and career books, looking for the pearls among the swine. I have done this because I like books and because each year I help select books for inclusion in a catalog of resource materials that JIST sends to institutions and professionals. I also edit career books written by others and write (in my spare time) my own books on job seeking. As if all that is not enough, I also have a role in selecting books that JIST publishes. I tell you all this so that you can put my comments on some books into context. Books published or distributed by JIST are among those listed here as are some that I have written and I tend to be more enthusiastic about those books, though I do try to be objective.

So now that you have been sufficiently warned, browse the materials that follow. I have organized them into categories and have provided comments on many of them. Since books are often revised periodically, I have not provided dates of publication nor have I always provided the author's or publisher's name. This in an informal list rather than a formal bibliography but I hope you find it helpful.

Other Books by Yours Truly

I have written several job search books that are primarily used in schools and institutions and a few that are in bookstores and libraries.

The Work Book — Getting the Job You Want: My first job search book. Published in 1981 and revised in 1987, it is still in print and has sold over

300,000 copies. Very popular in post-secondary schools and programs that are held accountable for helping their graduates find jobs.

Job Finding Fast: This is a thorough book that includes sections on career decision making as well as job seeking. It was written to support a full course or program at the post-secondary or college level.

Getting the Job You Really Want: A simpler book than either of the above that covers the same topics at a lower reading level.

The JIST Course — The Young Person's Guide to Getting and Keeping a Good Job: This one was written for use by high school students.

The Quick Job Search: A 32-page booklet covering the essentials needed for a successful job search.

Instructor Guides: I wrote instructor's guides for the books above to assist a teacher or trainer present a career planning or job search class or workshop.

The Right Job for You: Written to help people define a career and job objective. Available through bookstores.

Other Books Published by JIST

Here are some of the other books published by JIST that are available in libraries or bookstores. They may also be listed elsewhere in this appendix under appropriate sections. I have not included those titles primarily written for use in a school or a guided program. If you want to know more about them, you'll have to write to JIST for a catalog.

Note: JIST distributes career oriented books, software and videos from a variety of sources through its catalog, as well as materials that JIST produces itself. This catalog is available to qualified schools and institutions. Contact JIST (the address is in the front of this book) and ask for a catalog. The catalog is not available to individual job seekers.

America's Top 300 Jobs: This is a version of the *Occupational Outlook Handbook* published for the bookstore market. It has a different cover, title and a few other differences but its content is precisely the same.

America's 50 Fastest Growing Jobs: As its title suggests, this book provides information on the jobs that are growing rapidly as well as summary information on over 300 of the most popular jobs.

America's Federal Jobs: A guide to all the major federal agencies and what job openings they are likely to have as well as tips for applying.

The Job Doctor — Good Advice on Getting a Good Job, Phil Norris: A short and popular book that covers the basics of getting a good job. Phil has run a large and successful job search program and has a gift in making things simple and easily understood.

The Resume Solution — How to Write (and use) a Resume That Gets Results, David Swanson: Provides a step-by-step approach to producing superior resumes. Good sample resumes and worksheets.

Work in the New Economy, Robert Wegmann, Robert Chapman and Miriam Johnson: This is a well-researched and written book that reviews the research on labor market trends and how a job seeker is affected. I admire the work of Bob Wegmann and consider him THE expert on this topic. He died early in 1991.

Exploring Careers: An important book originally published by the U.S. Department of Labor to assist young people explore career alternatives. JIST revised and updated the original work.

Occupational Outlook Handbook: JIST publishes a clone of the same book originally published by the U.S. Department of Labor. Ours is the same in all ways as the original except for a different cover design and a lower price.

Dictionary of Occupational Titles: Another JIST clone of a Department of Labor publication, it describes over 12,000 jobs.

The Enhanced Guide for Occupational Exploration: Provides descriptions and cross-referencing systems to 2,500 jobs covering 95 percent of the workforce.

The Career Connection — A Guide to College Majors and Their Related Careers, Fred Rowe: Provides information on over 100 college majors and 1,000 occupations that are related to them. Includes information on salaries, course requirements, related high school courses and other details useful in planning a college major.

Career Connection II — A Guide to Technical Majors and Their Related Careers, Fred Rowe: Similar to the above but providing information on 70 technical training majors and 450 related occupations.

The Library as a Source of Career Information

A good library has a variety of specialized resources for job seekers on specific organizations. Here are some of the most important ones.

The librarian: That's right, your friendly librarian can be one of your best sources of specific information during your job search. If you can ask the question, he or she can probably give you some ideas on where to find an answer.

Finding Facts Fast, Todd: Perhaps the best book on finding out about anything at the library or elsewhere. Great research aid.

Trade magazines and journals: Most libraries will have one or more professional journals related to a variety of major career areas. Staying current on the publications in your field will help you in the interviewing process and they sometimes have job listings.

Business Newsbank, News Bank, Inc.: This service provides the narrative of articles from newspapers and business journals from 400 cities. It cross-references information by company name, individual's name, industry, or product category.

Business Organizations and Agencies Directory, Gale Research Co.: Provides a number of useful ways to look up business organizations by name, types of business activity, and others. It then provides information on each organization including address, phone number, contact person, and a brief description of the organization.

Business Periodicals Index: Cross-references business articles from over 300 periodicals by subject and company name.

Contacts Influential: A series of directories providing information on many smaller businesses. The directories allow you to look up organizations by name, or type of organization and learn various details of its operations and size.

Encyclopedia of Associations, Gale Research Co.: Lists over 19,000 associations representing more issues than you can imagine. It cross-references them in various helpful ways. Find out which professional organizations people in the occupation you are interested in are likely to belong to, then read their journal and get their list of members to contact during your networking. And consider joining one or more.

Million Dollar Directory, Dun's Marketing Services: Provides general information on over 115,000 businesses.

Moody's Industrial Manual: Provides detailed information on over 3,000 larger organizations.

Moody's Industrial News Reports: Provides articles related to each of the businesses listed in the related directory.

Polk's Directories, R.L. Polk & Co.: Each major city has its own *Polk Directory* that is created by way of a door-to-door canvass of individuals and businesses in the area. Cross-references by name, address, and type of business.

Reference Book of Corporate Management, Dun's Marketing Services: Provides information on the executives and officers of the 6,000 largest U.S. corporations.

Standard and Poor's Register of Corporations, Directors, and Executives: Provides brief information on over 40,000 corporations and their key people cross-references by names, types of businesses and other methods.

Thomas Register of American Manufacturers, Thomas Publishing Co.: Several related directories provide information on manufacturers and allows you to look them up by product, name, and by other means.

The Wall Street Journal Index: This is an important source of information on larger businesses and business trends.

Where to Find Business Information, Brownstone and Curruth: This one lists and describes the many newsletters, journals, computer databases, books, and other sources of business information.

The New York Times Index: A thorough index of all stories that appear in the *Times*.

America's Corporate Families — The Billion Dollar Directory: Describes the relationships of 2,500 large corporate "families" and their 28,000 subsidiaries. Also provides information on each and cross-references by location, business or product type and other methods.

Annual Reports: All publicly owned and many smaller organizations provide annual reports detailing earnings, trends, strategies and other information. If one is available, it can provide an excellent source of information.

Out-of-town *Yellow Pages:* Some libraries have out-of-town copies of phone books. If they don't, ask your local phone company.

Newspapers and magazines: Larger libraries have out-of-town papers. They often have stories related to a particular industry or even a specific business. Several excellent cross-referencing systems exist that can lead you to a topic of interest. You need only ask the librarian.

900,000 Plus Jobs Annually, Feingold & Winkler: Reviews over 900 periodicals which list openings and positions wanted in hundreds of fields. Well-done.

Directory of Executive Search Firms: Lists and cross-references hundreds of these businesses.

Professional & Trade Association Job Finder: By career category, details over 1,000 sources of information, referrals, and more.

Peterson's Business and Management Jobs: An annual listing of hundreds of employers plus essential background information on each.

U.S. Industrial Outlook: Another important book from the U.S. Department of Labor, it provides current trends and forecasts on over 350 industries. Arranged by SIC Codes, it easy to read and use, and provides good background on what is happening in any specific industry.

Where the Jobs Are — 1200 Journals with Job/Career Openings, Feingold & Winkler: A unique resource providing tips on responding to journal ads and cross-references to specific journals by job type.

Resume Writing Books

There are hundreds of resume books out there but most offer bad advice. They assume that a resume will help get an interview while the research clearly indicates that this is not an effective way to do so. And many offer poor or unnecessarily rigid advice about the resume itself. Clearly, the importance of a resume is overrated, yet they are a standard — and typically expected — part of the job search process. Here are a few resume books that I like:

The Resume Solution, David Swanson, JIST Works, Inc: I helped write this book and so am a bit biased. But it is a good book that covers the basics in a step-by-step manner with lots of worksheets and examples.

The Perfect Resume, Tom Jackson: A very helpful book on resumes that uses a workbook format. This approach makes it easy to identify skills, interests and achievements to support a clear job objective. Good examples.

Damn Good Resume Guide, Yana Parker: An irreverent title but it has many good examples and an easy-to-follow process for creating resumes.

Writing a Job Winning Resume, John McLaughlin & Stephen Merman: It goes right to the point to help someone structure a good resume. The examples display how each person covered up flaws and used their resume to present themselves well. A nice touch.

High Impact Resumes & Letters, Krannich & Banis: I like this book. In addition to the expected advice on constructing a resume, it provides worksheets on identifying skills and accomplishments, good job search advice and plenty of sample resumes and letters.

Your First Resume, Ron Frye: Tips for new graduates and others just entering the job market.

Who's Hiring Who, Richard Lathrop, Ten Speed Press: This has a very good section on what the author calls a "Qualifications Brief" that are a form of skills resumes. Good examples and methods for handling various problems.

Complete Resume Guide, Faux: Some good ideas and examples.

Developing a Professional Vita or Resume, McDaniels: Special resume advice for professionals with advanced education or experience.

Don't Use a Resume, Richard Lathrop: A booklet providing good examples and advice on writing a special resume that emphasizes skills.

How to Write a Winning Resume, Bloch: Good examples for college grads, more experienced job seekers, and professionals.

Liberal Arts Power — How to Sell It on Your Resume, Nadler.

Resumes for Technicians, Shanahan: Examples, tips for use, etc.

Resumes for Computer Professionals, Shanahan: Many examples.

Resumes for Executives and Professionals, Shy & Kind.

Resume Kit, Beatty: Much better than average advice on putting together effective resumes and cover letters.

Resumes for Paralegals and Other People with Legal Training

Resume Writing, Bostwick: Traditional job search advice but some useful resume and letter writing tips, 10 resume styles, and many examples.

Basic Career Reference Books

There are hundreds of books providing information on jobs, including a good variety at most large libraries. I consider the books listed here among the most helpful.

Occupational Outlook Handbook: Published by the U.S. Department of Labor, the OOH provides information on the 250 most important jobs in the United States. I consider this to be the most important and user-friendly source of career information available. I recommend it highly to job seekers and career changers. Most libraries will have a copy. JIST publishes a clone of the government's edition.

America's Top 300 Jobs: This is a special version of the *Occupational Outlook Handbook* that can be found in many bookstores and is published by JIST. Except for the title, cover design, and the first few pages, it has the exact same content as the *OOH* published by the U.S. Department of Labor.

Guide for Occupational Exploration: The "GOE" provides a method of narrowing down broad interests to the many specific jobs within each major occupational category. It lists over 12,000 jobs by occupational cluster, interests, abilities, and traits required for successful performance. In addition, each job is cross-referenced in useful ways. You can look up jobs by industry, types of skills or abilities required, values, related home/leisure activities, military experience, education required, or related jobs you have had. The U.S. Department of Labor published the earlier edition of this book and a later edition was published by a private source.

Dictionary of Occupational Titles: While the GOE allows you to locate thousands of job titles in a variety of helpful ways, it does not describe these jobs. The DOT does and is the only book to do so. Also published by the U.S. Department of Labor, the DOT can be found in most large libraries. It is a very large book (over 1,400 pages) and is not particularly easy to use but, combined with the GOE, provides the most thorough system of organizing jobs available.

The Enhanced Guide for Occupational Exploration: This book combines useful elements of both the GOE and the DOT. It uses the GOE's structure for organizing jobs into major interest areas and cross-references jobs in similarly helpful ways. But is also provides descriptions for each of the jobs it lists. It can do this within one book by excluding the many jobs that employ few people or are highly specialized. The 2,500 jobs it does include cover 95 percent of the jobs in the workforce and few people will miss those that are not listed. In fact, I think that the excluded 10,000 jobs tend to get in the way of finding the ones that most people actually work in. This book is published by JIST, the same people who published the book you are now reading.

Occupational Projections and Training Data: Published by the U.S. Department of Labor, supplements the *Occupational Outlook Handbook* with details on more jobs — over 700. Lists entry requirements, projected growth, etc.

Occu-facts: Provides one-page descriptions for over 500 jobs in an easy-to-read format. Jobs are arranged into groups of similar occupations which encourages its use as a career exploration tool.

Exploring Careers: This is an important career exploration book for young people that was originally published by the U.S. Department of Labor and revised and republished by JIST.

American Almanac of Jobs and Salaries, Wright: Provides the facts on various jobs and their compensation. A well-done resource covering most major occupational categories.

Encyclopedia of Careers, Ferguson Publishing: A series of books providing useful information on all major occupations.

Information on Specific Careers

A good library will have many books providing information on specific careers. The *Occupational Outlook Handbook* also lists free sources of additional information for the jobs it describes, though you have to send for them. Here are some books that provide information on specific careers or types of careers. You will find many others in a good library.

"Opportunities in" Series: This is a series of about 50 books that are published by VGM Career Horizons. It's incredible that so many books by different authors can be so consistently good. Most are recommended by the American Vocational Association or have received other awards. Each book covers a career or career cluster describing related jobs in that field, skills required, working conditions, pay, education required, and jargon. Some of the careers covered are Secretarial; Health & Medical Careers; Office Occupations; Data Processing; Computer Science; Travel Careers; Hotel & Motel Management; Cable Television; Accounting and many others.

Peterson's Engineering, Science and Computer Jobs: An annual update of 900 employers, lists types of jobs, and more.

High Paying Jobs in 6 Months or Less: For jobs requiring brief training.

High-Tech Jobs for non High-Tech Grads, O'Brien: Good ideas for those without technical training.

Career Finder — The Pathways to over 1,500 Entry-Level Jobs, Schwartz & Breckner: Checklists result in recommended jobs for more exploration. Lists salaries, openings, etc.

New Horizons — Education and Career Guide for Adults, Haponski: Methods of seeking and using education to get ahead. Good.

Career Planning/Job Search Books

There are now innumerable job search and career planning books and more are published all the time. Most are written by corporate recruiters, headhunters, social workers, academics and personnel experts who are well intentioned but have little practical experience in determining whether the methods they recommend work. Many books provide advice that would, if followed, slow down the job search process. Generally, I discard books that suggest sending out resumes and answering want ads as good job search methods or that do not include methods appropriate for approaching smaller businesses. The research clearly indicates the relative importance of these issues and anyone who is not aware of this should not be considered an expert. Here are some of the better books.

What Color Is Your Parachute?, Richard Bolles: This is the all-time best selling career-changing book ever. Well-written and entertaining, it is updated each year and includes a useful self-assessment section, "The Quick Job Hunting Map." Bolles is fun to read and the book is highly recommended.

Where Do I Go from Here with the Rest of My Life?, John Crystal & Richard Bolles: This book presents the innovative career planning process of John Crystal as written by Richard Bolles. John has since died but his techniques and insights into the career planning process helped start an important movement that came to be called "Life/Work Planning."

Who's Hiring Who, Richard Lathrop: Solid, practical information for job seekers. Good self-assessment sections and excellent resume advice (he calls them "qualifications briefs"). I particularly like this book and respect Lathrop's work.

The Complete Job Search Handbook, Howard Figler: Solid source for new ideas. Exercises to assess skills, values, and needs. Procedures for exploring careers and developing a job objective. Innovative job search and interviewing techniques. An excellent book that is loaded with innovative ideas.

The Job Doctor, Phil Norris: A very popular book that provides a quick review of the job search process. Provides practical advice that gets right to the point. The author has taught thousands of people to find jobs and has written a column titled "Ask the Job Doctor." Published by JIST.

Wish Craft, Barbara Sher: An upbeat book that provides activities and advice on setting goals and reaching your full potential.

Sweaty Palms — The Neglected Art of Being Interviewed, H. Anthony Medley: Fun and factual tips for job seekers at all levels. Covers illegal questions, problem interviews, appropriate dress and behaviors.

Job & Career Building, Richard Germann & Peter Arnold: A good choice for laid-off professionals, managers and others with more experience and training.

Work in the New Economy, Robert Wegmann, Robert Chapman, & Miriam Johnson: A very well-researched book. Covers where our economy is going and how we should adapt our career planning and job search methods to get better results. Considered by many to be essential reading for any well-prepared job seeker. Published by JIST.

Re-Careering in Turbulent Times, Ronald Krannich: Lots of good material including employment trends, selecting a career, getting training and education, communication skills, sources of job leads, interviewing, resumes, relocation, public employment opportunities, and career advancement.

Joyce Lain Kennedy's Career Book, Kennedy & Laramore: Joyce writes a column on careers that appears regularly in many newspapers. This is a very thorough book for young people and their parents, covering just about everything that a young person would need to know about career and life decisions. Highly recommended.

How to Make a Habit of Success, Bernard Haldane: Originally published many years ago, it was a best seller and is still available. Many consider Haldane one of the founders of the career planning movement that began in the 1950s. This is an important book that has much good advice.

Go Hire Yourself an Employer, Richard Irish: Lots of good stuff in this new revision. Covers skills identification, job search, resumes, interviews, the unemployment "blahs," succeeding on the next job and other topics.

Robert Half on Hiring, Robert Half: Written to help employers select better employees. Most of the advice is based on a series of employer surveys providing unique insight into how employers make hiring decisions.

Hardball Job Hunting Tactics, Dick Wright: From a trainer with lots of experience with the "hard to employ." Excellent sections on completing applications (a topic not often covered well) and resumes. Brief but good section on job search. Tips for people with various "problems" on how to overcome them.

The Three Boxes of Life and How to Get Out of Them, Richard Bolles: Introduces the concepts of "Life/Work Planning" and provides many good activities and ideas. Very thorough.

Job Power — The Young People's Job Finding Guide, Haldane & Martin: One of our favorite books for group process ideas on skills identification and selecting a job objective. Simple, direct, useful for any age.

Alternative Careers for Teachers, Beard: Good ideas on getting a job in another field using transferable skills.

Job Hunting for the 40+ Executive, Birsner: Provides good advice on the personal and job search needs of middle-aged executives.

The Right Place at the Right Time, Robert Wegmann & Robert Chapman: The labor market information is particularly good and the job search advice is sound.

Complete Guide to Public Employment, Krannich: Reviews opportunities with federal and local governments, associations, nonprofits, foundations, research, international and many other institutions. Well-done.

Alternative Careers for Teachers, Pollack / Beard: There are two books with the same title and both offer a different approach and good ideas.

Careers in Local and State Government, Zehring: Where they are, how to apply, take tests, internships and summer jobs. Includes job search tips.

Finding a Job in Your Field — A Handbook for Ph.D.'s & M.A.'s: Published by Anthony & Roe.

Foreign Jobs — The Most Popular Countries, Casewit: Profiles the most desirable countries and how to get jobs there.

Guerrilla Tactics in the Job Market, Tom Jackson: A popular book presenting a variety of good job search ideas.

Jobs for English Majors and Other Smart People: Good tips for liberal arts grads.

Moving Out of Education — A Guide to Career Management & Change, Krannich & Banis: Good tips for this special situation from an ex-educator who moved out.

Part-Time Professional: Good information on finding part-time jobs, benefits, negotiating with employers, converting full-time to part-time jobs, and other tips.

Selling on the Phone, Porterfield: Self-teaching guide for telemarketing and other sales approaches. Good ideas for reinforcing effective phone skills in the job search.

Getting a Job After 50, Morgan: Age discrimination is real and people over 50 need better than average job seeking skills to overcome this.

Do What You Love, the Money Will Follow, Sinetar: For those among us who seek meaning as our first priority, there is hope that we can also make a living doing the things we really want to do.

College & Technical Admissions, Information, Financing & Survival Books

More and more adults are going back to school to upgrade their career opportunities and any young person should consider getting as much education and training as possible. There are many ways to finance post-secondary training or education and that should not be a barrier. If you want to do it, seek and ye shall find a way. Here are some resources.

College Admissions Data Handbook, Orchard House: A four-volume set covering major geographic regions providing information on 1,600 schools. This data is some of the most up-to-date and valid information available. The books are expensive for individual purchase but should be available at libraries and high school guidance departments.

Technical, Trade & Business Data Handbook, Orchard House: Similar to the above but covers post-secondary technical and business training schools. Profiles on over 2,000 accredited schools and cross-indexed by subject.

The Career Connection — A Guide to College Majors and Their Related Careers, Fred Rowe: Provides information on over 100 college majors and 1,000 occupations that are related to them. Includes information on salaries, course requirements, related high school courses and other details useful in planning a college major.

Career Connection II — A Guide to Technical Majors and Their Related Careers, Fred Rowe: Similar to the above but provides information on 70 technical training majors and 450 related occupations.

College Majors and Careers — A Resource Guide for Effective Planning, Phifer: Good information on college majors, skills, related leisure activities, personal attributes and addtitional resource materials for major occupational interests. Well-done.

You Can Make It Without a College Degree, Roesch.

Bear's Guide to Finding $ for College: Well-written, readable, helpful.

College 101, Farrar: Primer for getting along in college.

Peterson's College Money Handbook: Provides costs, types of aid and other details from over 1,700 schools.

College Survival Guide, Mayer: Well-done new student orientation to the basics of making it.

Earn College Credit for What You Know, Simosko: On nontraditional college credit programs: types, application procedures, etc.

Essential Vocabulary for College Bound Students, Heller.

Peterson's Guide to Four-Year Colleges: Covers 1,900 schools and 400 majors. Organized to allow selection by many criteria plus tips on applying, etc.

Peterson's Guide to Two-Year Colleges: Provides selection information on over 1,400 schools with associate degrees.

Peterson's Guide to College Admissions: Student workbook on preparing and competing. Well-done.

Guide to Nontraditional College Degrees, Bear: Fun to read, well-done, and thorough.

Peterson's Independent Study Catalog: Guide to over 12,000 correspondence courses.

Peterson's Competitive Colleges: Data and tips on getting into the top 300 schools.

Peterson's SAT Success: Good preparation for this essential test.

Who Offers Part-Time Degree Programs?: Data on over 2,500 institutions. By Peterson's Guides

Winning Money for College: High school student's guide to scholarship contests.

Peterson's National College Databank: Data in over 350 categories, a major source of data for colleges of all descriptions.

Dress and Grooming Books

Initial impressions in the interview are very important. How you dress and groom is only one of the issues, of course, but it is one that most people can easily change and almost everyone can improve.

Dress for Success, Molloy: This is the standard on business dress for men. Good research and advice on how to dress in different situations to get different reactions.

Women's Dress for Success, Molloy: Same thorough approach as for men.

Always in Style with Color Me Beautiful, Pooser: By a noted color consultant, clothing styles, colors and make-up for women. Many photos.

Big and Beautiful, Olds: Larger women can be gorgeous too.

Color Me Beautiful, Jackson: Smash hit. Discover your "seasonal" colors and coordinate your look. Color photos. Well-done.

Professional Image, Bixler: One of few on dress, grooming, body language, and details for both men and women.

Entrepreneurial & Self-Employment Books

More and more people are working for themselves, starting small businesses or working in small businesses. So here are some books on that topic.

America's New Breed of Entrepreneurs: Presents collective experiences of 48 successful entrepreneurs and how they achieved their goals.

How to Start, Run, and Stay in Business, Kishel: Good primer for the school of hard knocks.

Inc. Yourself — How to Profit from Setting Up Your Own Corporation: Shows financial and other advantages, plus how to set up.

Making It on Your Own — What to Know Before Starting Your Own Business, Feingold.

Starting on a Shoe String — Building a Business Without a Bankroll, Goldstein.

Books on Future Trends

Work in the 21st Century, Isaac Asimov and others: Anthology of well-done articles on work trends for the future. As change accelerates 50 percent of all jobs are expected to be gone in 20 years, replaced by new ones. Stimulating.

Emerging Careers — New Occupations for the Year 2000 & Beyond: Based on years of research, details hundreds of new careers. Very good.

The Work Revolution, Schwartz & Neikirk: Economist and business writer team up. Thorough and well-done, Predicts retraining, education and other needs of rapid change.

Megatrends, Nesbitt: A best-seller that provides a review of where the economy is heading.

Books for Trainers & Instructors

Here are some books of specific interests to those providing career counseling and job search advice.

Counselor's Guide to Career Guidance Instruments, Kapes & Mastie: If you are looking for career-related assessment tests, this book contains popular and obscure tests objectively reviewed by experienced professionals.

The Job Market, Richard Lathrop: Presents brief, well-documented rationale for teaching people to find their own jobs. Much of the data on how people find jobs is very useful in presentations to job seekers.

Work in the New Economy, Wegmann, Chapman, & Johnson: I again mention this book here since I believe it is an essential book for a job search trainer or career counselor to read.

The JIST Chase, Mike Farr & Debbie Featherston: This anthology was written by JIST staff and provides background and operational details for an effective, self-directed job search program. Photocopied. Available from JIST.

Making Vocational Choices — A Theory of Careers, John Holland: There are few career theory books and this is one of the most influential. In plain and readable English, presents the research, rationale and practical uses of his theory of six personality types — the basis of most newer career assessment systems.

Job Search Instructor's Guides: I mentioned earlier that I have written various instructor guides that provide activities for presenting job search classes and groups. Guides of this kind are hard to find, so I mention them again here. Available from JIST.

The Business of Public Speaking: Good tips on business aspects of doing presentations.

Career Exploration Groups — A Facilitator's Guide, Garfield & Nelson: Includes group activities and exercises to aid in self-knowledge, career information and decision making.

Career Information Service, 4th Ed, Norris: One of the few texts for university level career counseling and development courses. Thorough book for career counselors.

Career Planning Workshop Manual: Instructor's guide for Life/Work Planning workshops. Includes group exercises, worksheets.

Developing Vocational Instruction, Mager & Beach: Easy to understand, step-by-step guidelines to developing good curriculum

How to Organize and Manage a Seminar — What to Do and How to Do It, Murray: Budgets, plans, staffing, promotion, etc. Very Good.

Louder & Funnier — A Practical Guide for Overcoming Stage Fright, Nelson: Getting over fear of groups is a major obstacle to success as a trainer or presenter. Excellent (and fun).

Making Successful Presentations, Smith: Good for the new or moderately experienced trainer.

Where to Start — An Annotated Career Planning Bibliography: Thorough, helpful. Organized by topic.

Interviewing Books

The Evaluation Interview, Richard Fear: Considered a classic for anyone who is, or wants to be a professional interviewer.

Out Interviewing the Interviewer, Merman & McLaughlin: Good exercises, case studies and tips for experienced and not-so-experienced job seekers. Includes salary negotiations, evaluating offers, getting off to a good start and more.

How to Make $1000 a Minute — Negotiation Your Salaries and Raises, Jack Chapman/ Sanders: Some interesting tips on getting more money and benefits during the critical part of a job offer.

Make Your Job Interview a Success, Biegeleisen: Contains a variety of good checklists, interview answers, grooming tips and other content.

How to Have a Winning Job Interview, Bloch: Good advice in a readable format, with lots of activities.

Getting to Yes — Negotiating Agreements Without Giving In, Fisher & Ury: Good negotiating tips for anything.

Interviews That Get Results, Vik: Good tips for job seekers.

Winning the Salary Game: Salary Negotiations for Women, Chastain: Good strategies for men too.

Job Success, Job Loss, Survival & Getting Ahead on the Job Books

Skills for Success, Scheele: Good advice on getting ahead in all sorts of careers.

Working Smart, Zehring: An emphasis for new managers but the content is good for almost anyone with advice on getting ahead, organizing time, dealing with people, developing leadership skills

Career Knockouts — How to Battle Back, Kennedy: Avoiding, learning and even benefiting from job failures.

Moving Up — How to Get High Salaried Jobs, Djeddah: Techniques to get promoted or move out to a new job.

Not Just a Secretary, Morrow & Lebov: Techniques for doing well and getting ahead.

Secretary Today, Manager Tomorrow — How to Turn a Secretarial Job into a Managerial Position, Marrs.

Termination Trap — Best Strategies for a Job Going Sour, Cohen: Excellent insights on avoiding or dealing with job loss.

Books on the Military

The military is the largest training institution in the country and is an important source of training and career experience for many people. Here are a few books on this alternative job and training source.

Practice for the Armed Forces Tests: Excellent series designed to improve scores. Drills, sample questions, test-taking tips, Armed Forces tests (general review for all service tests).

Resume and Job Hunting Guide for Present and Future Veterans, DePrez: Helpful book with some good techniques.

You and the Armed Forces, Marrs: Helps better understand career options and what to expect from military life.

Young Person's Guide to Military Service, Bradley: Covers pros and cons of going into the services. Good sections for minorities and women.

Your Career in the Military, Gordan: Reviews advantages of education, money and others plus enlistment options and procedures.

Books on Places to Live or Move To

Some people will be unhappy wherever they live, but living in a place you like does make life more enjoyable. Here are a few books that provide details.

Places Rated Almanac, Richard Boyer and David Savagean: Provides a thorough review of over 270 metropolitan areas including information on housing, education, climate, health services, recreation, arts, transportation, crime, and income.

Finding Your Best Place to Live in America, Bowman and Guiliani: Another good book providing information on good places to live.

Best Towns in America, Bayless: Describes 50 of the United States's most desirable places plus ways to evaluate all communities.

Greener Pastures Relocation Guide — Finding the Best State in the U.S. for You!

Books for Minorities and Other Special Populations

There are specialized materials written to help various segments of our population gain a competitive edge. Here are just a few.

Arthur Young's Pre-Retirement Planning Book: Very well-done book. Lots of worksheets.

Directory of Special Programs for Minority Group Members: Cites thousands of job banks, training opportunities, scholarships, loan programs, employment and training services and more. For Blacks, Hispanics, Asians, and Native Americans.

Job Hunting for the Disabled, Lewis & Marks: Interest surveys, programs, job descriptions and job search tips (mostly traditional).

Minority Organizations — A National Directory: The largest source of information available covering over 7,000 organizations and resources.

The Black Woman's Career Guide, Nivens: Provides good advice for any woman of any level of education. Covers over 50 good jobs, dress and grooming, skills ID, job search and more.

A Helping Hand, A Guide to Customized Support Services for Special Populations: Thorough guide for program operators who emphasize employment: JTPA, older workers, offenders, others. Practical tips for improved services.

Stepping Up — Placing Minority Women into Managerial and Professional Jobs: Based on a highly successful program that worked with unemployed minority women. Salaries went up dramatically as did advancement and retention. Tips to replicate results. This may be out of print, though JIST has a few copies remaining.

Helping the Dislocated Worker, Ashley & Zahniser: Summary of suggested services, model programs, implementation strategies. Very helpful for program planners.

Books on Tests & Test Taking

There are hundreds of career-oriented tests and here are some resources to help evaluate or prepare for them.

American College Testing Program (ACT): Over 450 pages of skills, reviews, sample questions, study tips and tips to raise ACT scores.

Guide to 75 Tests for Special Education: Up-to-date guide covering major tests, how to select, interpret and use.

Career Aptitude Tests, Klein & Outerman: Series of self-scored tests measuring aptitudes against over 250 jobs.

Civil Service Test Tutor: Practice drills and samples for government tests for beginning office jobs: accounting, file clerk, telephone operator, and similar jobs.

Counselor's Guide to Career Guidance Instruments, Kapes & Mastie.

How to Get a Clerical Job in Government: Hundreds of sample questions and answers covering major topics on federal, state and local exams.

How to Pass Employment Tests: Prepares job seekers to do well in tests they may encounter in their job search. Also has a section on tests often given to evaluate potential for advancement.

Making the Grade: A good book. Study habits and techniques for getting good grades by doing well on all sorts of tests.

Practice for Clerical, Typing, Steno Tests: Sample questions, drills, exercises to improve scores on most clerical tests.

Preparation for the SAT: Thorough preparation to increase scores.

Assessment Tests

Too many people think that there is a magical solution to their career planning problems that does not require effort — like taking a test that will tell you what you should do. Tests are only tools to provide you with information. I prefer assessment devices that encourage you to participate in the career decision-making process. If you have access to a career center or counselor, ask about taking a career interest test. But remember that it can only provide you food for thought, not an answer to what you should do. Here are a few that I recommend.

The Self-Directed Search, (SDS): By John L. Holland, Ph.D. This is the most widely used career assessment test available. Responses result in recommendations to consider occupations in one of six major clusters. Over 1,100 jobs are cross-referenced in a separate booklet in a logical and easily found manner. Self scoring and interpreted.

Career Decision Making System (CDM): By Thomas Harrington, Ph.D. & Arthur J. O'Shea, Ph.D. Another popular interest test that is self-scoring and interpreted. Easy-to-use. The Survey Booklet records stated occupational preferences, preferred school subjects, job values, abilities, plans for future education and training.

College Majors Finder: Cross-references Holland codes (which can be obtained from the SDS and CDM described in this section as well as from other sources) to over 900 college majors. Includes 2-year, 4-year, and advanced degree programs.

The World of Work: Published by JIST for use by young people, this is a 32-page book that provides activitites and narrative to assist in self-understanding and exploring career alternatives. It cross-references major occupational information sources including the *Occupational Outlook Handbook* and (in particular) *Exploring Careers*.

Books for Women

Some of the very best career counseling services over the years have been available through women's programs of various kinds. More women are in the workforce today than ever before and they tend to be better educated than average. But women without advanced education who are single heads of households are not doing well, on average. Special advice and resources are clearly needed and here are just a few.

Directory of Special Opportunities for Women: Over 1,000 resources for women entering and reentering the workforce. Recommended.

The Extra Edge, Mitchell: Success strategies for women, based on data from women grads of Harvard Business School.

Homemaker's Complete Guide to Entering the Job Market, Lussier: Useful techniques to transfer homemaking skills to the work world and find a job.

Time for a Change — A woman's Guide to Nontraditional Occupations: For women considering non traditional jobs: exercises and narrative plus a review of 10 growth-oriented jobs.

The Woman's Workbook, Ekstrom: Excellent for reentry women or women with children but little paid work experience. Exercises help identify skills from homemaking and other life experiences.

Developing New Horizons for Women, Ruth Helm Osborn: Very good text to improve self-esteem, identify strengths and develop long-range life and career plans.

Miscellaneous Good Stuff

These are listing of materials that are useful but that don't fit neatly into another category.

Liberal Education and Careers Today, Howard Figler: I dropped out of pre-med in my junior year of college (a long story) and got a degree in liberal arts. And I turned out OK. Figler makes the same pitch for a liberal arts education and provides research and lots of advice on how liberal arts is a good way to go.

Brushing Up Your Clerical Skills, Steinberg: For new and returning office workers. Exercises on spelling, punctuation, typing, business letters, filing, etc.

How to Get Control of Your Time and Your Life, Lakein: A very good time management and goal setting book. Simple and well-done.

Job Sharing Handbook, Smith: Provides guidelines for setting up a shared job, case histories, etc. Good.

Parents with Careers Workbook: Good worksheets and advice on getting organized, childcare, home management, single parents, dual careers, time use, etc.

Passages — Predictable Crises of Adult Life, Gail Sheehy: A great book in understanding ourselves and others as adults going through various stages.

Quick Typing, Grossman: For, of course, faster typing speed.

Computer Software

More and more people have access to computers and I see an increasing amount of software available to help people on one aspect or another of career planning and job seeking. I have included only software that is in a price range that might be attractive for an individual user and only those that I have tried and liked. Note that much of the better software is rather expensive and is designed for use by schools and other organizations rather than individuals. There is some near useless stuff on the shelves of software shops waiting for the unwary.

Career Compass: Users respond to 70 work activity questions with low/medium/high preferences. Computer delivers a six-page career interest profile which ranks and describes 14 occupational clusters. Interest area descriptions with details on the top three clusters and the major work groups in each. The type of work and where the work is done is briefly described for each major work group and cross-references likely jobs from a data base of over 400 occupations. (Meridian Education, $89)

Career Design: A thorough program that provides content to help identify skills, select career options, prepare a resume, interview, negotiate salary and more. Based on the career planning principles of John Crystal. A version for individuals is available for about $100. (Career Design Software, Atlanta)

Career Directions: Includes four modules: **Assessment:** Exercises define work preferences, skills, abilities, physical demands, occupational training time, etc. which result in appropriate career clusters; **Analysis:** A data base of 460 jobs searched for specific jobs meeting criteria set in first module. Can change responses to vary results; **Exploration:** allows review of occupational information on any job in data base, and **Planning:** aids in structuring specific plans for vocational training, college and/or job search. (Cambridge Career Products, $119)

Career Finder: One of the easiest programs to use. User answers just 18 questions with low/medium/high preference: 10 work related interests such as using words or numbers, understanding people, leading, dealing with details; 8 work characteristics such as willingness to work hard, travel, level of education. When done, responses are scored and compared to 21 occupational clusters. High scores indicate responses are close to those required in that field. User then sorts from over 400 jobs and gets the 20 closest matches. (Wintergreen Software, $189)

The Right Resume Writer: Brief, but helpful, tutoring on skills, chronological, and professional resume types. Skills identification section lets the user choose from 126 key skill words for use in the skills resume. Prompts for personal data, education, and employment history. Allows you to review and change information. After choosing a resume style, the computer formats automatically. (Career Development Software, $65)

The Right Resume Writer II: Similar to above, but with much improved formatting capabilities. (Career Development Software, $115)

The Perfect Resume Kit: Based on Tom Jackson's writings, this program is flexible, powerful and well-done. One of the best we've seen, it allows you to produce finely crafted resumes.

Letterwriter for Job Seekers: Nifty program with three sections: letters of applications, post-interview thank-you notes and creating your own letters. (Wintergreen Software, $65)

Notes

Other Titles Available from

JIST publishes a variety of books on careers and job search topics. Please consider ordering one or more from your dealer, local bookstore, or directly from JIST.

Orders from Individuals: Please use the form below (or provide the same information) to order additional copies of this or other books listed on this page. You are also welcome to send us your order (please enclose money order, check, or credit card information), or simply call our toll free number at 1-800-648-JIST or 1-317-264-3720. Our FAX number is **1-317-264-3709. Qualified schools and organizations** may request our catalog and obtain information on quantity discounts (we have over 400 career-related books, videos, and other items). Our offices are open weekdays 8 a.m. to 5 p.m. local time and our address is:

JIST Works, Inc. • 720 North Park Avenue • Indianapolis, IN 46202-3431

QTY	BOOK TITLE	TOTAL ($)
_____	*Getting the Job You Really Want*, J. Michael Farr •ISBN: 0-942784-15-4 • **$9.95**	_____
_____	*The Very Quick Job Search: Get a Good Job in Less Time*, J. Michael Farr •ISBN: 0-942784-72-3 • **$9.95**	_____
_____	*America's 50 Fastest Growing Jobs: An Authoritative Information Source* • ISBN: 0-942784-61-8 • **$10.95**	_____
_____	*America's Top 300 Jobs: A Complete Career Handbook* (trade version of the *Occupational Outlook Handbook*) • ISBN 0-942784-45-6 • **$17.95**	_____
_____	*America's Federal Jobs: A Complete Directory of Federal Career Opportunities* • ISBN 0-942784-81-2 • **$14.95**	_____
_____	*The Resume Solution: How to Write and Use a Resume That Gets Results*, David Swanson • ISBN 0-942784-44-8 • **$10.95**	_____
_____	*The Job Doctor: Good Advice on Getting a Good Job*, Phillip Norris, Ed.D. • ISBN 0-942784-43-X • **$8.95**	_____
_____	*The Right Job for You: An Interactive Career Planning Guide*, J. Michael Farr • ISBN 0-942784-73-1 • **$9.95**	_____
_____	*Exploring Careers: A Young Person's Guide to over 300 Jobs* • ISBN 0-942784-27-8 • **$19.95**	_____
_____	*Work in the New Economy: Careers and Job Seeking into the 21st Century*, Robert Wegmann • ISBN 0-942784-19-7 • **$14.95**	_____
_____	*The Occupational Outlook Handbook* • ISBN 0-942784-38-3 • **$16.95**	_____
_____	*The Career Connection: Guide to College Majors and Their Related Careers*, Dr. Fred Rowe • ISBN 0-942784-82-0 • **$15.95**	_____
_____	*The Career Connection II: Guide to Technical Majors and Their Related Careers*, Dr. Fred Rowe • ISBN 0-942784-83-9 • **$13.95**	_____

Subtotal _____

Sales Tax _____

Shipping: ($3 for first book, $1 for each additional book.) _____

(*U.S. Currency only*) *TOTAL ENCLOSED WITH ORDER* _____

(*Prices subject to change without notice*)

❑ **Check**   ❑ **Money Order**   Credit Card: ❑ **MasterCard**   ❑ **VISA**   ❑ **AMEX**

Card # (if applies)_____ Exp. Date_____

Name (please print) _____

Name of Organization (if applies)_____

Address _____

City/State/Zip _____

Daytime Telephone (   ) _____ —_____

Thank-you for your order!